THE
CHRISTIAN
FAITH

A Creedal Account

HANS SCHWARZ

Baker Academic
a division of Baker Publishing Group
Grand Rapids, Michigan

© 2014 by Hans Schwarz

Published by Baker Academic
a division of Baker Publishing Group
P.O. Box 6287, Grand Rapids, MI 49516-6287
www.bakeracademic.com

Printed in the United States of America

Originally published in 2010 in Erlangen, Germany, by Martin-Luther Verlag as *Der christliche Glaube aus lutherischer Perspektive*.

Library of Congress Cataloging-in-Publication Data is on file at the Library of Congress, Washington, DC.

ISBN 978-0-8010-4964-4

14 15 16 17 18 19 20   7 6 5 4 3 2 1

In keeping with biblical principles of creation stewardship, Baker Publishing Group advocates the responsible use of our natural resources. As a member of the Green Press Initiative, our company uses recycled paper when possible. The text paper of this book is composed in part of post-consumer waste.

CONTENTS

ABBREVIATIONS

ANF	*Ante-Nicene Fathers*
LW	*Luther's Works.* 75 vols. St. Louis: Concordia, 1955–.
NPNF[1]	*Nicene and Post-Nicene Fathers,* series 1
NPNF[2]	*Nicene and Post-Nicene Fathers,* series 2
WA	*Weimarer Ausgabe. D. Martin Luthers Werke: kritische Gesammtausgabe.* 72 vols. Weimar: Hermann Böhlau, 1883–2009.
WA BR	*Weimarer Ausgabe, Briefwechsel* (correspondence)
WA DB	*Weimarer Ausgabe, Deutsche Bibel* (the German Bible)
WA TR	*Weimarer Ausgabe, Tischreden* (table talk)

PREFACE

Christianity is an amazingly divided religion. In North America alone there are approximately four hundred different Christian denominations. In South Korea, to cite another example, the Presbyterians are split into at least one hundred different groups, some even consisting of just one congregation. None of the other major religions has had such a proliferation into so many different denominations. Is this a Christian disease that will split the body of Christ into more and more fragments? On first glance this seems to be true. But when we look more closely, this is not the case.

Yes, there are many different Christian church bodies. But they share one thing in common: the Bible. This book unites them in their witness to the Triune God, Father, Son, and Holy Spirit. Every Christian community that was founded with the premise just to be the church of Christ sooner or later issued a creedal account of its faith. Most enlightening is here the example of the Church of God of Anderson, Indiana. It had been founded in the nineteenth century with the explicit assertion that its only foundation was the Bible. But when it celebrated its centennial anniversary in 1979, the same church body issued a little booklet with its own confession so that people knew what this church stood for.[1] Every church body needs a certain creedal account of the faith it proclaims. But this account dare not exclude other Christians unless it disregards Paul's admonition about the oneness of the body of Christ, and unless it understands the great commission in an exclusive way as a commission to evangelize other Christians instead of the secular world.

Yet as our different denominations and church bodies show, the common creedal basis does not preclude that we accentuate this foundation differently

1. *We Believe: A Statement of Conviction on the Occasion of the Centennial of the Church of God Reformation Movement* (Anderson, IN: Publication Board of the Church of God, 1979).

depending on the traditions that have shaped us. Everybody sees the world from a different perspective depending on where one lives and under what conditions. This is already true for the New Testament. We have four Gospels. Each is different, but all four of them were received into the New Testament canon because the Christians at that time felt that they did not justify different books—a New Testament according to Matthew, another one according to Mark, and so on. They heeded Paul's admonition that there is just one body of Christ to which we all belong. His body is not to be divided.

This creedal account is written from a certain perspective that is influenced by the reformer Martin Luther (1483–1546) and his understanding of the Bible. Many of his insights are still valid today and have been picked up in different quarters of Christendom. This will become even more pronounced as we move closer to 2017, the five-hundredth anniversary of Luther's posting of his "Ninety-Five Theses."

One of Martin Luther's most important insights was that the Bible should not be read in a uniform manner, according the same weight to every page of the Bible. For instance, the instructions concerning sacrifices in Leviticus 1–8 are interesting to read, but they are without actual significance for us Christians. As Luther said, "They were only given to the Jews." He therefore distinguished between center and periphery in the biblical text. Some items are central and important while others are actually at the periphery for our Christian faith.

Jesus Christ is central. It was through Christ that God made God's own self known. We learn about Jesus only through the Bible, the Holy Scriptures. We learn in the Bible that we cannot come to God by our own merits but only through God's undeserved grace. Therefore we can only have hope in life beyond this life by trusting in God, that is, by faith. The foundation of the Christian faith is built on these four fundamental principles: by Scripture alone, by Christ alone, by grace alone, and by faith alone. We gain access to these principles in the Bible.

In the following chapters, I want to show what this faith is all about and how it can help us ascertain a solid foundation for our life in confronting the problems of our times. The references are kept to a minimum. But all quotations are referenced. It is my desire that this book will contribute to a deeper understanding of the Christian faith.

This book could not have been finished without the help of Dr. Terry Dohm, a former doctoral student of mine who improved the style and the content of these pages, and Hildegard Ferme, my long-time secretary who typed this manuscript as a farewell gift before entering well-deserved retirement. To her and her long-standing loyalty, which went far beyond the call of duty, I dedicate this book.

INTRODUCTION

Luther's Central Insights

Not long ago, a young man from South Korea who had just finished his doctorate with me sat in my study at the university to say good-bye. In the course of the conversation he asked me, "Is it all right to pray to become rich?" and noticing my bewildered look, he explained that many Christians in South Korea pray to get rich. "No," I replied, "because this would be a very selfish prayer, and besides, becoming rich is not that important. If you look at the really great people such as Moses, Buddha, Einstein, or Plato, none of them was rich." He told me that many people in Korea still consider God in a shamanistic way. If you perform the right actions, then you can, so to speak, use God for this or that purpose to obtain your goal. What lies behind this attitude is not just shamanism. It is the sinful human attitude that Augustine (354–430) described when he said that as a sinner a human being shows "apostatizing pride" and "covetousness."[1] In our self-assured pride, we seem to think only of ourselves, our well-being, and our own advantage, so that everything else, whether living or nonliving, will be at our service. This is also true of our approach to God. In our thinking, if God makes sense, God must serve our own purpose. If God does not do what we want, then we ask, "How can God act this way?" Yet a God who does what we want and who is at our disposal can easily become a construct of the human mind. Ludwig Feuerbach, the nineteenth-century critic of religion, therefore claimed that God is a projection of our human imagination. In contrast to that claim, Luther had discovered

1. Augustine, *On the Trinity* 12.9.14, in *NPNF*[1] 3:160.

1

three hundred years earlier that God is not a human construct, but God is God. This, I contend, is the first part of Luther's central Reformation insight.

God Is God

The British Methodist theologian Philip S. Watson wrote a book on Luther in 1947 titled *Let God Be God*. This sums up Luther's important discovery. If God is indeed God and not just some figment of the human mind, then God cannot be domesticated. It was the problem during Luther's time—and it still is in our own—that we attempt to domesticate God. Luther's question, and that of many sincere Christians today, "How do I obtain a gracious God?" expresses this attitude very well. At Luther's time human life expectancy was short, and when Luther died before reaching his sixty-third birthday, he was considered to be a very old man, and he certainly felt like one. Life on earth for people of that time was filled with toil and sorrow. One was virtually helpless against the plague, kidney stones, or high blood pressure, just to name a few afflictions. Human amenities were virtually nonexistent, and when Luther traveled from Wittenberg to Rome, he did so on foot, which took several weeks.

Since one could expect little from this life, one wanted to make sure that there was a gracious God who would at least provide one with a pleasant hereafter. To that effect, one did all one could, so to speak, to twist God's arm by going on pilgrimages, giving huge donations to the church, acquiring relics of famous saints, or, like Luther, joining a monastery and becoming a monk. It was not by accident that Luther joined the Augustinian Eremites, who were known as a very strict order. Luther thought that if he lived a disciplined monastic life, chances were better that he could dispose God favorably to him. Therefore Luther took the monastery's demands very seriously. If he missed one of the prescribed worship services, such as early morning or mid-morning or noon prayers, he made it up later. He once confessed, "If ever a monk entered heaven because of his monkish life, I too would have entered."[2] But Luther did not find spiritual comfort through his pious activities. To the contrary, they only sharpened his conscience, and he felt even more that he was a hopeless case in God's eyes. He could never come into God's presence, because he was human, and God was indeed God.

Following the Danish philosopher Søren Kierkegaard (1813–55), who called this insight the discovery of "'the infinite qualitative distinction' between time

2. Martin Luther, *Kleine Antwort auf H. Georgens nächstes Buch* (1533), in WA 38:143.26–27. Unless otherwise indicated all translations from German and Latin are my own.

and eternity," the Reformed Swiss theologian Karl Barth (1886–1968) said this shows that "God is in heaven, and thou art on earth."[3] If there is an infinite qualitative difference, there is no way for us to bridge the abyss between God and us. We can never reach God, nor can we twist God's arm to do our bidding. God is a sovereign and majestic God, the creator of the universe and everything in it. Modern cosmology has further shown us the immensity of the universe, with regard to both its extension and its age. Our universe is billions of light years in diameter and billions of years old. If there is a God above and beyond this huge universe, how could we ever think that we could manipulate God or dispose him graciously toward us? For Luther, such an attempt was sheer blasphemy, because it was a downgrading of God and an attempt to dethrone God. Yet when he looked around and saw all the things that were invented by pious and frightened people to dispose God graciously toward them, as well as all the ceremonies condoned and favored by the church at the time to obtain a gracious God (for example, to shorten the years one was to spend in purgatory, or to obtain the assurance of heavenly bliss), then Luther rightly became furious. Most of this stuff, he claimed, was an invention of the devil that led us away from the real God and created a god who was a human fabrication.

Luther concluded we can do nothing to dispose God favorably toward us. No prayers, good works, worship services, pilgrimages, or whatever else one could think of would suffice to turn God graciously toward us. As Luther well knew, Augustine once said that since we have forsaken God, we are "forsaken."[4] We cannot of our own power turn back to God. Such a reversal is impossible, because if we could do this, it would be an insult to God's sovereignty and majesty. Just imagine: For years we do not take God seriously. Our career, our family, and our earthly pursuits are more important to us than God, and we do not want God to interfere with them. But as we get older, we become pious and want to make God our priority. Now if we think that God rejoices because we finally take him seriously, we make a charade out of the God who rules the whole universe and is infinitely superior to us. God is not the senile old man in the sky who rejoices when we finally turn to him. No, God does not need us. God is truly God.

In his famous writing of 1525, *The Bondage of the Will*, Luther says it is not up to us to turn either to God or to the devil. It is the other way around. The two quarrel over us, and as a result we are either ridden by the devil or

---

3. Karl Barth, *The Epistle to the Romans*, trans. Edwin Hoskyns (London: Oxford University Press, 1933), 10.

4. Augustine, *On Rebuke and Grace* 11.31, in *NPNF*[1] 5:484.

guided by God. So, we might ask, what should be our attitude to such a God whose arm we cannot twist and who is superior to us in sovereignty? Are we simply puppets who must do what God wants us to do? The answer of most people, whether at Luther's time or today, is, "Not quite." Although God is indeed sovereign and powerful, they say, God will eventually reward us if we lead pious lives and do enough good works. Yet it was Luther's discovery—and this is the second point of his central insight—that God does not reward us.

God Does Not Reward Us

In 1098 the scholastic theologian Anselm of Canterbury finished a little book titled *Why God Became Man* (*Cur Deus Homo*). In this treatise he introduces the conviction that if God is indeed God, he must require us to lead a godlike life. Since we are human, however, even with our best endeavors we deviate from this godlike life at one point or another. As my son said when he was little and we wanted to scold him, "Nobody's perfect." But the problem is more serious than that because we cannot make up for any of our deviations. Each person has in his or her life deficiencies, the dark spots in one's biography that preclude us from being godlike. How then can we expect God to reward us for our life performance? We always fall short of the mark. None of us can ever meet God's expectations. This is exactly what Luther phrased so well in his famous hymn "A Mighty Fortress" when he wrote, "No strength of ours can match his might! We would be lost, rejected." Luther talks here about escaping the fangs of the devil. With this remark he focused on the right point. With our limited strength we can never make it to God. If God were to reward us for our efforts and for our blemishes, he would immediately condemn us. The blemishes are just too many.

This discrepancy between what we can accomplish and what God expects from us is the problem Luther encountered in Paul's Letter to the Romans. Paul writes: "For I am not ashamed of the Gospel; it is the power of God for salvation to everyone who has faith, to the Jew first and also to the Greek. For in it the righteousness of God is revealed through faith for faith; as it is written, 'The one who is righteous will live by faith'" (Rom. 1:16–17). Luther read here the important words "the righteousness of God." If God is a righteous God who will either reward or punish us for what we have done or left undone, then, Luther concluded, we have no chance to ever be accepted by God. Any good works that we do would only endanger the possibility of obtaining eternal bliss. They would underscore the naive idea that we can accumulate enough good works to obtain an eternal reward.

The problem is not only, as Anselm asserted, that there is always a deficit in all our endeavors, but also that we can never offer anything to God that is truly our own since God is the creator and sustainer of everything that is. Therefore the Lutheran liturgy rightly says, "We offer with joy and thanksgiving what you have first given us." If we think about it, we are so caught up in our existential deficiency and our inferiority to God that we cannot expect anything from God but his rejection. Augustine stated it fittingly by quoting Ambrose of Milan (339–397): "To be spotless from the beginning is an impossibility to human nature."[5] This means that we can neither offer anything to God nor expect anything in return. We have no bargaining power. But, like Augustine, Luther did not quit at this point. Shortly before his death, Luther summed up our situation in the famous words: "We are beggars. This is true."[6] It would be a misunderstanding and against everything we have said so far if Luther exhorted us here to beg God for forgiveness or for our acceptance. Here comes the third point of the central Reformation insight that Luther learned from Scripture, namely, that this hopeless situation is typical in God's script, because God creates out of nothingness.

God Creates Out of Nothingness

If God is indeed God, it is an impossible thought that we do our part and God adds his part. With anything that goes beyond our world, such as salvation, life eternal, or acceptance by God, cooperation between us and God is impossible. The reason for this is not only that God does not need our help but also that if we cooperated with God, we could never be sure that we did the right thing or did enough. While God's part would stand assured, since God is God, our part would always be in jeopardy. No assurance of salvation and of acceptance by God would be possible. Luther never condoned the idea that we have a free will toward our salvation. He was a realist who realized that regardless of how high we jump, we always fall back to this earth. We cannot save ourselves. Salvation is God's work alone. Luther claimed, in line with Augustine, that at the most we have a free will toward running away from God.

If we are accepted by God, it is not because of what we have done or left undone. It is not because God rewards us, because we never deserve a reward. If we are accepted, it is because of God's graciousness. God does it all without any necessity and without being coaxed into accepting us. Wherever there is

5. Augustine, *On the Grace of Christ* 50.55, in *NPNF*[1] 5:236.
6. Martin Luther, *Table Talk* (no. 5677, February 16, 1546), in *LW* 54:476.

cooperation between humans and God, uncertainty creeps in as to whether our part is sufficient and therefore whether God really accepts us. Luther experienced this when he questioned in his monastery cell whether he had done everything properly and pleasing to God. As mentioned, all his pious activities never soothed his conscience. Yet if it is God who does everything pertaining to our salvation, we can totally rely on God and can in this way trust his Word.

Luther also observed that God's accepting us out of free grace, this creation out of nothingness, is typical of the whole biblical history of salvation. Neither Moses nor David, neither Isaiah nor Amos was selected for the things he did or because he was so great. To the contrary, all these men had their blemishes, and it was God who made them the people they finally became. This example of creation out of nothingness again shows us the sovereignty of God and that God freely creates without any precondition. This was Luther's discovery with Romans 1:16–17. God is not a righteous God who rewards us for what we have done. If this were so, we could expect only divine punishment and ultimate rejection. Everything else would be wishful thinking. But Luther discovered that that is not what God does. God creates something out of nothing. God's righteousness is through faith for faith. Righteousness is attributed to us without any precondition. We are set into it through a new relationship with God. In the same manner in which God created the world, without any precondition, God now establishes a new creation, the new people of God.

If God is such a sovereign and gracious God at the same time, how can we react properly to this God? The problem contained in this question was enunciated by Jesus when he healed the ten lepers (Luke 17:11–18). Nine took the healing for granted, while only one returned and thanked Jesus for having been restored to new health. This story shows a typical human problem: thanking is not our strong point. Yet Luther was adamant about showing gratitude.

While he contended that a bad tree does not yield good fruit, he was equally assertive that a good tree cannot but yield good fruit; otherwise it is not a good tree. Or, as he put it, "Good works do not make a good man, but a good man does good works."[7] In the same way he also asserted that faith cannot be without many great and good works. Yet we should also take heed that good works are not those that we perform toward God but those we perform toward our neighbor. Jesus reminded his audience that at the end of these days God will say, "As you did it to one of the least of these . . . you did it to me" (Matt. 25:40). Once we have realized that God has done everything toward our salvation, for us and on our behalf, we cannot but rejoice. This rejoicing,

---

7. Martin Luther, *The Freedom of a Christian* (1520), in *LW* 31:361.

however, has a very concrete dimension. As the Lutheran theologian George Forell (1919–2011) put it in a book title, it is *Faith Active in Love* (1954). Good works, or our social involvement on earth, are not the precondition for our salvation. They would be far too insufficient to achieve that purpose. Yet they are the natural result of our totally undeserved acceptance by God, creation out of nothingness. The train of thought is: "Since God has been good to me, I will also be good to others. Since God has been gracious to me, I will also be gracious to others."

But how do we know that God is gracious? How do we know that God does not condemn us? Everything on our side would point in the direction that we have nothing good forthcoming from God. Is all of this not simply imagination, a figment of the human mind? The examples of Moses and David, Isaiah and Amos do not suffice. The Bible also tells us about the failure of King Saul and, despite all his wisdom, the still dubious figure of Solomon. That God is God and therefore infinitely superior to us, that God creates everything out of nothingness, that we cannot work our way to God but only God can bridge the gap between God and us—all these are insights that can be found in other religions too; and, as Luther drastically suggested, even the devil could come up with such insights. The crucial question, however, is how this God is disposed to me. How can I find the answer? It was evident for Luther that if God "would talk to me in his majesty, I would run away like the Jews did. But when he is clothed in the voice of human beings and accommodates himself to our capacity to understand, I can approach him."[8] Exactly this kind of accommodation has happened in Jesus Christ, because there God has shown us his heart.

God Has Shown Us His Heart

In Jesus Christ the infinite and the finite have come together. Through God's action the infinite qualitative difference between God and humanity has been bridged. As Luther wrote in his Christmas hymn "From Heaven Above":

> These are the signs which you will see
>   to let you know that it is he:
> in manger-bed, in swaddling clothes
>   the child who all the earth upholds.[9]

8. Martin Luther, *Vorlesung über Jesaia* (1527–29), in *WA* 25:106.44–45, in his *scholium* or comment on Isa. 4:6.

9. *Evangelical Lutheran Worship*, hymn 268, stanzas 5 and 3.

In the Christ-child the creator and sustainer of the whole world has come to us. And in another stanza of the same hymn Luther writes:

> This is the Christ, God's Son most high,
>   who hears your sad and bitter cry;
>   who will himself your Savior be
>   and from all sin will set you free.

Christ is our savior. He will set us free from our bondage to sin and open for us the gates of heaven. He can do this because he is the human face of God, the one in whom God shows us his heart. According to Luther, this is the major difference between the Christian faith and all other religions and philosophies. While they contain valuable insight into how God is in general, in Jesus Christ alone do we realize how God feels toward us. Through Jesus Christ we see that God is a gracious God, that God invites us to trust him, and that God spares nothing to save us from finitude and human self-deception.

The cross of Christ becomes the hermeneutical key to God's salvation history and more specifically to the Christ event. Nobody, Luther claimed, could have invented the cross as a means of salvation. If we had invented a sign of salvation, we would have naturally chosen something great and wonderful, not a shameful cross. But the cross shows God's characteristic way of creating out of nothingness. Since it could not have been invented, it reflects true history and God's working in that history toward our salvation. Therefore Luther asserted, "The cross alone is our theology."[10] And, "True theology is practical, and its foundation is Christ, whose death is appropriated to us through faith."[11] By practical theology Luther meant existential theology in contrast to speculative or theoretical theology. This practical aspect becomes clear in Luther's explanation of the second article of the Apostles' Creed in his *Small Catechism*. Once Luther asserts the true divinity and true humanity of Jesus Christ, he then shows the immediate consequences of this twofold nature for salvation. Salvation was accomplished by the innocent suffering and death of Christ. And this was done for our sake.

The emphasis on the cross is not some kind of negative theology, or a theology of the absurd, that Jesus must suffer and die. To the contrary, it is realistic, because it shows the characteristic working of God. While nobody would assume that anything good could come out of somebody dying on the cross, abandoned by all his companions, exactly this sign of defeat was used

---

10. Martin Luther, *Operationes in Psalmos* (1519–21), in *WA* 5:176.32–33, in his explanation of Ps. 5:12.

11. Martin Luther, *Table Talks*, no. 153 (1531/32), in *WA TR* 1:72.16–17.

as God's starting point for the victory of life. In his utmost compassion God turned around this sign of defeat and made it into the sign of the conquest of death and the beginning of a new creation. God is the one who provides salvation in and through Christ, without our doing anything.

How do we know that Christ shows us God's heart? Are not there many other embodiments or avatars of the Godhead? While Luther had no knowledge of the numerous gods of Hinduism and the various human embodiments of these gods, he was confronted in his time with the cult of the saints and of Mary. Luther said of Mary, "She is the servant because she has born to me God's son so that I can believe in him."[12] While he appreciated the saints insofar as they could provide us with exemplary godly lives and therefore serve a pedagogical function, he realized that they have no redemptive value. The reason was simple: God had not chosen to disclose God's self to us in any of them, but only in Jesus Christ.

Jesus Christ as the Ladder to God

Only through the human being Jesus can we approach God, because "the humanity is that holy ladder of ours, mentioned in Genesis 28:12, by which we ascend to the knowledge of God."[13] Only through the impression of the life and destiny of Jesus do we realize that God loves us. Only through Jesus do we obtain the appropriate understanding of God and God's activities. This means that Jesus is not important because he was such an effective preacher or because of the miracles he performed or the saintly life he led. Jesus is decisive for us because he is the mediator of God's salvational activity. This emphasis on Christ collapsed all the other ways in which medieval Christians approached God, understood God's will, or attempted to dispose God favorably to them. Christ alone was Luther's decisive insight.

As we have seen, the reason for Christ alone was founded in God's decision to disclose God's self only in Jesus. Yet Luther realized that this divine self-disclosure hinged on the unique relationship between God and Christ. To mediate God completely, Christ could not be just a saint or an avatar. He had to be completely and totally God. Otherwise he could not have mediated God. At the same time Christ had to be completely and totally human. Otherwise he could not have reached us and identified himself with us. Only as one being with the Father, a point that Luther affirmed with the Council of Nicaea,

12. Martin Luther, *Sermon on John 1:1ff* (1522), in *WA* 11:227.12–13.
13. Martin Luther, *Lectures on Hebrews* (1517/18), in *LW* 29:111, in his comments on Heb. 1:2.

could Christ mediate God. Therefore Luther claimed, "Christ does not consist of soul and body, but of humanity and divinity. He has not only assumed human nature, meaning that he consists of body and soul."[14] Furthermore, Luther affirmed "that that which Christ suffered can also be transferred to God, because they are one."[15]

In listening to tradition, especially to the church fathers, Luther did not put his trust in human words. He claimed that he would follow neither the writings of Augustine nor those of any other theologian if the Bible did not affirm their teachings. He even stated, "One can rather believe a simple lay person who quotes Scripture than the Pope or a council that does not quote Scripture."[16] Our knowledge of Christ cannot rest on theological deductions or human conclusions, but must ultimately be substantiated through God's Word as reflected in Scripture. Scripture alone is the ultimate foundation of our faith. Yet by emphasizing the Bible as our sole source of salvific knowledge, does not Luther introduce a printed pope, the Bible, instead of the pope in Rome? Luther would vehemently reject such a conclusion since the veracity of that which is contained in the Bible was never founded on the basis of its simply being printed there.

Luther was not a biblical literalist, and unlike John Calvin (1509–64) he did not expound one biblical book after the other. For him, there were central biblical writings and passages and there were peripheral ones. Central for him was whatever communicated Christ most clearly. Peripheral was everything else that had hardly anything to do with Christ, such as large parts of the Jewish ceremonial law or the Letter of James. Luther commented that though James "mentions Christ several times, he does not teach about him but promulgates a general belief in God."[17] Faith for Luther was no longer simply holding certain things to be true, such as the pronouncements of the church councils or of the pope, or even every letter of the Bible. Faith for him was a personal trust—trust in Jesus Christ, who is communicated to us through the Bible and who leads us to God the Father, from whom alone we can have salvation in the hereafter and guidance in the here and now. Therefore Luther returned to the central tenet of the Christian faith, God in Christ, who is both sovereign and compassionate, who accepts us without any precondition, and to whom we respond with a faith active in love.

14. Martin Luther, *Disputation on De divinitate et meritae Christi* (1540), in *WA* 39/2:110.22–23.

15. Luther, *Disputation on De divinitate et meritae Christi* (1540), in *WA* 39/2:121.1–2.

16. Martin Luther, *Contra Malignum I. Ecci judicium M. Lutheri defensio* (1519), in *WA* 2:649.2–3.

17. Martin Luther, *Vorrede auf die Epistel S. Jacobi und Jude* (1546), in *WA DB* 7:385.20–22.

PART 1

PRESUPPOSITIONS FOR THE FAITH

Three presuppositions are essential if we want to understand the Christian faith: theology, revelation, and the Bible. In contrast to Islam, the Christian faith is not a faith that requires foremost obedience. As we can gather from the story of the conversion of the court official of the queen of Ethiopia, Philip did not ask him, "Do you believe what you are reading?" but rather, "Do you understand what you are reading?" (Acts 8:30). The Christian faith is not an obedient faith but a discerning faith. Therefore it is necessary that we espouse our faith in a logically coherent manner without any contradictions. This is exactly the task of theology. The Christian faith is not an assortment of ideas according to one's gusto. It presupposes that God has made known God's self to us. This self-disclosure of God, not our own ideas, is the presupposition for our faith. Only when we have been exposed to this self-disclosure of God are our thoughts about God in order. Furthermore, we are not the first Christians. There is a long history of God interacting with humanity. This history has been reflected in the Bible, so to speak, as a faith witness. If we want to talk about our faith, we must compare it with this scriptural witness and correct our faith accordingly, lest we advance our own ideas instead of the historically validated Christian faith. But now let us first turn to theology.

THEOLOGY

As with many concepts of the Christian faith, the term "theology" comes from the Greek language, since Greek was the dominant language in the Roman Empire during the time of nascent Christianity. In this language, theology first meant a (mythical) narrative of the gods. This explains why Greek poets such as Homer (ca. 800 BC) and Hesiod (ca. 700 BC) were called theologians. A few centuries later Aristotle (384–322 BC), who was the most famous student of Plato (428/27–348/47 BC), wrote in his *Metaphysics* that there is a scientific philosophy that comprises all knowledge. He called this science "theology." For the Christians, therefore, theology was the science of the all-encompassing meaning of God.

Consequently, one can refer to the authors of the Gospels and to Paul as the first Christian theologians. But this designation would not fit these authors. They composed their writings to convince people of the truthfulness of the Christian faith and not primarily to espouse the Christian faith in a logically coherent fashion. They were most of all interested in proclaiming this faith. This is even true for the so-called apostolic fathers of the second (Christian) century, such as Clement of Alexandria (ca. 150–ca. 215) and the famous Bishop Polycarp of Smyrna (ca. 69–ca. 155).

Beginning and History of Christian Theology

Theologians in their own right appear only with the early Christian apologists of the second century, such as Quadratus (d. ca. 130) and Aristides of Athens

(d. ca. 125). The apologists attempted to defend Christianity against various attacks and tried to show that the Christian faith is no superstition but can be presented in a reasonable manner. This strategy of defense became necessary since in the second century more and more people accepted the Christian faith and the secular authorities became increasingly suspicious. Aristides, for instance, attempted to portray Christians as a new race that led humanity from its decay to new life. Justin Martyr, who died in Lyons in 165 during a persecution of Christians, showed in two apologies that the Christian faith is the true philosophy in contrast to the pagan philosophies in which one cannot sense God's Spirit at work.

The most important apologist of early Christianity was Origen of Alexandria, Egypt (ca. 185–ca. 253). Around 246 Origen attacked the eclectic Platonist Celsus, who had claimed that a reasonable Christian theology is a contradiction in itself because Christianity is hostile to all human values. Origen defended the Christian faith as intellectually credible and showed that Christians are at least as decent a people as pagans, or even better. While Christians at that time did not serve as soldiers of the pagan state and refused to function in various public offices, Origen emphasized that they helped the country by offering prayers and by teaching the people to lead honest lives. His work *On First Principles* was the first Christian systematic theology. In the introduction he showed that the apostles had rendered only that which was necessary for salvation, while the rest was up to later theologians to expound. Origen was convinced that the Christian faith offered a new and comprehensive understanding of the world that was superior to that offered by Hellenistic culture, but it was not necessarily opposed to that culture.

What Origen endeavored to do for the whole church was accomplished five centuries later by John of Damascus (ca. 650–749/753) for the Orthodox Church with his *Fountain of Knowledge*. In part three of this apologetic writing, John presented *An Exact Exposition of the Orthodox Faith*, which is often printed separately and contains a systematic exposition of the whole theological tradition. It gained virtually normative status in the Greek Church. John's intention was not to introduce new teachings but to answer—with the help of the church fathers such as Gregory of Nazianzen (ca. 329–390) and Basil the Great (ca. 330–379)—the most important questions about faith during his time. John's work is still influential for Eastern Orthodoxy.

Looking at Western Christianity, we must mention Augustine, bishop of Hippo Regius in present-day Algeria. In his voluminous work *The City of God* he demonstrated the superiority of the kingdom of God over the worldly kingdom, a notion that in the Middle Ages furthered the struggle between the emperor's and the pope's supremacy over Christianity. The reason for his book, however, was the pagan claim that the sack of Rome in 410 by King Alaric and his Visigoths was due to the wrath of the ancient gods over the conversion of so many people to Christianity. Augustine showed that the devastation of Rome was rather the result of God's wrath over the moral depravity of the pagans. As we saw in the introduction, Martin Luther learned as an Augustinian monk that one can obtain eternal bliss only through God's undeserved grace. As a sinful human being, one can only expect God's rejection. For Augustine it was important that an individual Christian always be part of an ecclesial community, the only institution through which one could hear about a gracious God. The Christian faith is not a private thing but is nourished and strengthened through the Christian community.

One could name many other theologians who contributed to an explanation of the Christian faith in an intellectually acceptable fashion. In the Middle Ages we must at least mention two, Anselm of Canterbury (ca. 1033–1109) from northern Italy and Thomas Aquinas (ca. 1225–1274) from southern Italy.

Anselm is still well known today because of three slim books. In his *Monologion* he deals with an issue still bothering many people today: how God's wisdom and justice can be reconciled with the existence of evil in this world. In his *Proslogion*, addressed to God, he deals with the so-called ontological proof of the existence of God. Anselm starts with the notion that God is the most perfect being and concludes that God's perfection entails God's existence, otherwise God would not be perfect. This kind of reasoning has often been misunderstood as an actual proof of God's existence. Yet Anselm confesses at the conclusion that so far he had only believed in God's existence, but now he understood that God must indeed exist. In this, Anselm wanted to show that God's existence can be intellectually credible. In his already mentioned work *Why God Became Man*, Anselm develops the so-called theory of satisfaction to show why God became human. Since a human can never do what God requires of a person, someone else must make up for that person's deficiencies so that those deficiencies can be equalized before God. Yet such a feat can never be accomplished by a human being but only by God's own self. Therefore God must become human so that this work can be attributed to a human person. From these writings we see that Anselm's whole theological work is dedicated to the intelligibility of the Christian faith, but not to replacing faith by reason. The point for him is that what one believes, one must also be able to understand.

The Roman Catholic Church holds Thomas Aquinas in highest esteem as a theological teacher and declared him at Vatican I (1869–70) to be the principal theologian of the Church. Thomas spent nearly ten years on his most important work, the *Summa Theologica*, in which he offered a comprehensive and clear exposition of the Christian faith in the framework of questions and answers. He achieved a reasonable exposition of the Christian faith with the help of Aristotle's philosophy. God is understood as the rational cause of the universe toward whom humans strive. The *Summa* is divided in three parts: (a) God, creation, and anthropology; (b) ethics; and (c) the person and work of Christ, which includes the sacraments. An envisioned fourth part concerning eschatology was never finished by Thomas but was by a later theologian.

Following Aristotle, Thomas considers God as the unmoved, or prime, mover and then arrives at five proofs for the existence of God: (1) God as the unmoved mover brings the world into existence. (2) As the necessary first cause of all things, God is the first cause of the chain of causes and effects. (3) As an absolutely necessary being, God endows all not-necessary beings with existence. (4) All imperfect beings are dependent on God as the absolutely perfect being. Finally, (5) God is the reasonable architect of the world. One can rightly ask whether such an unmoved mover is identical with the Father of Jesus Christ or only a lifeless construct. This and similar questions were raised by Martin Luther, often in direct contradiction to Thomas and Aristotle, whom he always called "the pagan."

Luther himself was not a systematic theologian who wrote a treatise on the Christian faith. His writings were occasioned by the problems people encountered in daily life or were a defense of his Reformation principles against attacks of his opponents. It was Luther's coworker Philipp Melanchthon (1497–1560) who wrote a textbook containing the theology of the Reformation. His *Loci* (general points of theological matters) was first published in 1521 and reworked several times. The doctrine of God and of humanity is only briefly noted. The salvational emphasis becomes clear when Melanchthon states at the beginning of his treatise that to know Christ means "to know his benefits and not as they teach to perceive his natures and the mode of his incarnation."[1] With this verdict he significantly reduced the medieval proliferation of theological items and the often minute distinctions and obscure applications. Important for him is what Christ has done for us.

John Calvin, the Reformer of Geneva, Switzerland, composed the *Institutes of the Christian Religion*. First issued in 1536 and reissued until 1559 in various improved editions, the *Institutes* is an attempt to explain the Christian faith. More than a thousand pages long, this treatise starts just like the Apostles' Creed with God the creator and Christ the savior and covers all

---

1. Philipp Melanchthon, *Loci Communes*, trans. Charles Leander Hill (Boston: Meador, 1944), 68.

significant aspects of the Christian faith. Calvin emphasizes the sovereignty of God as well as God's activity in history, which can be gleaned from the Bible. Through his activity in history God affects salvation for his people, whom he has chosen and even predestined. Calvin's emphasis on salvation through God alone and not through human cooperation shows that he is in line with the Lutheran Reformation.

Before we come to the present situation of theology, we must mention two important theologians of modernity. The first is Friedrich Schleiermacher (1768–1834), a Reformed theologian active at the beginning of the nineteenth century. In contrast to the Enlightenment period in which Christian religion was often reduced to morals, Schleiermacher argued that religion "is neither thinking nor acting but intuition and feeling."[2] Religion touches the inner human being and must be cultivated in the communion of a person with the universe. Humans have a capacity for religion, and in contemplating the universe one has the feeling of being touched by the infinite. Schleiermacher was influenced by Romanticism and also indebted to the Moravian piety in which he had been educated. In his dogmatics, *The Christian Faith*, he shows that the Christian self-consciousness issues from salvation achieved by Jesus. In Jesus of Nazareth the absolute dependence on God becomes visible in an unbroken way, and we become cognizant of our own dependence on God, a dependence strengthened by Jesus. The Christian faith is founded on Christ alone. Schleiermacher is often called the father of Protestant theology in the nineteenth and twentieth centuries. Although Schleiermacher was often too liberal for Karl Barth, since, according to Barth, he did not emphasize God's Word strongly enough, Barth still had Schleiermacher's picture hanging over his desk.

The Swiss Reformed theologian Karl Barth, whom we have already mentioned, is the second important theologian of modernity. He is famous for his *Church Dogmatics*, which comprises more than six thousand pages and, like Thomas Aquinas' *Summa*, was never finished. He is also the founder of the so-called dialectic or neo-Reformation theology. In contradistinction to the liberal theology of the nineteenth century, and similar to Søren Kierkegaard, Barth emphasized the infinite qualitative difference between God and humanity. If we want to know something about God, he argued, we cannot obtain this knowledge through reason, but through God's Word alone. Therefore any talk about God as expounded in the religions of the world is a human fabrication and sinful. In his theological writings Barth attempted to strictly

2. Friedrich Schleiermacher, *On Religion: Speeches to Its Cultured Despisers*, trans. and ed. Richard Crouter (Cambridge: Cambridge University Press, 1996), 22.

delineate his insights from God's self-disclosure in Jesus Christ. Since this was also the concern of the Reformation, the designation of this movement as neo-Reformation is fitting. The most important Protestant theologians of the second half of the twentieth century, such as Jürgen Moltmann (b. 1926) from the Reformed tradition and the Lutheran Wolfhart Pannenberg (b. 1928), took God's self-disclosure as the starting point for their theological deliberations.

But where was Lutheran theology during the past few centuries? In Germany, one must think of the nineteenth-century Erlangen School and its founder Adolf von Harless (1806–79). In this school of thought, theology has to be related to the church. Contrary to Schleiermacher's view, theology is not a discipline for church governance, since it has its origin in the faith experience within the church. Therefore true Christian theology must stem from the ecclesial faith of the Christian community. Under Johann Christian Konrad von Hofmann (1810–77), Erlangen theology reached its climax. In his most well-known publication, *The Proof of Scripture: A Theological Investigation*, he attempts to establish a biblical foundation for the Christian doctrine. The starting point for him is "Christianity, the communion of God and humanity, personally mediated by Jesus Christ."[3] Theological assertions can be attested to by the personal experience of a theologian. This theology is also called the Erlangen theology of experience, a movement that cannot deny its pietistic influence. Outside of Erlangen one must mention Ernst Wilhelm Hengstenberg (1802–69), the guardian of Lutheran confessional identity. A son of a Reformed pastor, he embodied ever more strongly a Lutheran theology. As editor of the *Evangelische Kirchenzeitung* (Protestant church gazette), he exerted significant influence on church and theology. Influenced by the awakening in northern Germany, he endeavored to stem the tide of an alleged pantheism caused by Schleiermacher and representatives of a rationalistic theology. His main strength and his merit were in a critical apologetics and in showing that the Old Testament was an actual disclosure of God, in contradiction to what one often heard from rationalistic exegetes.

But now let us return to the twentieth century. Jürgen Moltmann in the second half of the century wrote his seminal publication *Theology of Hope* (1964), in which he refuted Karl Barth's approach. For Barth, God's self-disclosure occurred, so to speak, vertically from above, resulting in a static understanding of history. According to Moltmann, however, God is a history-making God, and therefore history is always directed toward the goal predestined by God. With his emphasis on the future-directedness of God's activity,

---

3. Johann Ch. K. von Hofmann, *Der Schriftbeweis. Ein theologischer Versuch*, 2nd ed. (Nördlingen: C. H. Beck, 1857), 18.

Moltmann rediscovered the eschatological structure of the Christian faith. He continued this approach in numerous publications, always emphasizing the social relevance of the Christian faith. As a result, he became one of the most influential theologians of the World Council of Churches.

When Wolfhart Pannenberg published in 1961 his "Dogmatic Theses on the Doctrine of Revelation," he immediately received the attention of the theological world. Pannenberg argued that God's self-disclosure had not occurred in a historical salvation ghetto but in the context of world history and therefore must be accessible to anybody who has eyes to see. With this approach he freed the Christian faith from the ecclesial ghetto of pious people into which Barth had steered that faith. While Barth had emphasized the opposition of worldly knowledge and faith knowledge, for Pannenberg there is only the commonly accessible arena of world history since faith and reason belong together. Faith does not mean to believe certain things or certain statements, but to trust that the God who has proven to be trustworthy in the past will also be trustworthy in the future. Pannenberg has also had a decisive influence in the ecumenical dialogue with the Roman Catholic Church, since in Roman Catholicism the congruence of faith and reason has always been important.

In addition to the theological approaches discussed above, there are many other ways of doing theology today. This is evident in the many "theologies of," such as theology of liberation, theology of the environment, theology of the underprivileged, and so on. These approaches show that theology often concerns itself with issues that are neglected in the world.

Three Essential Functions of Theology

We have seen how theology has changed through the centuries as a result of the context in which it originated and the new questions and issues constantly being raised. Examples of this are the discussion of indulgences during the time of the Reformation and the endeavors of the church in the fourth century to correctly determine the relationship between Father, Son, and Holy Spirit and to phrase it in acceptable terminology. Nevertheless, Martin Luther's assertion in his *Commentary on Galatians* that love should issue from faith is timeless when he says, "This is the perfect doctrine of both faith and love. It is also the shortest and the longest kind of theology—the shortest so far as words and sentences are concerned; but in practice it is wider, longer, and deeper, and higher than the whole world."[4] Theology comprises both dogmatics

4. Martin Luther, *Lectures on Galatians* ([1531] 1535), in *LW* 27:59.

(the doctrine of faith) and ethics (the doctrine of love). How then should we expound the doctrine of faith? The German American theologian Paul Tillich (1886–1965) writes, "Theology, as a function of the church, must serve the needs of the church. A theological system is supposed to satisfy two basic needs: the statement of the truth of the Christian message, and the interpretation of this truth for every new generation."[5] Theology is concerned with the truth of the Christian message, and this message must be pronounced anew in every generation so that it satisfies the demands of its time. The Lutheran theologian Christian Ernst Luthardt (1823–1902) writes, "While the church simply has to proclaim God's salvational revelation to humanity, theology has the task to justify academically the proclamation of the church."[6] This proclamation must be justified before the one who proclaims, meaning the church; then before the people who hear the proclamation; and finally before God, whose proclamation is being heard. This proclamation involves the three functions of theology: (1) to be critical of itself in propounding an ecclesial theology, (2) to be apologetic in expounding its content to the world in a logically coherent way, and (3) to be oriented doxologically before God, whom it praises with its work.

The *critical function of theology* is often misunderstood. In contrast to the attitude of many critical and liberal people, a theologian's purpose is not to show what we can no longer believe today. The opposite is true! The function of theology is to critically construe the content of our faith. Thoughtful Christian faith is founded on God's activity in history. Lest it degenerate into superstition, it must always critically reflect on its own history. As humans we can reflect on our actions and thoughts and do not primarily live instinctively as animals do. So, for instance, when a synod of the church convenes, it should ask how we can most effectively proclaim the gospel in word and deed under the changed conditions of the church and world. The conclusion of our deliberations cannot be that we must say something different. In so doing we would abandon the gospel. Yet often we must say the same thing differently so that the gospel does not sound antiquated.

The world does not stand still, and we should answer the questions not of yesterday but of today. The answer, too, should not be in a language of yesteryear, but of the present. If the critical dimension is missing, we are in danger of becoming anachronistic and a stumbling stone for people instead of a beacon that points to the way of the future. We would also overlook the

---

5. Paul Tillich, *Systematic Theology*, vol. 1, *Reason and Revelation: Being and God* (Chicago: University of Chicago Press, 1951), 3.

6. Chr. Ernst Luthardt, *Kompendium der Dogmatik*, 14th ed., ed. Robert Jelke (Leipzig: Dörffling & Franke, 1937), 5.

admonition of Paul: "For now we see in the mirror, dimly, but then we will see face to face. Now I know only in part; then I will know fully, even as I have been fully known" (1 Cor. 13:12). Since we are not yet in heaven, we must endeavor to explain the gospel in the most convincing way.

This critical dimension is not only directed in a self-critical way against ourselves; it is also at work in our association with those who are fellow sojourners. For instance, it was one of the great discoveries of the Roman Catholic Church at Vatican II (1962–65) that Christians of other traditions also have a serious interest in the gospel. The representatives of the Vatican Council recognized that these others are sisters and brothers in Christ, and therefore ecumenical cooperation is not the private hobby of some Christians but intrinsically belongs to every Christian. While listening to these other Christians, Vatican II rediscovered, among other things, how important the knowledge of the Bible is for all Christians and that the laity has a very important function in the church.

In ecumenical dialogue we become aware of how others see us, and we learn that things we take as a matter of fact are not necessarily so. Lutherans, for instance, take for granted that Christ is really present in, with, and under bread and wine at the Lord's Supper. In ecumenical dialogue, however, Roman Catholic partners questioned this belief, to the surprise of the Lutherans. They concluded that since Lutherans do not say how Christ is actually present in the Lord's Supper, they did not believe in the real presence of Christ. Only the assurance by the Lutherans that it is Christ's own business how he is present convinced the Roman Catholics that Lutherans take the bodily presence of Christ as seriously as they do. Therefore a presumed difference was abolished, and both parties grew closer together.

The *apologetic function of theology* is also often misunderstood. It does not mean that Christians should apologize that we are still around, but that we should heed 1 Peter 3:15–16: "Always be ready to make your defense to anyone who demands from you an accounting for the hope that is in you; yet do it with gentleness and reverence." Apologetics also does not mean throwing mud at each other. But we should explain to everyone who wants to know, in an intellectually convincing way, what we believe and why we believe it. It is of utmost importance to explain our faith in an understandable and convincing manner, because Christianity is often rejected out of ignorance or misinformation. There are many people, especially natural scientists, who believe that faith in the God who created the world and still maintains it excludes a biological understanding of the development of life, and vice versa. Yet even Charles Darwin (1809–82), who promulgated the theory of evolution, thought that God had created everything from one species or from several species.[7] Therefore it comes as no surprise that the American popular scientist John Fiske (1842–1901) claimed, "Evolution is God's way of doing things."[8]

In our apologetic endeavors we relate God's self-disclosure to our world and ask which conceptuality is most appropriate for today. Since the world continuously changes, this is an ever new task. We can discern this, for example, in the creation narratives in Genesis 1 and 2. The narrative in Genesis 2 mirrors the experience of the Israelites in the climate of the steppe in Palestine. The Israelites depended on God sending rain for something to grow and thrive. The red earth reminded them of their own skin, which was tanned by wind and weather, and also of the fact that they came from dust and returned to dust. Nevertheless, they were commanded to cultivate the earth and to integrate the animals into their own sphere of life by giving the animals names. Yet the drudgery of daily life eventuated through human sinfulness and therefore could not be attributed to God.

When the Israelites entered the Babylonian captivity, this creation narrative no longer sufficed to explain the Israelite faith in God the creator. The Babylonians were convinced that the stars, sun, and moon had considerable influence on the destiny of every person. Furthermore, they thought that the god Marduk had created the earth by killing the goddess Tiamat and forming the world from her body. It was the task of humans to be servants of the gods. Against these ideas the Israelites affirmed in Genesis 1 that the world could have come into being only through their God, who in unique sovereignty had created everything through God's word, including the sun, the moon, and the stars. These heavenly bodies were not powers in their own right but only fulfilled the functions for which they were designated by God. Moreover, humans were not servants of God but were created in God's image and as God's representatives. In God's name and according to God's intentions, they were to become stewards of creation. In this new situation of the Babylonian exile, the confession of God the creator had to be reformulated in confrontation with the Babylonian creation myths.

The apologetic function of theology does not demonstrate that the Christian faith is true, because faith is always founded on trust and not on empirical knowledge. But this function attempts to explain the faith in the most convincing way so that everybody can understand what this faith in God is all about. Therefore apologetics invites all kinds of questions that move human hearts

7. Cf. Charles Darwin, *On the Origin of Species* (1859), in *The Works of Charles Darwin*, ed. Paul H. Barrett, and R. B. Freeman (London: Pickering, 1988), 15:346–47.

8. As quoted in Lyman Abbott, *Reminiscences* (Boston: Houghton Mifflin, 1897), 460.

and minds. By so doing it need not be afraid that it surrenders to unbelief. Since God has endowed humans with reason, Christians are always summoned to understand their own faith in order not to indulge in credulity.

The *doxological function of theology* results from the very exposition of the Christian faith. We are to glorify God with all that we do, which includes our exposition of what and in whom we believe. Though God does not need us, he accepts our service to explain in the best possible way God and God's working. From the very beginning, the Christian faith was no private enterprise but was transmitted into the world in word and deed. This missionary activity serves to glorify God and to make him known to all humanity. Theological reflection is not conducted to glorify us or to increase the influence of Christianity; it is conducted only for God's sake and for the sake of the gospel. Theology therefore is fundamental to being a Christian. It belongs essentially to the Christian faith and to the glorification of God. As Christians we owe it to God to make God and God's deeds known to everybody in the best possible way.

Our whole life is intrinsically theological, whether we think so or not. We may do something in a certain way because we have always done it that way, or because we have fun doing it, or because it is the simplest way of doing it. Each of these motivations has theological consequences. We always act theologically, and the question is whether our actions are congruent with God's will.

Theological considerations show us what kind of theology is behind our activities and those of the church. Theological thinking therefore is the intentional attempt to raise into consciousness the motivations behind our actions. For instance, we can fall prey to working for righteousness' sake without knowing why this approach is wrong. Yet when we realize the problematic aspect of this attitude through theological reflection, we can attempt to avoid working for righteousness in our actions. This means that theological reflection does not automatically make us better people, but in applying it we can at least attempt to avoid mistakes. Even our best theology is not perfect, because we are sinful people living in the sinful context of this world. Theology is always on the way—on the way to articulating more convincingly the unchangeable gospel. Since theological work is always fragmentary, we are dependent on God's assistance and on God's forgiveness of our theological mistakes. This saves us from self-assuredness. As theologians we live by God's grace to be granted the right insight into God's activities. But theology remains a barren shell if it is not filled by God's self-disclosure as its norm and content.

Yet how can we still talk about God's self-disclosure in a world shaped by reason? Here we turn to the topic of revelation.

2

REVELATION

Revelation has become problematic because our world is shaped by the factual. The concept of revelation implies something of a surprise, while the transcendent content of revelation seems to avoid a precise description. How can we as humans talk about God, who is neither detectable nor describable in the space-time continuum of our world? Can revelation even mediate something otherwise inaccessible to us? Finally, why should we prefer the revelation of Christ to other revelations?

Strictly speaking, revelation is never revelation about something but self-mediation. Even when I say that something has been a revelation to me, I mean that I have realized something. Revelation means that something or someone has encountered me. In God's revelation God does not impart to us this and that information, but God imparts God's self. God, who is not limited by space, time, and matter, imparts God's self in these limiting categories. On the one hand, these categories facilitate God's self-mediation, but on the other hand, God makes God's self dependent on our interpretation because God's self-mediation becomes a phenomenon occurring in our world. Our interpretation, which always occurs through us human beings, naturally can contain mistakes. Therefore the documents speaking of such a revelation always contain contradictory assertions. For instance, the New Testament witnesses claimed that Jesus is the expected Messiah, while the Pharisees and the scribes denied this. Such contradictory explanations are especially noticeable in general revelation.

General Revelation

Paul writes concerning the heathens, "For what can be known about God is plain to them, because God has shown it to them. Ever since the creation of the world his eternal power and divine nature, invisible though they are, have been understood and seen through the things he has made" (Rom. 1:19–20). For Martin Luther it was a matter of fact that by employing one's reason one could recognize God in nature. The intelligent design movement claims in a similar way that there is a designer behind the creation with its finely tuned natural laws. The psalmist, too, confesses, "Fools say in their hearts, 'There is no God'" (Ps. 14:1). In the philosophical tradition one also talks about an almighty, omnipresent, and eternal God. The philosopher Immanuel Kant (1724–1804) admitted, "Two things fill the mind with ever new and increasing awe and admiration the more frequently and continuously reflection is occupied with them; the starred heaven above me and the moral law within me."[1] God's existence is therewith not proven, but at the most assumed. As Luther always emphasized, the recognition of God from creation or through human reason cannot lead to certitude. The philosopher Ludwig Feuerbach, for instance, claimed that the philosophical attributes that we ascribe to God are only human designations projected onto God; they express our desire to overcome our human limitations. General revelation does not lead to a certainty about God. At the most it leads to the feeling that there must be a God.

Karl Barth rejected the possibility of general revelation and called it unbelief. The Roman Catholic Church represents the opposite position and asserts in its *Catechism*, citing Vatican I, "Our holy mother, the Church, holds and teaches that God, the first principle and last end of all things, can be known with certainty from the created world by the natural light of human reason."[2] If we concede that with our reason we can know that God is, we still cannot know who this God really is and how God relates to us. To gain that knowledge we need God's self-disclosure in Jesus Christ.

It is not insignificant that all religions avoid giving the impression that revelation is only a human discovery, as is suggested by the saying, "That was a real revelation for me." In the religious context revelation is not just a new and surprising experience but also something that transcends our own possibilities. If we take this transcendence seriously, then any natural revelation is denied. Something or someone that cannot be reached by us is revealed in our world,

1. Immanuel Kant, *Critique of Practical Reason*, in *The Philosophy of Kant: Immanuel Kant's Moral and Political Writings*, ed. Carl J. Friedrich (New York: Random House, Modern Library, 1993), 288 (conclusion).
2. *Catechism of the Catholic Church* (New York: Doubleday, 1995), 20 (par. 36).

in our space-time configuration. For instance, when at the first Pentecost the Holy Spirit was poured out on the disciples, Scripture reports that "a sound like the rush of a violent wind" came, and "divided tongues, as of fire, appeared among them, and a tongue rested on each of them" (Acts 2:2–3). The Holy Spirit, who is not contained in space and time, now becomes visible in our space-time configuration in material objects, in those tongues of fire. Immediately the question arises whether these material objects are the only reality and whether that which is revealed, meaning the Holy Spirit, is not rather wishful thinking. Therefore some of those present could sneer and say, "They are filled with new wine" (Acts 2:13). This skeptical response is at least logically justified, since we are confined to our space-time configuration and must attempt to explain all our experiences within the categories of that configuration.

In his antinomies or contradictions of pure reason, Kant shows that such a judgment that limits itself purely to this world dare not exclude other possibilities of interpretation. For example, reason can prove on the one hand that our world had a beginning in space and time, and on the other hand it can prove the opposite, that it had no beginning in space and time. The thought of a beginning of space and time goes beyond our space-time configuration by claiming a beginning of that configuration. Since our human reason is the measure only of all *things*, it cannot transcend the world of things, meaning our space-time configuration. Any assertions that go beyond this—for instance, the claim that the tongues of fire were manifestations of the Holy Spirit, or the opposite claim that they were not—cannot be empirically proven. With the instruments available to us, we can prove neither that revelation has occurred nor that it has not occurred. Denying revelation is as much an assertion of faith as affirming revelation.

With this conclusion we are not confronted with an either/or as if, for instance, we threw a coin in the air that would land either heads or tails. When God discloses God's self in Jesus, he confronts his listeners with the claim that "the time is fulfilled, and the kingdom of God has come near; repent, and believe in the good news" (Mark 1:15). God's self-disclosure confronts those who are met by it and demands that they make a decision for or against this self-disclosure. This means revelation does not occur in neutral objectivity but always confronts us in an existential encounter. This is not surprising, because if revelation is really the self-disclosure of God and not human self-deception, it leads to an encounter with God as the ground of our being. A decision against it would lead to estrangement from God, but a decision for it would mean a closer relationship with God. But is reason then left out?

Reason comes in at two points. First, any claim of a self-disclosure must be carefully investigated. Often the claim has been made that a miracle occurred, which then turned out to be a hoax. Similarly, the claim of self-disclosure can be a pious fraud or self-deception. To rule out such possibilities, reason must do its job. Once one has reached the conviction that a divine self-disclosure really has occurred, then reason must draw the necessary conclusion. In contrast to the possibility of a self-disclosure, however, the actuality of a self-disclosure cannot be proven or rejected on grounds of reason. Here we encounter the limits of our human reason.

Special Revelation

What is the place value of God's self-disclosure in Jesus Christ? According to John 14:6, Jesus says, "I am the way, and the truth, and the life. No one comes to the Father except through me." Does this mean that besides the Christian religion all others are only unbelief as Karl Barth claimed? This certainly cannot be the case with the pious Israelites, because Paul does not just call Abraham "our ancestor according to the flesh" (Rom. 4:1) but also holds him up as an "example of the faith" (Rom. 4:12). Martin Luther even mused that the Muslims know much about God—for instance, that God is creator, redeemer, and judge. Luther then specified, however, that this knowledge was outside knowledge of God. In Jesus God has disclosed his heart, so we know how God relates to us. Jesus as the Son of God, as the human face of God, shows us the way to the Father. This Christocentric approach, knowledge of God through God's self-disclosure in Jesus Christ, is central to Lutheran teaching. Barth, however, in his voluminous *Church Dogmatics*, starts with the doctrine of the Word of God and then continues with the doctrine of God. The Lutheran theologian Paul Althaus (1888–1966), who alongside Werner Elert (1885–1954) and Walter Künneth (1901–97) is a representative of the Erlangen School of the twentieth century, starts in his *Christian Truth* with considerations of primal revelation in history, human thinking, and nature. Althaus then continues with the actual salvational revelation that focuses on "God's saving activity in Jesus Christ."[3] Werner Elert in his *The Christian Faith* presents a similar Christocentric approach.[4]

The encounter with Jesus and his message is central and normative for our knowledge of God and for knowing "that we are from the truth" (1 John 3:19). God's self-disclosure in Jesus Christ therefore becomes normative for

3. Paul Althaus, *Die Christliche Wahrheit. Lehrbuch der Dogmatik*, 5th ed. (Gütersloh: Gerd Mohn, 1959), 102–47.

4. Werner Elert, *Der christliche Glaube. Grundlinien der Lutherischen Dogmatik*, 4th ed. (Hamburg: Furche, 1956).

any other claim or any self-disclosure. The authors of the New Testament were convinced that the God of the Old Testament identified the self-disclosure with Jesus of Nazareth and vice versa. They then concluded that the self-disclosure of God has unsurpassable significance because God has disclosed God's own self in an unsurpassable way, namely, in a human being. For us human beings, God cannot mediate God's own self to us in any better way than in a human being. Therefore we must deny the allegation that there are further revelations beyond Jesus. This does not mean that God has ceased to make God's self known today, but that God's self-disclosure today does not go beyond what we have experienced in Jesus of Nazareth. If there were further revelations, the revelation in Jesus Christ would be relativized; it would be one among others.

The question of whether this self-disclosure is exclusive, ruling out any other revelations, cannot be easily answered. For instance, the British philosopher of religion John Hick (1922–2012) talks about a "Copernican revolution," saying that because God and not the Christian faith is at the center of the universe, we must recognize that all religions, including the Christian faith, focus on God. The various religions are answers to the ultimate, answers that are conditioned by cultural factors. With this claim, Hick has certainly made an important point. As the eminent church historian Adolf von Harnack (1851–1930) asserted, it was the task of Jesus to point to God the Father. It is also important to recognize that religions are influenced by their environment and, conversely, that they have an impact on their environment. In the West we are influenced by the analytical Latin medium, as shown, for instance, in the emphasis on the doctrine of justification. In Eastern Christendom, where Greek was the dominant language, the unifying process is emphasized, as we see in the notion of *theosis* (in the process of salvation the human being becomes more and more divine). Yet when Hick concludes that in the interchange between religions and their environment the religions are merely different answers to the ultimate, to God, he goes beyond the verifiable.

Admittedly, every religion has knowledge of God. Yet this knowledge is not equally emphasized. The Roman Catholic theologian Karl Rahner (1904–84) talked about "anonymous Christians." By this he meant non-Christians who conduct themselves in their faith in such a way that, as Rahner said, God is present in them toward salvation.[5] Yet one should not reduce God's history with humanity to the present time, as Hick and other pluralists do. As the Letter to the Hebrews reminds us, "Long ago God spoke to our ancestors in many and various ways by the prophets, but in these last days he has spoken

5. Karl Rahner, "Christianity and the Non-Christian Religions," in *Theological Investigations*, vol. 5, *Later Writings*, trans. K. H. Kruger (Baltimore: Helicon, 1966), 131.

to us by a Son, whom he appointed heir of all things, through whom he also created the worlds" (Heb. 1:1–2). There is a long history of God with humanity, as we can perceive in the Old Testament. First, the Israelites venerated other gods; then God gave knowledge of God's self through material items such as the burning bush, through dreams as with Jacob and the ladder, through a voice as in the call to Isaiah, through an angel as with Abraham, and through animals as with Balaam's encounter with God. But now, as Hebrews states, the situation is different, because God has made known God's human face through God's Son.

In the apocalyptic period of early Judaism, as the centuries around the time of Christ are often called, many thought the end of the world was near. Many figures besides Jesus made messianic claims, such as the Jewish liberation fighter Simon ben Koseba, better known as Bar Kokhba (meaning "the son of a star"), who led a rebellion against the Romans in AD 132–135. Yet only in the life and destiny of Jesus can we discern that the long-expected end time has commenced. Jesus, for instance, claimed that through him "the blind received their sight, the lame walk, the lepers are cleansed, the deaf hear, the dead are raised, the poor have the good news brought to them" (Luke 7:22). Here Jesus took the Old Testament promises connected to the time of salvation (see Isa. 35:5–6) and turned them toward himself. He revealed in his words and actions that the time of salvation had begun. What had been expected for such a long time and had always been projected into the future was actually dawning in Jesus. Therefore Jesus could say that the kingdom of God was in the midst of his audience. He was the turning point of history. This fact is also evident in the beginning of the Christian community. Jesus' followers did not remember him out of pious feelings. Rather, under the impression of the Easter events, those who had encountered the proclaimer now suddenly proclaimed. Jesus was recognized and made known as the Messiah.

In the apocalyptic period the resurrection of the dead was understood to be the beginning point of the end-time events, and therefore the resurrection of Jesus gained central importance. We read in the New Testament that through Christ the Holy Spirit is "the pledge of our inheritance toward redemption" (Eph. 1:14), meaning the inheritance of life eternal. With the resurrection of Christ, the apocalyptic hopes were not simply verified; they became the presupposition of our own resurrection and thereby the hope that "all will be made alive in Christ" (1 Cor. 15:22). Therefore the apocalyptic *idea* of the resurrection was transformed into the Christian *hope* of the resurrection. Christ is not only the turning point but also the goal of history, because at the end nothing more can occur than that which has already begun in Christ. Christians, too, though they still live under the conditions of this world, already participate in this new reality: "If anyone is in Christ, there is a new creation: everything old has passed away; see, everything has become new!" (2 Cor. 5:17).

The emphasis on the unsurpassability of God's self-disclosure in the person and destiny of Jesus of Nazareth does not contradict the insight that God has also made God's self known in other religions. Yet the history of religion outside the Judeo-Christian history does not simply come out of that particular history, nor does the history of human sinfulness. Rather, the history of humanity, despite its sinful separation from God, is moved toward God, to whom humanity owes everything. Though some religions emphasize human activity to overcome our existential separation from God, all religions somehow retain the knowledge that we cannot save ourselves.

In addition, the emphasis on the unsurpassability of God's self-disclosure in Jesus Christ does not imply a rejection of other religions. The Christian proclamation expects those who encounter that proclamation to make a decision; and as far as we know, such a decision has consequences beyond this life. But the Christian faith is not a doctrine concerning the destiny of other people. Since God has shown in Jesus Christ that God is holy and merciful, we may hope—though we do not know for sure—that those who have never completely experienced God's self-disclosure in Jesus Christ will not be eternally separated from God. This means that God's self-disclosure becomes a source of hope for all and brings clarity to our understanding of God. Why God's self-disclosure occurred the way it did, we cannot discern by reason. It remains a secret of God's providence.

3

SCRIPTURE

The Bible, or Holy Scripture, is normative for all of Christendom. It is the wellspring from which faith lives and by which faith is strengthened. Next to Scripture are other sources, including tradition and confessional writings. Tradition is important because it shows us that we live in a historical context, one that we must acknowledge. Furthermore, we learn through tradition that many of our own questions were posed and often answered long ago. Yet tradition must always be measured against the Bible, the source that made possible the Christian tradition. Confessional writings can also serve as a guide for the Christian faith, helping us to distinguish important points from less important ones. Yet these writings cannot become substitutes for the Bible. As the Lutheran confessional writings state, "We believe, teach, and confess that the only rule and guiding principle according to which all teachings and teachers are to be evaluated and judged are the prophetic and apostolic writings of the Old and New Testaments alone."[1]

The writings of the Bible are far from uniform. They contain poetry (such as the Psalms), letters (such as Paul's), legal prescriptions (such as the laws of purity), and narratives (such as the exodus from Egypt). Luther called the Old Testament law "the *Sachsenspiegel* of the Jews," that is, the law that primarily concerned the Israelites, just as the Saxon law applied chiefly to the Saxons. Therefore Luther distinguished between the Bible's *center*—that

---

1. *The Epitome of the Formula of Concord* 1, in *The Book of Concord: The Confessions of the Evangelical Lutheran Church*, ed. Robert Kolb and Timothy J. Wengert (Minneapolis: Fortress, 2000), 486.

which gives impetus to the Christian faith—and its *periphery*—items which have little or nothing to do with the Christian faith. Nevertheless, taken as a whole, all biblical writings are a witness to God's self-disclosure in history. Since the biblical writings are so different, having been composed for very different occasions, one must explain them historically if one wants to discern their proper meaning. Against the fourfold use of Scripture (allegorical, a meaning in the nonliteral sense; moral, a meaning for practical life; anagogical, a meaning for eternal life; and historical, a meaning from its historical perspective), Luther emphasized only its literal and historical significance. A scriptural passage can be properly understood only in its respective historical context. One cannot take a passage out of its historical context and combine it imaginatively with other scriptural references and still claim that its proper meaning has been discerned. Scripture is not a crossword puzzle but must be understood in a contextual way. There it confronts us with the claim that it is God's Word. In this way the Bible is not a book like any other.

The Formation of the New Testament

At the time of Jesus the New Testament did not yet exist. When Jesus talks about the Scriptures (Matt. 21:42; 22:29), he is referring to the Old Testament writings. Sometimes he specifically mentions "the law and the prophets" (Matt. 5:17; 7:12; etc.), referring to the Pentateuch (the first five books of the Bible) and the prophetic writings. But the New Testament is not a commentary on the Old Testament. Its content is Jesus of Nazareth as the Christ. This confession of Jesus as the Christ, the anointed one or Messiah, is the origin of the New Testament and the connecting link with the Old.

In New Testament scholarship there is no agreement as to what extent the New Testament preserves the person and message of Jesus. On one end of the spectrum are minimalists, who claim that one can discern, at most, only some precepts of Jesus' proclamation and his violent death; on the other end of the spectrum, literalists assert that each word uttered by Jesus in the New Testament was actually spoken the way it is written and that each of the actions reported took place exactly as they are narrated. Both minimalists and literalists agree that Jesus and his proclamation are the focal point of the New Testament and its origin. One must remember that the New Testament Scriptures presuppose faith in Jesus as the Christ and attempt to convey that to their listeners or readers. Though these writings contain historical facts about the life and activity of Jesus, they were written not with the intention of providing a news report or a biography but to convince the listeners of the truthfulness of the faith in Jesus as the Christ.

From the beginning of the church there existed an oral tradition that, if we are to believe Papias of Hierapolis (d. ca. 140), was possibly accorded higher value than the already existing written sources of the second century.[2] As both the apostles and the disciples of the apostles died and many pseudo-Christian (predominantly Gnostic) writings claimed apostolic authority, the New Testament writings were gradually canonized. The New Testament canon (rule or measuring stick) evolved to protect against mistaken renderings or even intentional distortion of the gospel. For instance, Marcion (ca. 85–ca. 160) had eliminated among other things all Old Testament references from the New Testament. The intention of canonization was to include only those writings that "measured up" to the teaching of the church at large. A decisive criterion of canonization was therefore that a writing be read and recognized by the whole church and used in the worship service. Another criterion for inclusion in the canon of the New Testament was authorship by an apostle or the disciple of an apostle. The Muratorian Canon, named after its discoverer Lodovico Antonio Muratori (1672–1750), is a copy of the first known list of canonized New Testament writings. The list can be dated to the end of the second century and does not include 3 John, James, and 1 and 2 Peter. It also contains some writings that are not in our New Testament today, including the Apocalypse (Revelation) of Peter, which the canon states was not being used in worship. The first time we encounter a list of the twenty-seven New Testament writings in our canon today is in 367, when Bishop Athanasius of Alexandria (ca. 295/98–373) circulated his thirty-ninth Easter letter. Yet into the fifth century the church in Syria used as a canonical book a synopsis of the four Gospels, the *Diatessaron* by the Syrian theologian Tatian (ca. 125–ca. 185). This most likely was done out of a certain loyalty to their local theologian.

Origin of the Christian Bible

The Christian designation *New Testament* or *New Covenant* presupposes an Old Testament or an Old Covenant. This designation implies both continuity and discontinuity. The New Testament emphasizes that God made a new covenant that replaced the old one (2 Cor. 3:6). This covenant was established through the blood of Christ (Mark 14:24). At the same time, the early

---

2. Eusebius, *Church History* 3.39.4, in *NPNF*[2] 1:171, where he quotes Papias. Yet some surmise that by "written sources" Papias means "interpretations" of the Gospel accounts.

Christians did not discard the Hebrew writings but accepted them as the Old Testament. They saw God's covenant with Israel as the predecessor of the new covenant and saw themselves as the new Israel in continuity with the Israel of old. It was a matter of course that in the mid-second century the ideas of Marcion were rejected since he renounced the "Jewish god" and "purified" the New Testament by eliminating all of its Old Testament references.

For Christians, the references to the Old Testament were indispensible because the God of the Jews, the God of the Old Testament, was the Father of Jesus Christ, and the Hebrew Scriptures pointed to Christ, as Jesus himself had claimed (John 5:39; Acts 10:43). Therefore the Old Testament was seen as containing the promises, and the New Testament as containing the fulfillment of those promises. We must keep this intention in mind when we encounter Old Testament passages that the early Christians claimed referred to Christ and that are difficult for us to understand today (e.g., Gal. 4:22–32). Giving up the term Old Testament in favor of Hebrew Bible or Hebrew Scriptures, as is often suggested today, is a dangerous move. Not only is the concept of the New Testament no longer understandable, but the suggestion is also made that there are several writings or bibles which are of equal value. By understanding the Hebrew Scriptures as the Christian Old Testament, the church avoided the implication that it was an alternative to the Jewish faith or a rival religion to Judaism. By accepting the promises given to Israel and seeing them as fulfilled in Jesus as the Christ, the church maintained continuity between the old and the new and also created a dynamic structure in the Christian faith. If one forgoes the concept of the Old Testament, not only is the continuity endangered, but so also is the claim of fulfillment in the New Testament.

Scripture and Tradition

As noted above, the oral tradition existed at the beginning of the Christian faith. This tradition was largely identical to the *kerygma* (the Christian proclamation, or the gospel of or about Jesus Christ). Paul refers to tradition at two decisive points, with reference to the institution of the Lord's Supper and the actuality of the resurrection of Christ (1 Cor. 11:23; 15:3). Though he claims that both traditions came directly from the Lord, it is clear that they were handed on by humans. Ultimately, tradition is always from the Lord, whether it is mediated through humans or not. It is so reliable that neither Paul nor "an angel from heaven" (Gal. 1:8) could have more authority.

Once this oral tradition gained canonic authority, another practice became more and more important. To remove the authoritative character of Gnostic wisdom literature, the Christians delineated the Christian truth and its authority by pointing to an unbroken chain of tradition. For instance, in the second century Clement of Rome (ca. 50–97 or 101) wrote, "The apostles have preached the Gospel to us from the Lord Jesus Christ; Jesus Christ [has done so] from God. Christ therefore was sent forth by God, and the apostles by Christ. Both these appointments, then, were made in an orderly way, according to the will of God" (1 Clem. 42). In this, continuity was maintained and nothing new could be taught. Another guarantee is mentioned by Vincent of Lérins (d. ca. 450). He wrote in his *Commonitory* (*Admonition*), "Moreover, in the Catholic Church itself, all possible care must be taken that we hold that faith which has been believed everywhere, always, by all."[3] This does not mean that faith can never change and is static, but rather that it cannot grow in a unilateral way. Its growth must be approved by everybody, by the church at large. Until the high Middle Ages there was common agreement that the faith of the people must always be measured by Scripture.

When the Reformation came, it claimed Scripture as its sole base and norm, and rejected tradition altogether. John Calvin, for instance, went to such extremes that he outlawed church organs because they were not mentioned in the Bible. In contrast, the Council of Trent (1545–63) claimed that tradition must be received and held in veneration with an equal affection of piety and reverence as Scripture itself. As the council stated, it clearly perceived "that this truth and instruction [pertaining to faith and morals] are contained in the written books and in the unwritten traditions . . . as having been dictated either by Christ's own word of mouth, or by the Holy Spirit."[4] Tradition was therewith accorded the same value as Scripture.

This position was maintained in Vatican II. Although we read in the *Dogmatic Constitution on Divine Revelation* that the gospel "is the source of all saving truth and moral teaching," we read in the same document: "Consequently, it is not from sacred Scripture alone that the Church draws first certainty about everything which has been revealed. Therefore both sacred tradition and sacred Scripture are to be accepted and venerated with the same sense of devotion and reverence."[5] Here the formulation of Trent is repeated. But then we read in the same paragraph: "For both of them, flowing from the same divine wellspring, in a certain way merge in a unity and tend toward

3. Vincent of Lérins, *Commonitory* 2.6, in *NPNF*[2] 11:132.

4. Council of Trent, *Session IV* (April 8, 1546), no. 1501/783 according respectively to the new and old numbering system in Denzinger-Schönmetzer, *Enchiridion Symbolorum*, 34th ed. (Freiburg: Herder, 1967). http://www.catecheticsonline.com/SourcesofDogma8.php.

5. *Dogmatic Constitution on Divine Revelation* 7, in *The Documents of Vatican II*, ed. Walter M. Abbott (New York: Guild Press, 1966), 115.

the same end."[6] This could still mean that tradition is somehow contained in Scripture. But we remember the Roman Catholic dogmas of the bodily assumption of Mary into heaven (1950) and papal infallibility (1870), which cannot be deduced from Scripture. This means that Vatican II's identification of Scripture and tradition can also lead to separate doctrinal decisions.

As mentioned earlier, the explanation of Scripture can never be absolutely objective or neutral. Baptists as well as Jehovah's Witnesses and Lutherans call Scripture the only source and norm of faith. But the Bible is always read and understood from a certain angle or with a certain hermeneutical key. We encounter the same in everyday life. No two people see something exactly the same way. Does this mean that the traditions in which we stand or our viewpoints lead to an unavoidable biblical relativism, as some postmodern people claim? This danger arises when our interpretations are no longer measured by Scripture and we become independent agents. Then our own perspectives become the infallible center, and whoever contradicts us is excluded. This was the case in the major schisms in the Middle Ages between the church of the East and the church of the West and in the time of the Reformation between the churches of the Reformation and the so-called old believers who did not join the Reformation. One's own perspective was accorded normative value, and the common truth of the gospel was relegated to secondary status. This means that neither "Scripture alone" nor "Scripture plus tradition" can protect us against error.

In this situation Martin Luther found a way that we can still pursue today. On the one hand, he emphasized Scripture alone. But he did not view everything in Scripture as on the same level; instead, he distinguished between the center and the periphery. Unbeknownst to him, he went back to that which had led to the formation of the canon. We remember that most important Scriptures were first accepted into the canon, and then gradually those that were more on the fringe. In determining what was at the center, Luther started with that which had led to the formation of the New Testament Scriptures, namely, the proclamation of Jesus as the Christ, or as Luther said, the writings that "inculcate [*treiben*] Christ."[7] That which proclaims Christ most clearly is central; that which proclaims Christ less clearly moves toward the periphery; and that which does not proclaim Christ at all, Luther argued, does not belong in the canon. Therefore Luther was very harsh concerning the Letter of James because, as Luther asserted, this letter preaches the law and does not mention Christ's teachings even once.

6. Ibid.
7. Martin Luther, "Preface to the Epistles of St. James and St. Jude" (1522), in *LW* 35:396.

With this hermeneutical principle Luther could be very open to the tradition as long as it proclaimed Christ. He often referred to the church fathers, and especially to Augustine, not just because Luther had once been an Augustinian monk, but because Augustine emphasized that we have a future beyond this life only by grace and not through our own merits. This shows that for Luther the proclamation of Christ includes the affirmation that Christ offers salvation through grace alone. The apocryphal gospels, which often depict Jesus as a powerful miracle worker but are less interested in the salvation of humanity, have no right to be considered as proclamations of the gospel. Therefore they were not received into the canon.

But what is the place of the Old Testament? Here Luther made a very fitting remark: in the Old Testament "you will find the swaddling clothes and crib in which Christ lies."[8] Whoever does not know the promissory history of the Old Testament does not understand its fulfillment in the New Testament. Yet many passages in the Old Testament no longer pertain to us directly— for instance, how to build an altar or which animals are clean and unclean. Therefore Luther could call the Old Testament the *Sachsenspiegel* or the civil law of the Jews. Even concerning the Ten Commandments, or the Decalogue, Luther mused that God had inscribed on the heart of every person what God gave to the Jews through Moses on Mount Sinai. Indeed, we find similar commandments in many cultures because no community can survive, much less thrive, if commandments such as "you shall not kill" and "you shall not steal" are not followed by most people. But Luther thought that since the Ten Commandments came directly from God, they are better and less corrupted than the so-called natural law. Luther went on to show in his *Small Catechism* and in his *Large Catechism* how we should apply the Ten Commandments today.

We are separated from Luther's time not only by five hundred years but also by the Enlightenment. This movement brought about the historical-critical discovery and exposition of the Bible. Many people today do not regard the Bible as God's Word but as a literary document like any other. When we read Luther's *Lectures on Genesis*, which kept him busy for more than ten years (1535–45), we notice that at least in his worldview Luther was a child of his time. He held the same cosmology and prevalent superstitions as his peers. He never thought of himself as an infallible church father, even if he put forth his theological convictions with utmost emphasis. Nevertheless, we can still learn from him even with respect to the so-called historical criticism of the Bible. We remember that Luther translated the Bible into German from its original languages, Hebrew and Greek. If the Bible is God's Word, then it

8. Martin Luther, "Preface to the Old Testament" (1523), in *LW* 35:236.

would not suffice for him to translate the then popular Latin Vulgate edition of the Bible into German. Luther endeavored instead to translate the Bible from the original text to know exactly what this original text meant, here showing his historical understanding of the Bible. Furthermore, he did not read the Bible in a nonhistorical or fundamentalistic way, but distinguished between that which still pertains to us as Christians and that which no longer applies, as we saw for instance with his remark on the Old Testament law as the *Sachsenspiegel* of the Jews. The Old Testament showed for him the prehistory of the New Testament leading up to Christ (cf. the swaddling clothes and the crib). The New Testament must be interpreted from its central point: God in Christ.

The proper criterion of all books of the New Testament is whether they teach Christ. "What does not teach Christ is not apostolic, even though St. Peter or St. Paul does the teaching. Again, whatever preaches Christ would be apostolic, even if Judas, Annas, Pilate, and Herod were doing it."[9] Not all parts of the New Testament are of equal value. For a long time Luther had doubts about the relevance of the Revelation of John because it talks about Christ in such a mysterious way. He finally recognized its value as a document of church history that witnesses to the victory of the gospel. In all biblical criticism it is important that a text or a book be examined with regard to its relevance or its witness to Christ. If this Christocentric perspective is missing, then a historical-critical investigation has missed its mark. As Luther contended against the humanist Erasmus of Rotterdam, "Take Christ out of the Scriptures and what will you find left in them?"[10]

With regard to Scripture Luther presupposed that the Bible is not an unintelligible book. This is seen in his debate with Erasmus where Luther defended a twofold clarity of Scripture. First, there is an *external* clarity, which means that "nothing at all is left obscure or ambiguous, but everything that is in the Scriptures has been brought out by the Word into the most definite light, and published to all the world."[11] This means that Scripture is accessible to everybody, and everybody can understand it. There is no need for a special ecclesial teaching office to explain the Bible. Moreover, there is an *internal* clarity, because "no man perceives one iota of what is in the Scriptures unless he has the Spirit of God." The Word (of God) contained in the words discloses itself only when we are addressed by God. Though it was important for Luther and the other Reformers that we all have equal access to Scripture, we cannot

---

9. Luther, "Preface to the Epistles," in *LW* 35:396.
10. Martin Luther, *The Bondage of the Will* (1525), in *LW* 33:26.
11. Luther, *Bondage of the Will*, 33:28, for this and the following quotation.

command Scripture. As the Word of God it must disclose itself to us so that we understand its significance for our faith.

As mentioned above, Luther came to reject the fourfold use of Scripture popular in his time, which he had followed earlier in life. Especially in the controversy over the Lord's Supper with the Reformed wing of the Reformation (1525–29), Luther exclusively employed the literal use by asking what the literal significance of a certain passage was. In reading the Bible this way, one could slide into a literalistic view unless one remembers that each biblical text was written in a certain context and had a particular audience. For instance, the writer of the Gospel of Matthew wanted to show his readers that Jesus is indeed the fulfillment of the Old Testament promises. Luke, however, endeavored to point out that Jesus cares especially for those who are shortchanged in life. To understand a text we must first of all understand it in its original context. This type of reading does not suffice, however, because by doing this alone, we would be stuck in that original situation. The text also addresses us today, and most of us already have an idea what the text wants to say. As New Testament scholar Rudolf Bultmann (1884–1976) stated, "This preunderstanding is not closed but open, so that there can be an existential encounter with the text and an existential decision."[12] If the Bible is God's Word, we dare not violate it ideologically by adhering to the motto of some preachers: "I already know what I am going to preach, but I have not found the right text for my message." We must go to the text and be open to letting the Word convert our views by showing us that it is a living Word and not a dead text.

12. Rudolf Bultmann, "Is Exegesis without Presuppositions Possible?" in *New Testament and Mythology and Other Basic Writings*, ed. and trans. Schubert M. Ogden (Philadelphia: Fortress, 1984), 151.

PART 2

GOD THE CREATOR

The Old Testament witnesses to a God who not only acts in history but pushes history forward. God is not an idle God who has backed off from creation, but remains in and with it. During Old Testament times the fact that there is a God was taken for granted; therefore the psalmist says, "Fools say in their hearts, 'There is no God'" (Ps. 14:1). Yet today this is no longer the case. Whether in our own home or in nature, we tend to recognize only our own achievements and nothing of God's doing. Moreover, when confronted with the tragic events in nature and history, whether tsunamis or the Shoah (Holocaust), many people question whether there really is a God. Therefore we must first come to an understanding of what we mean by God.

4

GOD

It was simply taken for granted by Martin Luther and his contemporaries that there is a God and that this fact can be attested to by reason. But this assured assumption has dissipated today in the minds of many people. Many ask the question, if there is a God, then where or what is he? Is God a result of human imagination as Ludwig Feuerbach (1804–72) claimed and as Karl Marx (1818–83) and Friedrich Engels (1820–95) promulgated? Of course, God does not come into view in our world, nor is God part of this world. Immanuel Kant had already distinguished the world of the phenomena from the world of the noumena (things as they are in themselves). He asserted that reason can only research the phenomenal realm. This means that reason cannot by itself perceive God. Once we go beyond the phenomenal realm of things and ideas (attempting for instance to see whether the world had a beginning), then, so Kant asserted, reason can prove both possibilities: the world had a beginning and the world had no beginning. This antinomy or contradiction even applies to God, because we cannot answer by reason alone the question of whether there is a God. So what do the so-called proofs of the existence of God actually mean?

The Limits of Natural Reason

Whether we think of Plato or René Descartes (1596–1650), or Kant and Gottfried Wilhelm Leibniz (1646–1716), the most important representatives of the intellectual history of humanity have always concerned themselves with God and the possibility of proving God's existence. Yet they did not start in a neutral fashion. They always presupposed God's existence and then sought to explain that God's existence is agreeable with human reason. Typical of this approach is the famous scholastic theologian Anselm of Canterbury, whom we saw in chapter 1. Anselm states at the conclusion of his investigation in the *Proslogion*, "I thank You, good Lord, I thank You that what at first I believed through Your giving, now by Your enlightenment I also understand."[1] Therefore Anselm conducted his so-called ontological proof of God's existence in order to recognize the God in whom he already believed.

As we saw earlier, Anselm's *ontological proof* emphasizes that God is the one beyond whom nothing greater can be imagined. Such a God must exist by necessity, because God's existence pertains to God's perfection. Otherwise God would not be the one beyond whom nothing greater can be imagined. In contrast to Feuerbach, who centuries later claimed that God exists only in our desires, Anselm affirmed that actual existence necessarily pertains to God's perfection. Yet this claim was not without rebuttals. Immanuel Kant showed especially in his *Critique of Pure Reason* that Anselm had mixed up the logical predicate with the real one. Unlike God's omnipotence and omniscience, existence and being are not real predicates of God. One cannot make the transition from the idea of God's existence to the reality of God by attributing to God the predicate "existence," which God would need to be perfect. Kant's simple objection was this: "A hundred actual thalers [silver coins] do not contain the least [coin] more than a hundred possible thalers. . . . In the state of my assets, however, there is more in the case of a hundred actual thalers than in the case of the mere concept of them (i.e., the mere possibility)."[2] But Anselm had already considered this difference, acknowledging that there are things that can be thought of as either existent or not existent, for example, the one hundred thalers. Yet when one thinks of God as the one beyond whom nothing greater can be thought, then God's existence necessarily pertains to God because to think of God as nonexistent would be a contradiction in itself. For Anselm, these considerations were not strict proofs of the existence of God, and he conceded that one could think of God inappropriately, and then God's existence would not necessarily follow. Yet the person who thinks of God in a logically consistent way understands that nothing greater than God can be thought of, and therefore it follows that God is such a God "that not even in

---

1. Anselm of Canterbury, *Proslogion* 1.4, in *Anselm of Canterbury*, ed. and trans. Jasper Hopkins and Herbert Richardson (Toronto: Edwin Mellen, 1974), 95.
2. Immanuel Kant, *Critique of Pure Reason* (A 599 / B 627), unified ed., trans. Werner S. Pluhar, intro. Patricia Kitcher (Indianapolis: Hackett, 1996), 584.

thought can he be posited as not being."[3] Again, this theological argument served to clarify the God in whom Anselm really believed.

The *cosmological proof* starts with the notion that there is no effect without a cause, and therefore there must be a first cause that started everything. Thinking along these lines, Plato arrived at the notion of a "world soul" that set itself in motion and consequently moves everything else. His disciple Aristotle, however, believed that something in motion cannot be the initial cause of a chain of movements but rather is itself part of this chain. Therefore he asserted that at the beginning there must be an unmoved mover that sets everything in motion. But in order for this unmoved mover not to receive a reaction from the movements, Aristotle contended that there can be no bodily contact with this first mover, which must move everything by thought and desire. Aristotle's thought was so influential that Thomas Aquinas pursued the cosmological proof in four of his five proofs of the existence of God in his *Summa Theologica* (1266–73). Thomas wants us to consider that so far we have not seen anything in our world that has its existence in itself. Everything depends on something prior. Since everything in space and time is limited, there must be something unlimited that posits a beginning for these things. Even Kant admitted that the cosmological argument is the most natural and "the most convincing, not only for common sense, but even for speculative understanding."[4] Yet Kant also showed that neither through experience nor through pure reason can we decide whether there is such a first causation of a movement and an unmoved mover.

Another argument for God's existence is the *teleological proof*. This proof recognizes the beauty and harmony of the world and reasons that the world must have an intelligent creator because all of this could not have just accidentally arisen. Today this argument is continued in the so-called anthropic principle, which claims that through the fine-tuning of the natural constants and the laws in nature, everything is arranged in such a way that carbon-based life could arise at the end of the development.[5] In the intelligent design movement, this assertion is transformed into the argument that a designer must be behind the creation. The argument from design was already made at the conclusion of the eighteenth century by the British apologist and physico-theologian William Paley (1743–1805) in his best seller, *Evidences*.[6] Physico-theology

3. Anselm, *Proslogion* 4.

4. Kant, *Critique of Pure Reason* (A 604, B 632), 285.

5. John D. Barrow and Frank J. Tipler, *The Anthropic Cosmological Principle*, 2nd ed. (Oxford: Clarendon, 1987), 16.

6. William Paley, *Natural Theology: Or, Evidences of the Existence and Attributes of the Deity, Collected from the Appearances of Nature* (Boston: Gould and Lincoln, 1860), 10.

attempts to find a creator in nature by looking at the magnitude and beauty of creation. Kant said of this proof, "It is the oldest, the clearest, and the most accordant with common reason of mankind."[7] Paley compared nature with a clockwork so that we are to assume that the creation was made by a creator just like a clockmaker makes a clock. If things in nature are so precisely correlated to each other as are the cogs in a clockwork, then there could be at the most a world architect but not necessarily a God behind creation. Yet Kant himself confessed that "two things fill the mind with ever new and increasing admiration and awe, the oftener and more steadily we reflect on them: the starry heavens above me and the moral law within me."[8] This leads us to the next so-called proof.

Though Kant criticized the traditional proofs, he himself introduced the *moral proof*. Martin Luther already was convinced that everybody knows there is a judge whom we must all face. Kant, however, understood God as a proposition of practical reason. Since we all know how we ought to conduct ourselves in this world but never reach moral perfection, the discrepancy between knowledge and action must somehow be overcome. Therefore there must be a further development to perfection beyond this life. And for this to be the case, we must presuppose God because only God can grant us immortality and eternal perfection. Kant says, "As a consequence, the postulate of the possibility of a highest derived good (the best world) is at the same time the postulate of the reality of a highest original good, namely, the existence of God."[9] Without a God, everything in our world would remain unfair and incomplete. Naturally, each human being wants to believe that in the end everything will come out well and be in harmony. But Kant knows that he cannot really deliver a proof of God's existence. It remains a proposition, an assertion of something he hopes to be true.

Finally, the *historical proof* of God's existence proceeds from the fact that all people at all times have believed in the existence of God. But to deduce from that fact that there must be a God is unconvincing. One cannot conclude that the One believed in by faith indeed exists. Furthermore, we must consider that especially in the twentieth century Marxism promulgated an ideology, though of limited duration, that deliberately denied God. The almost universal materialism of our present time has also led many people simply to forget about God. Therefore we could conclude from the historical proof that people

7. Kant, *Critique of Pure Reason* (A 623 / B 651), 293.
8. Immanuel Kant, *Critique of Practical Reason*, in *The Philosophy of Kant: Immanuel Kant's Moral and Political Writings*, ed. Carl J. Friedrich (New York: Random House, 1993), 288 (conclusion).
9. Kant, *Critique of Practical Reason* 2.5 (A 226).

once believed in God but that this faith diminished more and more, so that in the end there is atheism, life as if God did not exist.

What can we conclude from the so-called proofs of God's existence? First of all, we have seen that one cannot prove God. As limited beings we can prove only that which is on our own level, that is, that which is limited. Conversely, God's existence cannot be disproven by empirical means, be it by science or pure reason. If there is a God, as Christians and many other people believe, then we cannot grasp God unless God allows God's own self to be grasped.

Who or What Is God?

When we ask who or what God is, we could adduce the so-called attributes of God, which say that God is omnipotent, omniscient, omnipresent, and eternal. These attributes are very rarely found in the Bible. We detect God's omnipotence, for instance, in the promise of God to Abraham and Sarah that they would have a son. God asked the doubting Sarah, "Is anything too wonderful for the LORD?" (Gen. 18:14). Similarly, in announcing the birth of Jesus, the angel says to Mary, "Nothing will be impossible with God" (Luke 1:37). In both cases, the emphasis on God's omnipotence serves only to assure that God can fulfill the promises God has made, but not to state that God can do or wants to do whatever God pleases. Mostly, the aforementioned attributes of God are taken over from the philosophical understanding of God. They became popular through the Neoplatonic philosopher Pseudo-Dionysius the Areopagite (ca. 500), who argued that one could talk about God not directly but in a negative way (*via negativa*). One starts with human possibilities and then denies them (such as mortal/immortal) or exceeds them in a superlative way (such as mighty/almighty, knowing/all-knowing, etc.) to attribute them to God. When we start with human possibilities and confer them in one way or another to God, how can we still avoid the charge of Feuerbach that God is a product of our human desires? Here the Bible has a very different approach. Since it is largely a document rendering the reflection of people who experienced God's activity in history, we can participate in these people's experiences.

The first and continuous experience of God in the Bible involves God's personal quality. God is not a person that one can depict. The Israelite prohibition of making pictures of God (Exod. 20:4), a prohibition taken over by the Muslims, attests to this. Yet God is an addressable and a responding "Thou," as we clearly see in the Psalms. This experience of God is rendered predominately with male attributes, but feminine attributes are interspersed— for example, in the verse, "All people may take refuge in the shadow of your

wings" (Ps. 36:7). Since God was not considered a fertility god, a sexual defi-
nition of God was foreign to the Israelites. Since God can be experienced in
a personal way but is no actual person, God cannot be limited like persons
are. As Psalm 139 poetically expresses, God is from eternity to eternity, and
from God nothing is hidden; God is everywhere present, and in the majesty
of God, God is experienced as holy.

God's holiness can be understood from Leviticus 11:44: "Sanctify yourselves
therefore, and be holy, for I am holy." Holiness is an attribute of God that we
should emulate, not a projection of a human attribute. Of course, in every
religion holiness is considered a trademark of God's majesty. In Leviticus,
however, it does not serve to demarcate God from us, but it should incite us
to godlike conduct. God's holiness also implies that we are not equal to God,
and therefore we dare not encounter him in a casual way. We must always
be mindful that in God we are confronted with the Creator and Lord of the
universe. Holiness also means that God is just.

The biblical emphasis on God's justice is not so much on the penal or judi-
cial aspect, though God will mete out what is right, but that there is a certain
divine way of action that we should emulate. The psalmist therefore says, "For
the LORD is righteous; he loves righteous deeds; the upright shall behold his
face" (Ps. 11:7). Justice is paired with God's wrath, primarily over those who
are unjust. Therefore we read in the New Testament, "It is a fearful thing to
fall into the hands of the living God" (Heb. 10:31). Yet something decisive has
occurred: "In Christ God was reconciling the world to himself, not counting
their trespasses against them, and entrusting the message of reconciliation
to us" (2 Cor. 5:19).

This readiness of God toward reconciliation is not something totally new.
Already the psalmist recognized, "But you, our Lord, are a God merciful and
gracious, slow to anger and abounding in steadfast love and faithfulness" (Ps.
86:15). It is a thoroughgoing characteristic of God's history with humanity that
God is merciful. The Old Testament history can be seen as one of the apostasy
of God's chosen people, yet God, even in threatening Israel with the day of
wrath, ultimately does not reject them. Instead, God promises to make "an
everlasting covenant" with Israel (Isa. 55:3). The Christians realized that this
promise found its fulfillment in Jesus, who was called the Christ, the human
face of God. Through his sacrificial death Christ made a new covenant, a new
testament, with humanity (cf. Mark 14:24).

If God is the one according to whose will everything ultimately occurs, how
can there be so much evil in this world? This issue of theodicy, of God's justice,
has always occupied the minds of people. In the Old Testament Job already
posed the question as to why so many bad things can happen to a good person.

He finally arrived at the insight that in confrontation with God's majesty it makes no sense to demand that God should justify his own actions (cf. Job 38–40). God is God, and this means he cannot be judged by our categories of good and evil. Kant, too, recognized that theodicy "is essentially nothing but the issue of our arrogant reason which thereby forgets its limits."[10]

In his treatise *The Bondage of the Will* (1525), Luther talks about the unsearchable will of God, or the hidden God who does not want to be known by us and whose ways are none of our business. "God must therefore be left to himself in his own majesty, for in this regard we have nothing to do with him."[11] The distinction between the hidden and the revealed wills of God, which comes out most clearly in *The Bondage of the Will*, is closely connected to Luther's understanding of the Godhead and the hiddenness of God's actions. Since God is God, we cannot discern God's activity unless he points us to that activity. God is active in a way that we do not expect or understand. Luther writes, "For the works of God must be hidden and never understood, even when it happens. But it is never hidden in any other way than under that which appears contrary to our conceptions and our ideas."[12] If we ponder why and how God has done this or that, or why he allows this or that, then we always end up in despair. We should not search for the hidden will of God. "This will is not to be inquired into, but reverently adored, as by far the most awe-inspiring secret of the Divine Majesty, reserved for himself alone."[13] Instead, we should cling to the preached and revealed will of God, through which we experience God as gracious and merciful. With these thoughts Luther wants to put an end to all the speculations about God and point to the gospel alone.

As Paul Althaus emphasized, the hiddenness of God "presupposes his self-attestation."[14] The God question is present in every human being because everybody needs something to which he or she ultimately clings. As limited beings we need something that has unlimited validity. Therefore Luther writes in his *Large Catechism*: "Anything on which your heart relies and depends, I say, that is really your God. . . . A 'god' is the term for that to which we are to look for all good and in which we are to find refuge in all need."[15] But then he adds: "If your faith and trust are right, then your God is the true one.

10. Immanuel Kant, *Über das Misslingen aller philosophischen Versuche in der Theodizee*, in *Werke in zehn Bänden*, ed. Wilhelm Weischedel, 9:105

11. Martin Luther, *The Bondage of the Will*, in *LW* 33:139.

12. Martin Luther, in a *scholium*, or comment, on Rom. 8:26, in *LW* 25:366.

13. Luther, *Bondage of the Will*, 33:139.

14. Paul Althaus, *Die christliche Wahrheit. Lehrbuch der Dogmatik*, 5th ed. (Gütersloh: Bertelsmann, 1959), 93.

15. Martin Luther, *The Large Catechism*, in *The Book of Concord*, 386, in his explanation of the first commandment.

Conversely, where your trust is false and wrong, there you do not have the true God." Decisive here is not that everybody has a God or something or someone that is regarded like a god, but that this God can be at our side regardless of what comes and therefore be a right God, or rather *the* right God.

In conclusion, returning again to the issue of theodicy, when we ask why there is so much evil in this world, it is actually of little value to know that God will ultimately overcome all that is evil. The recognition of God disclosed in Christ goes a decisive step further. As Paul joyfully proclaims, in Christ the new era has already dawned (cf. 1 Cor. 15:55–57). Therefore we sing in a hymn:

> Jesus comes, reason for eternal joy!
> Alpha and Omega, beginning and end stand there.
> Divinity and mankind unite both;
> Creator, how have you come so near to us humans!
> Sky and earth, tell the nations:
> Jesus comes, reason for eternal joy.[16]

---

16. *Evangelisches Gesangbuch*, hymn 66:1, Engl. trans., http://www.virtuallybaroque.com/trak1459.htm.

5

CREATION

Though creation is mentioned at the beginning of the Bible, it was not the most important topic in the Israelite faith in God. Similarly to us today, the Israelites had an existential interest in God. For them, the primary question was whether God was interested in their lives. Therefore the narratives of the patriarchs, which tell of God's care for Abraham, Isaac, and Jacob, the rescue of the Israelites from the slavery in Egypt, and the covenant of God with God's people, are actually the oldest part of the Old Testament. First, God was recognized as the one who acts in the history of individual people and in the history of the people Israel. Especially during Babylonian captivity, when the Israelites were confronted with the creation mythology of the Babylonians and their gods, the necessity arose to ponder who had actually created the world.

God the Creator

There is no logical necessity for the creation narrative that Old Testament scholars frequently call the priestly creation account (Gen. 1:1–2:4a) to come at the beginning of the Bible. Israel had been conquered by the Babylonians, and its intellectual elite had been led into exile. There the Israelites were astounded by the culture of this imperial power with its imposing mythologies and multitude of gods. Even in their best time the Israelites had nothing of comparable splendor. It would only have been logical for the conquered Israelites to adopt the creation mythology of their conquerors. But something totally unexpected occurred. The Israelites realized that if the world had been created, then its creator could only be the one God who had made God's self known to the Israelites. God did not create the world after a battle, as the Babylonians said about their god Marduk; rather, God created the world simply through God's action-causing Word. Even the Babylonians' magnificent devotion to the moon and the stars made no sense to the Israelites, who knew that God had banished the moon to shine at night and had simply glued the stars to the firmament. Furthermore, humans were not made to be servants of the gods, as the Babylonians thought, but were created in the image of God. Humans have the important task of administering the creation as God's representatives. Thus the priestly creation account was from beginning to end polemically directed toward the creation mythologies with which the Israelites were confronted in Babylonia. The Sabbath, the day of rest at the end of the seven days of creation, is to remember God. It has nothing to do with a chronology of how much time God needed to create the world.

Next to the priestly narrative is the so-called Yahwist creation account (Gen. 2:4b–25), which derives its name from the fact that God is always designated with the name Yahweh. It is commonly considered to be older than the priestly account since the dry steppe is presupposed there. First, God must grant rain so that something can grow. It is interesting that the garden depicted there is by no means a fool's paradise. Adam is immediately charged with tilling the garden. In a picturesque way we hear that God made the first human being (Hebrew: *adam*) out of dust (Hebrew: *adamah*) to indicate the similarity between the reddish brown skin of the Israelites and the reddish brown earth. In a similarly picturesque way we hear that the woman was created from the rib of a man, indicating that the man (Hebrew: *ish*) and the woman (Hebrew: *'isha*) are of equal material and of equal value. When the woman is designated as "a helper" of the man (Gen. 2:18), this does not mean that she is, so to speak, the domestic servant of the man, but shows that she is an appropriate supplement to the man, and vice versa the man to the woman.

Other biblical references to God's creative activity include the so-called creation Psalms (8, 19, 104, 139, and 148) and Job 38–42. But the two creation narratives at the beginning in Genesis are the most elaborate ones and have drawn the most attention.

Creation Out of Nothingness (*Creatio ex nihilo*)

In Genesis 1:1–2 we read: "In the beginning when God created the heavens and the earth, the earth was a formless void and darkness covered the face of the deep." One could think that this statement excludes a creation out of nothingness, because there was already "a formless void." This means that in Genesis 1 we seem to be on the same level as a scientific explanation of the origin of the world, because that explanation also starts with something already assumed. Indeed, it is not until 2 Maccabees 7:28 that we read: "I beg you, my child, to look at the heaven and the earth and see everything that is in them, and recognize that God did not make them out of things that existed." In evaluating these two seemingly conflicting assertions, we must look at their respective contexts. Even for us it is still difficult to think simply of nothingness. It was only Greek philosophy that allowed such thought. For the Israelites, as for many peoples who lived in nature, something that had no clear outlines was at the same time not yet created. The "formless void" (Hebrew: *tohu wa bohu*) designated for the Israelites a state that was not yet created. Similarly, in Genesis 2 God must first cause the rain to come so that something can grow. It is the intention of both creation narratives to assert that God did not use something already available to create the world. With this insight, the biblical understanding of creation is different from scientific theories of the origin of the world. These theories always start with something already there to explain how the world assumed its present state. The biblical creation narratives, however, emphasize who created the world in the very beginning and who is behind the whole course of world history. This brings us to the relationship between God and the world.

God's Relationship to the World

The British physicist Stephen Hawking (b. 1942) has said that God determined at the most the original conditions of the course of the world. Martin Luther, however, emphasized, "God has not created the world in such a way as a carpenter builds a house and then leaves it to stand by itself as it is, but he stays with it and maintains it because he has made it."[1] God is not withdrawn from the world but continues to work in it. Often this conviction leads to a pantheistic view of God in which God and the world are virtually identical. God then becomes another term for nature. According to the biblical understanding, however, though God usually works through the natural processes in the world, God is strictly distinguished from it. But where can we localize God? If we can no longer think of God as being somewhere, God nearly evaporates.

American process theology, which dates back to the philosopher Alfred North Whitehead (1861–1947), has often proposed in a picturesque way that

1. Martin Luther, *Caspar Crucigers Sommerpostille* (1544), in *WA* 21:521.20–25, in a sermon on Rom. 11:33–36.

the world is God's body, whereby spirit (God) and body (world) influence one another. This notion denies both the absolute priority of God over the world, since God no longer creates out of nothingness, and God's absolute sovereignty, since God is no longer almighty. It avoids the misunderstanding that God is a cosmic dictator at whose command everything occurs. It argues instead that God can move the world toward the future only by persuasion and that God's ability to create new things is limited by the world. Since we often notice that the spirit is willing but the flesh is weak, one must ask whether this approach can really convince us that there will be an actual salvation and a new world of God's liking.

It makes little sense when we assume that God is above us, so to speak, on a higher level. Above us there are other solar systems and other galaxies, but there is no "space" for God. Outside of our universe there are no further spaces, because, as Einstein has shown us, space and matter are intimately connected. A way to understand God's "space" was, however, promulgated by the Tübingen theologian Karl Heim (1874–1958) with his dimensional understanding. If we go from one dimension to a higher one, Heim argued, the possibilities contained in the lower remain, but new ones are added. For example, in a two-dimensional configuration, a plane, one can circumvent a point B situated between A and C by turning either left or right. In a three-dimensional configuration, a cube, one has the additional possibilities of circumventing B above and below. We can envision God in a higher dimension than the one of our world. God would then have all the possibilities of this world plus additional new ones. While we cannot enter God's dimension from our side, for God it would always be possible to enter our (lower) dimension. This dimensional distinction between God and world or God and us would make it possible for God to be present and active in our world as God pleases. God could use in this way the possibilities available to us plus the additional ones. Then it would be intelligible that God is not tied to the possibilities of our world even if usually God makes use of them.

If we follow these considerations, then God has not only set apart our world from God's own dimension, but God can also be continuously at work in it and lead it to new and unforeseen possibilities. God is not tied to the laws that we discover in our world. This insight is important as we now consider that God usually governs the world according to general providence.

General Providence

For many people the decisive question today is no longer whether there is a gracious God who will grant them eternal life but, much more pragmatic, whether there is a God who cares about them in the here and now. In this way they are like the Israelites who, as we remember, were primarily interested in God's activity in history. Yet history does not proceed in empty space, but in our world and in nature. If we want to talk about God's general providence, we must consider God's activity in nature, in human conduct, and in history.

Natural Orders

When God made a covenant with Noah, God said, "As long as the earth endures, seedtime and harvest, cold and heat, summer and winter, day and night, shall not cease" (Gen. 8:22). Through the orders of preservation, God maintains nature and provides for us stability and predictability. This is shown in a threefold way:

1. The cycles of day and night and of the seasons. These cycles are indispensable for life on earth and, as far as we know, are completely reliable. Since they are derived from our own experience, they cannot provide complete security, but they minimize the possibility of alternative natural occurrences.

2. Biological, chemical, and atomic processes. We encounter these processes in chemical and atomic reactions and in the biological functioning of our bodies' cells. They are indispensable for life on earth, and the Bible reminds us of their dependability. Jesus, for instance, says that without God's doing no sparrow falls from the sky and every single hair on our head is counted (Matt. 10:29–30). Consider how often cells divide in our bodies and how many things could go wrong in this process. It is truly astounding how precise this biological process is and how rarely cancerous distortions develop.

3. The evolutionary process. As in every developmental process that is not totally determined, this process is not automatic but open-ended; it can go in different directions. But once an evolutionary step has occurred, certain consequences follow and all earlier possibilities are forever excluded. This idea is summed up in the title of a book by the French Nobel laureate Jacques Monod (1919–76), *Chance and Necessity*. The evolutionary process is dependable because it continues and never by necessity ends.

This openness, however, does not mean that we can take evolution into our own hands and shape it in whichever direction we want. We notice this limitation, for instance, when we meddle with nature and introduce foreign animals to a relatively isolated geographical territory such as Australia. Often these new animals endanger endemic species. This is similar to monocultures, which often facilitate the fast spread of diseases and threaten native populations of animals that depend on a variety of plants for food. Nature always has a certain equilibrium or balance, and a disturbance on one side leads to a corresponding disturbance on the other.

Again, we have an important reference to this reliability in nature. We read in the first creation narrative, for instance, that God spoke his creative word, "and it was so" (Gen. 1:7, 9, etc.). Then we read that humans are supposed to assume a certain responsibility (Gen. 1:28). Finally, we read that "the LORD God made garments of skins for the man and for his wife, and clothed them" (Gen. 3:21). Neither the created order by itself nor human endeavors within these processes are sufficient for humans to survive. God must continue to be actively present in God's creation.

Moral Orders of Preservation

While the processes in nature illuminate the continuous creative activity of God, the moral process highlights the preservation of humans. God gives to humans and other living beings certain norms of conduct that allow them to survive. Empirical philosophers such as John Locke (1632–1704) emphasized that humans attain their norms of conduct by experience. In contrast, Luther stated, "What God has given the Jews from heaven through Moses, he has inscribed on the hearts of all people."[2] Contrary to what some people think, human conduct is not without norms. Indeed, behavioral research has discovered that almost all cultures have norms for conduct similar to those of the Decalogue. If there were, for instance, no prohibition on killing other people, humans could not live together. It is similar with stealing. Even the command to honor father and mother goes in this direction. If we have no respect for the older generation, we waste resources of knowledge that an older generation has accumulated, and we must, so to speak, invent the wheel anew. Certain norms of conduct must be obeyed by the large majority of people so that a human community can thrive. Discoveries show that this also applies to some extent to the animal kingdom. How, for instance, could a beehive survive if each honeybee intentionally lied to the others about the place where it found food?

Lutheran theologians such as Werner Elert and Paul Althaus spoke in this context about orders of creation that God instituted with the original creation.

---

2. Martin Luther, *Predigten über das 2. Buch Mose* (1524–27), in *WA* 16:380.19–20, in a sermon on Exod. 19.

Yet we no longer live in the original creation because our world is marred by sin. Therefore it makes more sense to follow Walter Künneth's idea about orders of preservation through which God preserves us from destructive tendencies. These orders or norms are not static and unchangeable, but aim at the preservation of the human species. If circumstances change, these orders must change accordingly to maintain their intention of preservation. For instance, it is the intention of the sixth commandment, "You shall not commit adultery," to maintain durable pair relationships. When we think of marriage at the time of King David or in the Middle Ages or in the present, we recognize that that which endangers marriage has changed through the ages.

Therefore we must continuously examine moral norms to see whether they still fulfill their intention to protect humanity against possible self-destruction. This is evident in the Sermon on the Mount when Jesus connects the Ten Commandments to their original meanings. It is also evident in Luther's explanation of the Ten Commandments in his *Small Catechism* and *Large Catechism*. For instance, with the seventh commandment, "You shall not steal," in his *Small Catechism* Luther no longer focuses on taking things illegally as one would expect from the Jewish tradition or on the casuistry of what stealing actually means as was still the case in the Middle Ages. Luther goes beyond prohibitions and unfolds the positive content, showing in the newly won freedom what it means to be a good neighbor. He writes, "We are to fear and love God, so that we neither take our neighbors' money or property nor acquire them by using shoddy merchandise or crooked deals, but instead help them to improve and protect their property and income."[3] These norms and their positive unfolding serve to preserve humanity, and they must always be observed by the majority of people. If most people neglected them, the survival of humanity would be endangered. These norms are part of the common human tradition. Atheists can recognize them as derived from human experience, either through tradition or through our own reason. Christians, however, recognize in them God's preserving hand with which God guards humanity against destructive powers. Therefore Luther says dramatically, "If God would withdraw his protective hand, you would become blind, or an adulterer and murderer like David, you would fall and break your leg and drown."[4] With moral orders God maintains and preserves creation toward its end-time fulfillment. At that time, these orders will become a matter of course and will be unrestrained.

3. Martin Luther, *The Small Catechism*, in *Evangelical Lutheran Worship*, 1161.
4. Martin Luther, *Predigten des Jahres 1531*, in WA 34/2:237.3–4, in a sermon for the feast of St. Michael.

Preservation in History

In theology it is common to distinguish between salvation history, as for instance documented in the Bible, and world history, as in the secular world. With this distinction it is evident that God governs salvation history. But what is the case with world history? Is it only a product of human endeavors? Karl Barth referred to salvation history as *the* history which encompasses all other history and toward which all other history serves only as an illustration. Wolfhart Pannenberg, however, rejects the idea that God is at work only in salvation history and that one needs faith to recognize God's activity in history. He writes, "It belongs to the full meaning of the incarnation that God's redemptive deed took place within the universal correlative connections of human history and not in a ghetto of redemptive history, or in a primal history belonging to a dimension which is 'oblique' to ordinary history."[5] Indeed, in the Bible God's activity always occurs in the context of world history, for instance, when the Babylonian Empire brought an end to the Jewish state or when the Romans crucified Jesus. Therefore one does not need a special faith to recognize these historical facts. Though Pannenberg argues that God has proven the Godhead in the language of (historical) facts, he concedes, "*Mere* historical faith, which is satisfied with the establishment that the event happened and does not allow itself to be grasped by this event, thus has precisely not understood aright the inherent meaning of this history, but has diminished it. . . . But the *mere* acknowledgement of the history was not enough. It had to be grasped instead as an *event* that has a *bearing on me*."[6] One must be open to God's work in history to recognize, so to speak, God's fingers in that history. If we deny in advance such activity, we need not be surprised that we cannot see it at the end. This reminds us of the Lutheran conviction that there is a living voice of the gospel (*viva vox evangelii*) that addresses us not only through the Bible but also through history. With this admission we do not open the door to an un-Lutheran theory of two sources of revelation, because whatever encounters us in history must be measured against the Bible. Nor should this be confused with some kind of biblicism; rather, it reminds us that the God whom we discern has disclosed God's self unsurpassably in Jesus Christ. Therefore we must always return to that revelation and compare our insights with that revelation. This is all the more important because events in the history of humanity are often interpreted as God's providential activity.

5. Wolfhart Pannenberg, "Redemptive Event and History," in *Basic Questions in Theology: Collected Essays*, trans. George H. Kehm (Philadelphia: Fortress, 1970), 1:41–42.
6. Pannenberg, "Insight and Faith," in *Basic Questions*, 2:36.

We can see how differently historical events can be interpreted with the aforementioned destruction of Rome in 410 by the Visigoths under the leadership of King Alaric. Many held that this destruction was the result of the wrath of the old gods because people had abandoned the pagan cults and joined Christianity. Augustine, however, argued in *The City of God* that the sack of Rome was the result of the moral depravity of paganism. A generation later, Salvianus of Marseille (ca. 400–ca. 480) introduced a third version by interpreting the sack of Rome as divine judgment over the Christians who were not true enough to their Christian faith. From this example we can learn how through pious self-justification a historical event can easily be understood as a result of God's activity. Therefore we should never perceive an event as the result of God's providential activity in an atomistic way, taking the event out of its context. Adolf Hitler (1889–1945) committed this mistake several times when he talked about providence after surviving unhurt an attempt on his life (though we should note that Hitler talked only about "the providence" without any reference to God). Nor should we talk about history as a whole as a result of God's activity, because history would then be the result of divine determinism.

As we have seen with reference to God's promise of a son to Abraham and Sarah (Gen. 18:14) and to Mary and Joseph (Luke 1:35), the omnipotence of God is only adduced to show that God can fulfill the divine promises. When Jesus was asked for an explanation of why Pilate had slain the Galileans or why eighteen people perished through the collapse of a tower at Siloah (Luke 13:1–5), he did not interpret these events saying that God had punished these people by death. Even with the blind man whom Jesus cured (John 9:3), Jesus did not affirm that his blindness was the result of divine punishment on account of his parents' sins. This kind of reasoning would have been customary in Judaism at that time. In the first two cases Jesus emphasized in an existential manner that these events remind us of our own mortality and sinfulness, and in the latter case he stated that this event had occurred to show God's works.

Historical events have no meaning in themselves. They are also not just part of the larger context of world history. Ultimately, they have eschatological significance. Though Christians are often convinced that history finds its fulfillment in the eschaton, we should not yield to the temptation to equate God with the causes of the historical process or with one of the causes. Rather, we should agree with the Lutheran theologian Friedrich Gogarten (1887–1967), who reminded us that God made us heirs and administrators of this world and therefore granted us freedom without curtailing this again through general providence. An administrator without freedom would be a puppet, not a responsible person. In contrast to Gogarten, we must emphasize that responsibility does not preclude providence but is its precondition. As administrators of God we need God's guiding providence to fulfill our responsibility. Through general providence God gives us order and grace as a frame of reference for our existence through which we and our environment can be preserved. In this way our existence is open to the future. But is this existence only a continuation of presently discernible tendencies, or is there also something new occurring as indicated by the category of fulfillment?

Special Providence

Through general providence, presently discernible tendencies are continued. Yet we noticed with God's general providence that there occurs a necessary continuation and at the same time an unpredictable surprise—Monod's chance and necessity. This pattern shows itself also in special providence, most pointedly in the salvational activity of God in history. On the one hand, there is continuation, for instance, through God's covenant with humanity and in the interplay of promise and fulfillment or of law and gospel. On the other hand, something unforeseen occurs, such as the crossing of the Red Sea, the election of David, and the miracles of Jesus. The unexpected is often a trademark of God's activity. In special providence, not only does God give history an unexpected turn, but the unexpected points to, and to some extent even anticipates, the new quality of life that has been promised for the eschaton. Through general providence we are chaperoned toward the eschaton by the orders of preservation, while in special providence we are granted a glimpse of the end-time fulfillment. This becomes especially noticeable with the New Testament miracles.

In their narrative form the miracles of Jesus are similar to non-Christian miracle narratives as they were reported in antiquity of so-called miracle workers, such as the neo-Pythagorean philosopher Apollonius of Tyana (ca. 40–ca. 120). Even the New Testament does not hesitate to talk about such miracle workers (cf. Acts 8:9–11). Yet the intention of New Testament miracles is very different from these miracles. They are not miracles per se. As we can gather from the commentary, "The Lord worked with them and confirmed the message by the signs that accompanied it" (Mark 16:20), the miracles of Jesus and of those who performed them in his name are illustrations of Jesus' message. We can discern this also in Jesus' reaction to the question of disciples of John the Baptist as to whether Jesus was the promised Messiah. Jesus answered, "Go and tell John what you hear and see: the blind receive their sight, the lame walk, lepers are cleansed, the deaf hear, the dead are raised, and the poor have the good news brought to them" (Matt. 11:4–5). Jesus' proclamation and activities belong together and interpret each other. They are signs of the commencing kingdom of God and thereby have an eschatological function.

The miracles of Jesus, however, were only momentary signs of a new eon in which there is no longer sickness, hunger, and death. The healed persons became sick again, and in the end they died. It is important here to realize that these miracles pointing to the future cannot be separated from the final destiny of Jesus in his resurrection. Through this miracle that was accorded permanent status, Jesus did not die again, because he had been resurrected to a new and imperishable form of life. With this miracle all other miracles obtain their legitimacy. They are not mirages or temporary wishful thinking that dissipates once our everyday life has caught up with us. They are pointers to and individual anticipations of a new reality that has shown itself already in permanence in Jesus Christ.

But miracles also seem to be stumbling blocks in our world because they cannot be coordinated with our everyday experience. For instance, traditional Roman Catholic theology has considered miracles a proof of a supernatural activity in which the secondary causes of our world are suspended for a moment by the supernatural activity of the divine prime cause. By a miraculous act of God the secondary causes are then continued. Such a disruption of our reality has always drawn skeptical attention and raised the question of whether this is even possible. Luther, however, emphasized that in principle nothing is impossible for God. But then he continued that God "could give children without using men and women. But he does not want to do this. Instead he joins man and woman so that it appears to be the work of man and woman, and yet he does it under the cover of such masks."[7] This means that a miracle is not a disruption of natural laws or of anything else. Since God has created the world with its laws, God has no need to break these laws but could change them at any time. Moreover, natural laws are laws that we derive from our experience of the natural processes. They are valid only until proven wrong.

Miracles are exceptions since they contradict the life experiences we have gathered so far. This means one cannot predict miracles. Consider, for instance, the crossing of the Red Sea by the Israelites. According to some affirmations in the Bible, this was a totally natural event in which a strong wind pushed back the shallow waters so that the Israelites could cross. The "miraculous" part of this event was that the wind commenced just when the Israelites were on their flight and that it changed its direction exactly when their pursuers were crossing the sea. Even many miracles of healing are possible, though not predictable, as we learn from modern medicine. Therefore it is wrong to

---

7. Martin Luther, *Psalm 147* (1532), in *LW* 14:114, in his exegesis of v. 13.

talk about a disruption of the natural laws with miracles. Miracles are rather highly unusual experiences.

Prayer is also part of God's special providence. In the Bible the faithful are frequently encouraged to pray to God and to present all their problems to God. Therefore we read in the Psalms: "Call on me in the day of trouble; I will deliver you, and you shall glorify me" (Ps. 50:15). Besides prayers of thankfulness and praise, the most frequent ones are intercessory prayers. Here is the possibility to enter into dialogue with God and to cooperate in prayer with God concerning the future direction of the world and therewith participate in special providence. Yet as Dietrich Bonhoeffer (1906–45) warned, "God does not give us everything we want, but he does fulfill all his promises."[8] Jesus did not heal all the sick—he never conducted healing services. Instead, he healed only a few people to illustrate his message. A prayer will never remain unheard, but it will not always be fulfilled the way we want. A prayer can never serve to degrade God to be our emissary. Though it should be brought forth with utmost confidence and conviction, prayer must always be uttered in the way that Jesus prayed in Gethsemane, that ultimately not our will but God's will may prevail (cf. Matt. 26:39).

8. Dietrich Bonhoeffer, *Letters and Papers from Prison*, rev. ed., ed. Eberhard Bethge, trans. R. Fuller (New York: Macmillan, 1967), 213.

$$\boxed{6}$$

HUMANITY

So far we have only mentioned humanity implicitly, such as in our discussions of creation and the relationship of God to the world. But now we must focus on humanity, namely, on our created existence, our position in the world, and our ability to enter into dialogue.

The Created Aspect of Humanity

In the last 150 years, scientists have discovered more and more about the gradual development of living beings and have also brought humanity into the context of developmental history. For many the name of Charles Darwin has provoked controversy. Two of Darwin's books, *On the Origin of Species by Means of Natural Selection* (1859) and *The Descent of Man* (1871), have attracted much attention and been the cause of many misunderstandings, especially the claim that humans descended from apes, a claim that Darwin never made but that is often attributed to him. In *The Origin of Species* Darwin assumed that life "was imbued by the creator in some species or in one. . . . Because it agrees better with what we know through the laws which have been imprinted in matter through the creator that the origin of past and present inhabitants of the world must be traced back to secondary causes."[1] In this developmental context we must also see humans. It is interesting that in the priestly creation

1. Charles Darwin, *The Origin of Species* (1876), in *The Works of Charles Darwin*, ed. Paul H. Barrett and R. B. Freeman (London: Pickering, 1988), 16:446–47. It should be mentioned,

narrative not even a special day of creation is reserved for humans. On the sixth day God commands the earth, "Let the earth bring forth living creatures of every kind" (Gen. 1:24), and subsequently God creates humans. Humans and animals even share the same plant food. This shows how closely humans are associated with other living beings. In the Yahwistic creation narrative we hear in a picturesque way how God brought one animal after another for the first human being to name, "but for the man there was not found a helper as his partner" (Gen. 2:20). Here the thought is even expressed that a human being would find a partner in an animal.

In Genesis 1:27 we hear three times that God created the human beings. Humans are first of all God's creatures and not independent beings. The Yahwistic creation narrative says even more dramatically, "The LORD God formed man from the dust of the ground, and breathed into his nostrils the breath of life; and the man became a living being" (Gen. 2:7). A human being is a creature whose life is owed to the breath that God breathed into his or her being. A human being has no self-existing life. Therefore we read nothing about a soul that could exist independently from the body. To the contrary, in Genesis 2:7 there is a close connection between the human being (Hebrew: adam) and earth (Hebrew: adamah), as we noted earlier. The reddish brown skin reminds the Israelites that after death they will return to the reddish brown earth and become part of it: "You [will] return to the ground, for out of it you were taken; you are dust, and to dust you shall return" (Gen. 3:19).

Though in the Bible we often encounter the distinction between body and soul or body, soul, and spirit, the human being is understood as a unity. For instance, a human being never sins only with the body, but sins as a human being. A human being receives life from God alone and not through a godlike soul that resides in the body. Only in Hellenism and later on in Gnosticism, a religious movement that took its wisdom from many different sources, do we hear of a higher soul and a perishable body. In the Bible human life is a gift of God that we return to God at the end of life. Therefore we hear nothing of nature simply bringing forth humans, as occurs with other living beings, but God is the source from which the first human being originates. Modern biology has indirectly attested to this. It could not adduce any evidence that human life is, so to speak, preprogrammed by evolution. According to scientific knowledge, it is "purely accidental" that human life originated. But for Christians who believe in God's activity, this "accident" expresses the will of God. We see this in the book of Job: "Your hands fashioned and made me;

---

however, that in the first edition of 1859 the mention of a creator is missing, though in his train of thought it must be added.

and now you turn and destroy me. Remember that you fashioned me like clay; and will you turn me to dust again? Did you not pour me out like milk and curdle me like cheese? You clothed me with skin and flesh, and knit me together with bones and sinews. You have granted me life and steadfast love, and your care has preserved my spirit" (Job 10:8–12). Though the writer of these lines knew exactly the procreative process, he evaluated this process as God's activity. The Bible perceives nature never as an independent entity but always as a servant of God. Regardless of where a human being ultimately emerges from, it is always from God and God's work. This is reemphasized in baptism when a human being officially becomes a child of God.

Though humans and animals enjoy the same food and may share the same living space, they are not on the same level. We read in Genesis that animals were brought by God to Adam so that he would name them and exercise dominion over them. Yet a human being needs a personal thou, and therefore at the conclusion of creation the woman is created. She is later called Eve (Gen. 3:20), which in Hebrew means "the living one" or the mother of all living, and becomes the primal mother of all of humanity. For us it is strange to hear that she was created from a rib of Adam. Perhaps this vivid narrative wants to explain why most of the vital organs of human beings are protected by ribs, except in the abdomen. But this assertion also has an important theological significance, because the woman does not simply arise from dust but is fashioned from the same material as the man. This *man* (Hebrew: *ish*) notices this new being immediately and calls the female person *wo-man* (Hebrew: *'isha*), indicating that the two belong together and are created by God for each other. But then comes the strange assertion: "Therefore a man leaves his father and his mother and clings to his wife, and they become one flesh" (Gen. 2:24). Perhaps this is a reference to an earlier culture in which a man left his family and moved to the kindred of the woman. In Israel, however, the custom was just the opposite. Therefore this assertion does not describe a present situation but rather a natural urge. As they were once one flesh and the woman was created from the substance of the man, so it is their natural urge to achieve this unity again.

Responsibility for Creation

From the very beginning the human being is entrusted with a special task: "The LORD God took the man and put him in the garden of Eden to till it and keep it" (Gen. 2:15). The man is not in the garden for himself or his own pleasure, but with being human comes the task to cultivate and preserve the earth. This task has nothing to do with exploiting the natural resources or the animal kingdom. How badly humans have failed in this regard is shown by the many animal species that have been eradicated through human interference or threatened by it. Humans have treated nature in a similarly irresponsible way. Already Plato writes in his *Critias*: "In the first place the Acropolis was not as now. For the fact is that a single night of excessive rain washed away the earth and laid bare the rock. . . . The Acropolis . . . was well covered with soil, and level at the top, except in one or two places."[2] Erosion and environmental problems, including today's climate change, have human causes. Instead of cultivating and preserving the earth, we have misused it in various ways in opposition to our position as God's representatives on earth.

In the priestly creation narrative God says, "Let us make humankind in our image, according to our likeness." Then we read, "So God created humankind in his image, in the image of God he created them" (Gen. 1:26–27). The plural chosen here ("let us") shows that humans are not a direct replica of God but an image of both God and the whole heavenly court. This is exemplified in Psalm 8:5, which says, "You have made them a little lower than God, and crowned them with glory and honor." Humans belong, so to speak, to God's heavenly court, and because of this they are entrusted with certain tasks.

What does it mean to be created in God's image? The answer to this question does not involve characteristics such as upright posture, use of reason, or other human capabilities. The emphasis in the priestly creation narratives does not lie in the fact that we are created in God's image. Rather, it is on the purpose for which this image is given. Therefore we read, "God blessed them, and God said to them, 'Be fruitful and multiply, and fill the earth and subdue it; and have dominion over the fish of the sea and over the birds of the air and over every living thing that moves upon the earth'" (Gen. 1:28). Similarly, as we have seen in the second creation narrative, humans are entrusted with certain responsibilities, namely, to populate the earth, to subdue it, and to have dominion over the animal world. But what does this have to do with being created in God's image? We must remind ourselves that to this day it is the custom in most government buildings to have a picture of the president or governor in whose name the civil servants conduct their business. The same is expected from us as human beings. In the name of God and as God's representatives, we are to assume God's activities on earth. Therefore everything we do on this earth must be evaluated by God's standard. Selfish activities, without regard for God's will, contradict this obligation. The misuse of nature and the animal world and the exploitation and subjugation of people or certain races are contrary to our divine obligation.

2. Plato, *Critias* 112a.

Immediately after we hear that humanity is created in God's image, we read, "Male and female he created them" (Gen. 1:27). Neither the bodily strength of a man nor the procreative capability of a woman better represents God. Only in cooperation between man and woman, whether in the family or in the larger human community, can we meet the task entrusted to us, to represent God. The sexual differentiation given by creation should lead not to a mutual opposition but to a mutual cooperation. How the respective division of labor in the human community occurs is left to the respective communities, albeit under the presupposition that man and woman are of equal value in their service. Luther, for instance, said in his *Lecture on Isaiah*, "Everyone should lead such a life so that he knows that it is well pleasing to God, even if it is a despised and lowly life. A male servant, a female servant, a father or a mother, are such forms of life that are instituted by the divine word and are sanctified and well-pleasing to God."[3]

All human activities should always be seen as divine service, as a service to God. Yet the question arises whether humans can do justice to that mandate. As the prophets point out over and over again, Old Testament history is an example of the history of human misconduct over against God. One can also hardly think about Jesus' sacrifice in the New Testament without thinking of human misconduct. We are confronted with the divine mandate to live according to the will of God and to be God's representative, but we constantly experience the fact that we are not capable of accomplishing this high task. The command to subdue the earth has led humans to put themselves in the center of everything and to use the whole world according to their own liking and advantage. In seeing only ourselves and nothing else, we regard other people and the environment as nonexistent. This anthropocentrism should be rejected because of the very fact that we have been created not in our own image but in the image of God as representatives who are responsible to God. Once God is totally eliminated, as happened, for instance, in the French Revolution at the end of the eighteenth century or in Marxism and National Socialism in the first part of the twentieth century, indescribable crimes can result. Being related to God prevents us from placing ourselves at the center.

Our Dialogical Structure

The Greek historian Herodotus (ca. 490–ca. 425 BC) reports that the Egyptian king Psammetichus tried to discover the original language of humanity.[4] He

3. Martin Luther, *Vorlesung über Jesaja* (1527/29), in *WA* 25:385.26–29.
4. Herodotus, *The Histories* 2.2, trans. Aubrey de Sélincourt, rev. A. R. Burn (Harmondsworth: Penguin, 1972), 129–30. It is difficult to determine who that king was.

commanded a shepherd to take two newborn infants and let them grow up with
a herd of goats without saying one word to them. After two years the shepherd
opened the door to the place where the children lived, and they called out to
him, "*Becos*," raising their hands toward him. This occurred again each time
the shepherd came, and he reported it to the king. The king ordered a search
to be conducted to discover the language in which this word *becos* could be
found. When it was discovered that the Phrygians called bread *becos*, it was
concluded that the Phrygians spoke the original language of humanity. No one
had noticed that the children were simply imitating the baaing of the goats.
Emperor Frederic II (1194–1250) conducted a similar experiment, but with
more dire consequences. He, too, wanted to discover what language children
would speak if they grew up in total isolation. So he commanded that a group
of newborn infants be raised by surrogate mothers who would bathe, clothe,
and feed them but were not allowed to have any other contact with them or
talk to them. The experiment ended as a total disaster because gradually all
the children died. Today science has found the reasons for this. Behavioral
psychologists tell us that severe developmental damage called hospitalism
occurs if a newborn does not have lasting social contact with a caregiver after
the second month of life. A human being cannot live forever in isolation. This
is true for prisoners who are kept in solitary confinement and often fabricate
pseudo-worlds to escape from their isolation.

Humans must continuously interact with their environment. While animals
are highly specialized beings who have adjusted in order to live comfortably
in certain environments (such as a camel in the desert and a polar bear in the
arctic region), human beings are much less specialized and also less restricted.
We can live almost everywhere, but we need an artificial environment to do
so, for instance, heating in the winter or air-conditioning in the summer and
appropriate clothing. This means we can transform our environment so that
we can live comfortably in it. While we do not have the excellent hearing of
a dog, the superb eyes of a falcon, or the strength of an elephant, we are able
to do a greater combination of things than any animal. Moreover, humans
have developed many aids, so that, for instance, in an airplane they can fly at
the height of thirty thousand feet, and with a car or train they can travel in
one day the distance between Budapest and Paris. We must also think of the
huge libraries in which humans have stored immense knowledge. Not only
can humans change their environment according to their needs, but they can
see it from very different angles. A hunter sees the world very differently than
does a forester or somebody jogging through the woods. These perspectives
can be changed at will, so that at one time I can be a hunter, another time a
forester, and another time a jogger. Yet with animals this perspective is much

more engrained through instincts. For instance, if a dog senses a deer while walking in the woods, immediately the dog will attempt to find the scent of the deer and follow it. But if a man sees another person in the woods, he can either ignore that person, greet him or her cordially, or simply enjoy that he is not alone in the forest.

While a proverb says that you can't teach an old dog new tricks, it is characteristic of humans that until old age we can interact with our environments and learn new things. Animals, however, are confined in their conduct and in their ability to learn, and when their growth phase is completed, learning slows greatly. This is different with adult people, who remain open to new things and strive to increase their horizons. This continuous pushing forward, shown especially in our quickly changing times, also entails sorrow when we must leave behind accustomed ways. If changes occur too fast, there is the danger that we will lose our orientation and discover that something we have relied on is no longer reliable. For instance, what we learn in school or in college often becomes outdated within a few years because of new discoveries and insights, and one of our biggest challenges is keeping up on the current state of affairs. When we remember how rapidly this continuous progress diminishes our nonrenewable natural resources, we can rightly ask whether modern progress, which takes place largely on a material basis, is sensible and can be maintained in the long run.

These problematic developments notwithstanding, we must keep in mind that humans have always striven forward to transcend that which is at hand. This is most obvious with material progress where that which we possess is discarded in favor of something new. We are reminded here again of Augustine's insight: "Thou hast formed us for Thyself, and our hearts are restless till they find rest in Thee."[5] While the phenomena of steadily learning something new and trying to go beyond that which is presently available belong fundamentally to our human existence, rapidly increasing progress is a phenomenon of modernity. As humanity separated itself more and more from God and asserted its autonomy, it needed something that would give its limitation unlimited value. Therefore humanity even more frantically searched for a point of orientation and significance for this life. Such a reference point seems to be unavailable in our limited world, because the more material things we accumulate, the emptier our lives seem to become. The rediscovery of God as the point of orientation that endows our limited existence with infinite value could prevent us from falling prey to the world with its ever-increasing rapid progress and its exploitation of us and our finite, nonrenewable resources, and

5. Augustine, *Confessions* 1.1, in *NPNF*[1] 1:45.

could show us instead that we can live our lives in a more relaxed manner. We
need not continuously seek after the latest invention, because we know that
we are protected by the hand of the Almighty. Therefore we can regard the
persons and things that surround us as reminders of God's mandate not only
to subdue the world but also to protect it. In rediscovering ourselves as God's
representatives, we will notice that the dialogue in prayer with the one whom
we represent frees us from being enslaved to things and also from the necessity
to assert ourselves continuously through our actions. We will discover that
we belong to God, who leads and protects us, and that we are responsible to
God for that which we commit or omit.

So we return to the dialogue with God our creator. This dialogue is totally
different from the dialogue between people because in human dialogue often
something is expected in return. But when we dialogue with God whom we
know as a loving God, we discover that God does not want anything from us
but rather that we are on the receiving end. This is nowhere better expressed
than in prayer. Luther rightly claims that "God's orders or command and the
prayers of Christians . . . are the two pillars that support the entire world"
and without which the world would disintegrate.[6] God has promised us that
he will always be mindful of the content of our prayers in his preserving and
creative activity. Through prayer we are on God's side, cooperating with him
with regard to the future of our world.

---

6. Martin Luther, *Sermons on the Gospel of St. John* (1537/38), in *LW* 24:81, in his explanation of John 14:12.

7

SIN

While God's existence or at least God's activity in the world has often been questioned, there is no doubt about the fact of human sinfulness. In analyses of the human situation, the conviction is often expressed that we could free ourselves from our fate if we just had the right insights and the right conduct. There is an abundance of self-help books and of people who promise to be our guide to a positive and fulfilled life. Nevertheless, the deficit in individual human lives and in interpersonal relationships is noticeable everywhere. Therefore one must question whether we can really arrive at a fulfilled life through our own efforts or whether there are not powers stronger than us that must intervene if we are to be freed from the strictures of evil into which we continuously fall. Moreover, all of our personal efforts end with our deaths, and we can have no direct influence on what comes after us.

The Cause of Evil

If the cause of our defective life lies within the human sphere, then perhaps we can eliminate it, be it through education, genetic manipulation, or preventive measures. Yet if the cause is outside us, it could be too big a task for us to eliminate. The Judeo-Christian tradition is unanimous that the origin of our deficits and the evil we encounter does not come from outside external powers.

The origin of evil seems to lie in the structure of human existence. We notice this at once in the Old Testament narratives. Though the story of the fall in Genesis 3 is nowhere else picked up in the Old Testament, it is no isolated case. It is part of human history and the first link in a whole chain of sinful events. Immediately after Adam and Eve's disobedience and expulsion from the garden, Cain kills his brother Abel (Gen. 4:1–16), and Lamech kills a man and speaks of being avenged (Gen. 4:22–23). Then comes the marriage between sons of God and daughters of humans (Gen. 6:1–4), followed by the great flood (Gen. 6:5–9:29), and finally the building of the Tower of Babel (Gen. 11:1–9). Yet the event of the fall in Genesis 3 is not one incident among many but is the first sinful act of the first female human being (Eve) and the first male human being (Adam), whose names from then on are used as proper names. By designating Adam and Eve as individual human beings, the writer wants to point out the exemplary character of this first sin. It is not only a trespassing of God's command, but in the center is distrust in God. Before this act, both humans had a childlike trust in God, but now the harmony with God is broken. Yet the writer does not want to show how the once good creation became so bad. Rather, he wants to point to the cause of our present human situation.

Following the thinking of idealistic philosophy, one could see something positive in the fall. Similar to a child who asserts her independence by growing up, the first human couple won their independence from God. But this kind of reasoning results from a misunderstanding. While a child must separate herself from her parents to gain adulthood, the exact opposite is true in the relationship between humans and God. God is not only the one to whom we owe everything, but he is also the origin of life. If we separate ourselves from God, we may be free, but we lose our connection to the origin of life. Therefore the psychoanalyst Carl Gustav Jung (1875–1961) wrote, "There is deep doctrine in the legend of the fall: it is the expression of a dim presentiment that the emancipation of ego-consciousness was a Luciferian deed."[1] If we tear ourselves away from God, we do not immediately die, but our lives are restricted to this earthly realm. We cannot expect something positive beyond death, because we have cut our "umbilical cord" that connects us to the source of life. Furthermore, we must secure our orientation from within this world, which is difficult since everything in this world is relative and finite. This means we must fabricate something as absolute, such as an ideology or religious worldview, and establish it as a point of orientation.

1. Carl Gustav Jung, "The Phenomenology of the Spirit in Fairytales" (1948), in *Collected Works 9.1: The Archetypes and the Collective Unconscious*, trans. and ed. R. F. C. Hull (New York: Pantheon, 1959), 230 (par. 420). Jung continues his comments on the fall when he perceptively says, "Man's whole history consists from the very beginning in a conflict between his feeling of inferiority and his arrogance."

In the story of Adam and Eve, we see that sin cannot be derived in a causal way from God's good creation. When God inquired about Adam's conduct, Adam attempted a causal excuse: "The woman whom you gave to be with me, she gave me the fruit from the tree, and I ate" (Gen. 3:12). Eve responded to God with a similar excuse: "The serpent tricked me, and I ate" (Gen. 3:13). But God did not accept either of those explanations. Adam and Eve had to shoulder the consequences of their own conduct. The origin of evil cannot be causally explained. Humanity was not sinful from the very beginning, and even the serpent is considered as a creature and thereby part of God's good creation. Why a part of God's good creation became a tempter is a speculative matter and does not interest us in this context because it does not contribute anything to the description of human sinfulness.

Yet why did the first humans allow themselves to be tempted? We read that they wanted to be like God and that they wanted to know the difference between good and evil. It is difficult to assume that God would have created a humanity that had the potential to become God's possible rival, even to become like God. No, this would make little sense. But we may assume that humans wanted to be like the heavenly beings. Instructive here is the reference that humans wanted to know what is good and what is evil. We are not confronted here with the difference between good and evil, but with the knowledge of everything that comprises good and evil. Already at that time and even today humans have an urge to know everything and to know everything better. This urge should not be misunderstood as mere human curiosity since that is evidenced in science and has been instrumental in promulgating progress. It is rather the destructive desire to deprive others of their private spheres and to regard others as objects without respecting their individuality. This human hubris to penetrate into the most private sphere of the other so that he or she stands before one without any protection effectively destroys the relationship to God. Only God has such all-comprehensive knowledge as we can gather from Psalm 139. If we usurped such penetrating knowledge we would transgress our position as limited beings and assume a godlike stature.

God does not react against this sinful hubris like an annoyed tyrant. Surely the harmony with God is broken, and the couple must leave the garden of innocence. But the threat that the humans would die on the day they ate from the tree of knowledge (Gen. 2:17) was not realized. They were only told that they would return to the dust from which they came. Not even the reference to work outside the garden can be understood as an actual curse because already in the garden the humans had a certain mandate. Since the harmony with God was broken, however, the relationships between humans and nature and between man and woman became tenuous. The text suggests that their lives were filled with hatred and passion, and yet they still had the desire for harmony. Life became a burden. But life did not come to an end, because God did not forfeit humanity though they had forfeited God. God continued to provide for the human couple (cf. Gen. 3:22). Even humans in their fallen state owe their lives to God, on whom they are ultimately dependent.

If we search for the cause of evil outside the narrative of the fall, we arrive at the following conclusion: Initially the Israelites understood God as the source of both good and evil, but they developed an ever stronger tendency to see God's action with regard to evil primarily as punishment of humans for their evil deeds. Therefore the cause of the evils committed by humans is to be found outside God, first in the temptation by something within God's good creation, then in the image of the heavenly accuser (as Satan, for instance, is depicted in the book of Job), and finally in the increasingly independent figure of an evil devil (e.g., 1 Chron. 21:1). This means that the Israelites gradually gained a clearer understanding of God, which culminated in God's complete self-disclosure in Jesus Christ. We must remember one important point: Regardless of where evil comes from, this does not diminish human beings' responsibility for their own deeds. Even when the temptation appears to be irresistible, humans ultimately bear the responsibility. We can see this, for instance, in the depiction of David's temptation in 1 Chronicles 21. David confesses, "Was it not I who gave the command to count the people? It is I who have sinned and done very wickedly" (1 Chron. 21:17). And yet in verse 1 of this chapter we are told that Satan incited David to count the people of Israel. The point is that we cannot excuse our own mistakes by blaming others, whether because of wrong advisers or the persuasion of the media. Ultimately, we are responsible for our own actions.

The most significant references to Satan (Zech. 3:1; Job 1:6–12) appear during the time when the Israelites had returned from Babylonian exile. It would be highly unusual if the encounter with the prominent culture of Babylonia had not influenced the Israelites in their thinking. Indeed, we notice that the Babylonian court ceremonies influenced the Israelite ideas of Satan. For instance, in Babylonia a royal official traveled throughout the country and reported to the king the conditions prevailing there. We see a similar trait in the function of Satan in the book of Job and also in Zechariah. Moreover, there are parallels to the teachings of Zoroaster, whose sphere of influence extended from Eastern Persia in present-day Iran to Babylonia in present-day Iraq. According to Zoroaster, a highest god governs the whole world. Under him are two other gods, his sons. The one is responsible for evil, and the other for good. We remember that the Israelites originally gave God the credit for everything that happened, both good and evil. Only later did they attribute all evil to Satan. This exclusion of evil from God seems to be influenced by Zoroastrian thought. Yet we must also note that in the Old Testament the claim had never been made that Yahweh was the father of Satan, whereas in Zoroastrianism one of the sons of the highest god carried the responsibility for all the evil in the world. The encounter with other religious ideas need not turn into a dependency, and it can be instrumental in clarifying problems in one's own religion.

In early Judaic writings, which influenced the thinking of people at the time of Jesus, world history is described as a battle between good and evil powers. While God's sovereignty rules supreme, humans must decide in this battle between the sphere of influence of light and that of darkness, between the law of God and the work of the Evil One. Therefore we read in the Testament of Judah: "So understand, my children, that two spirits await an opportunity with humanity: The spirit of truth and the spirit of error" (Test. Judah 20:1). But humanity is not helplessly thrown into this battle between light and darkness; rather, it receives its ultimate destiny from the hand of God. Though world history is understood as a struggle between good and evil forces, God rules supreme. This situation results in an ethical dualism of decision, whereby humanity must decide for or against God. A compartmentalization of the world into a sphere of influence of evil and another one of God was foreign to the Jews because they were convinced of the incomparable might of God.

In the New Testament we encounter an absolute and unconquerable opposition between God and Satan. Jesus' mission can be understood as a continuous confrontation with Satan. Satan appears at the decisive point in Jesus' life and destiny, beginning with the temptation at the start of Jesus' mission (Mark 1:12–13), all the way to the betrayal by Judas Iscariot (Luke 22:3). The episode of Beelzebul (Mark 3:21–27) shows that the whole demonic realm is under the control of Satan. When Jesus expels demons, this is a manifestation of the greater work to expel Satan. This means that the New Testament depicts the position of Satan in two very different ways:

1. The Synoptic writers, meaning the writers of the first three Gospels, report that Satan wants to destroy humanity and especially Jesus of Nazareth as the one who will usher in the kingdom of God. This destructive power of Satan should not be underestimated. He causes everything evil in the world, though the New Testament rejects the idea that each human destiny is caused by some personal sin (cf. Luke 13:1–3). Though the people at the time of Jesus thought that there was a causal connection between one's own conduct and the good and evil consequences

that followed, Jesus refused to admit such a causal connection. For him the aspect of salvation was decisive out of this negative constellation.

2. The New Testament writers report also the defeat of Satan caused by Jesus Christ. The narrative of Beelzebul (Mark 3:21–27) shows that Satan had found his conqueror in Jesus. This is attested to by each subsequent action of Jesus, including his sacrificial death (1 Cor. 15:57). Satan still wants to accuse humans before God, but Jesus intercedes for them so that their "faith may not fail" (Luke 22:32). Satan has even lost his prominent position and his access to heaven, as Jesus explained: "I watched Satan fall from heaven like a flash of lightning" (Luke 10:18). This agrees with the assertion in the book of Revelation: "The accuser of our comrades has been thrown down, who accuses them day and night before our God" (Rev. 12:10). Since Satan has been overpowered, the disciples are promised to have "authority to tread on snakes," which means they have authority over the evil and seductive anti-godly powers (Luke 10:19).

While in Gnosticism the world is divided into an evil cosmos ruled by Satan and a heavenly realm in which the faithful rule with their Father, such a division is foreign to the New Testament. When we read in the writings of John that there are two spheres of influence, one ruled by Christ and the other by Satan, the world is still God's creation, created through the divine Word. Also in contrast to Gnosticism, the New Testament does not divide between two classes of people, those who can be redeemed and those who are destined to perdition. In John 3:17 Jesus says, "God did not send the Son into the world to condemn the world, but in order that the world might be saved through him." Even if now two powers fight for supremacy in this world, this will not continue, because "the world and its desires are passing away, but those who do the will of God live forever" (1 John 2:17). This is the hope that endows the New Testament faith with strength.

All of this shows that there is an increasing conviction in the biblical writings that the cause of evil cannot be attributed to God. Since the Israelites understood God as creator of everything, the cause of evil must come out of this creation. Especially in the postexilic time, which in many ways was a tumultuous period, more and more people rightly looked to God as the one from whom all good is derived. From the very beginning, however, the power of evil was not understood as something that could come from humanity alone, whether from an individual person or the human community. This necessity to assume an evil outside humanity and outside God did not diminish human responsibility for one's own deeds. Yet to determine in a speculative way why part of God's good creation denied its origin was of little interest for the biblical authors. They also had little interest to determine exactly what evil was. Though evil was often understood as something that diminished the life-increasing processes, mostly it was understood as that which intended to hinder the extension of God's kingdom. Even biological phenomena such as diseases, and problems in the physical world such as earthquakes, fell under the category of evil. Because one did not distinguish in a dualistic way between two primal principles—God as the cause of all good and Satan as the cause of all evil—one also did not differentiate between natural evil and spiritual evil. In whatever form evil arises to hinder the fruition of the good, ultimately it will be overcome and will serve to glorify God.

The Anti-Godly Reality

If we pursue the question of whether the cause of evil has any personal traits, we dare not slide into some kind of pagan polydemonism like the Christian Middle Ages with belief in witches, devils, archdevils, and all kinds of evil spirits. Yet the cause of evil cannot simply be attributed to humans or be considered as part of the natural processes. Even the philosopher Immanuel Kant admitted the existence of radical evil. For him, evil is a natural inclination that people voluntarily follow. Yet what is behind this evil to which humans always yield? Is it only human imperfection? If this were the case, we could eliminate it through education or genetic manipulation. Yet no genetic constellation for evil has been found. All the efforts for a good education notwithstanding, each generation has to battle anew with evil and its consequences. This means that evil seems to exist outside humanity and at the same time influences it. If we equate evil with the devil, who supposedly has a stunted leg and horns on his head, this picture is more fitting for fairy tales than for a concrete human situation. We cannot describe evil, but only its dynamics, as evil is directed against God and against the good. Since evil appears in such different ways, it is better to introduce here the concept of "anti-godly powers," which shows on the one hand the thrust of evil and on the other hand its multiplicity of appearance.

While philosophers have wrestled with the question as to why there is something and not just nothing, theology has focused on the issue of why there is evil if there is God. Even Luther concerned himself with this issue, especially in his treatise *The Bondage of the Will*. There he likens humans to a beast of burden. "If God rides it, it wills and goes where God wills. . . . If Satan rides it, it wills and goes where Satan wills. . . . The riders themselves contend for the possession and control of it."[2] This means that God and Satan fight with each other for supremacy in the world. This kind of reasoning could lead to a dualism, and ultimately we would not know who would win in the end. Yet in the same writing Luther distinguishes between the preached God and the hidden God, that is, between God's Word and God's self. Luther explains with regard to God's will:

> He does not will the death of the sinner, according to his word, but he wills it according to that inscrutable will of his. It is our business, however, to pay attention to this word and leave that inscrutable will alone. . . . It is enough to know simply that there is a certain inscrutable will in God, and as to what, why, and how far it wills, that is something we have no right whatever to inquire into, hanker after, or meddle with, but only to fear and adore. It is therefore right to say: "If God does not desire our death, the fact that we perish must be imputed to our own will."[3]

Ultimately God is behind everything and is greater than all the anti-godly powers. There is, then, a seeming paradox between the conviction that God, in the struggle with Satan over the rule of the world, is greater than all the anti-godly powers, and that God in God's unsearchable power and majesty ultimately stands behind Satan. This paradox we cannot solve. It must be left unresolved. At the same time Luther emphasizes that God's majesty cannot serve as an excuse for us when we conduct ourselves in the wrong way. We are responsible for our own actions.

As we gather from the New Testament witness, the anti-godly powers are in continuous rebellion against God, attempting to fight God's omnipotence. The human rebellion that follows in that train is not a sign of human depravity or a predetermined necessity. When we consider, for instance, the biography of Hitler or Stalin, we notice that these men voluntarily followed the destructive path of the anti-godly powers. Similar to these powers, they wanted to dethrone God and enthrone themselves in total autonomy as new gods.

In the narrative of Jesus' temptation we discern both the might and the intention of these powers (Matt. 4:1–11). They attempt to draw Jesus onto their side so that he will worship and adore them instead of God. As compensation they promise unlimited influence. Elsewhere in the New Testament the anti-godly powers recognize that Christ has come to destroy them and their influence (Mark 5:7; cf. 1 Cor. 15:57). As Luther says of the Prince of Darkness in his hymn "A Mighty Fortress Is Our God," "One little word can

2. Martin Luther, *The Bondage of the Will*, in *LW* 33:65–66.
3. Ibid., 140.

fell him [the Prince]." When we join Christ, we can participate in his victory over these powers.

In conclusion, we must note that these destructive forces do not confront us like an impersonal *it*, but are attempting to come across as an overwhelming *thou*. The personification of these powers helps us to understand them. Since the Bible has no uniform name for them, and since we often get the impression that there is a multitude of them, the term "anti-godly powers" seems to be most appropriate. As we have seen, this term counteracts the misunderstanding that we are dealing with a devil or a Satan as is portrayed in fairy tales.

The Power of Sin (Original Sin and Actual Sins)

Having tried to fathom the cause and reality of evil, we now want to trace its influence on humans in how far they are free to do or not do what they want. The narrative of the fall notwithstanding, we must first note that we still live in God's good creation. Humans are created in the image of God and are commanded to act as God's representatives on earth. Yet we do not accomplish this mandate, and therefore we sin against God. While we must distinguish between actual sins and so-called original sin, which is attested to by every subsequent sinful act, according to the biblical witness both aspects point in the same direction. Both are understood as a turning-away from God, an action from which ensues sinfulness as humanity's unnatural nature.

Turning Away from God

While in the Bible sin is depicted in many different ways, one of its fundamental characteristics is the turning-away from God. We notice this already in the narrative of the fall. When God asked Adam why he hid himself, Adam answered, "I heard the sound of you in the garden, and I was afraid, because I was naked; and I hid myself" (Gen. 3:10). Humans turn away from God, and in the subsequent encounter with God they are anxious and insecure. Whether a person violates certain norms, rejects all norms, or simply makes a mistake, all this is subsumed under the concept of sin against God. For instance, when David eliminated Uriah the Hittite so that he could have his wife, Bathsheba, and the prophet Nathan challenged him, David confessed, "I have sinned against the LORD" (2 Sam. 12:13). God wants us to live in congruence with God's will, and if we deviate from that, this is sin. This means that everything is sinful which does not issue from our trust relationship with God. The apostle Paul phrases it this way: "Whatever does not proceed from faith is sin" (Rom. 14:23). Since sin is always related to or measured against God, it cannot be empirically proven. For instance, the people of Sodom and Gomorrah did not understand their behavior as sinful. Only in relating it to Yahweh was their conduct determined to be sinful (Gen. 18:20; cf. Ezek. 16:48–50). Since sin is a turning-away from God, we need not be surprised that a person who sins shall die (Ezek. 18:4). If one turns away from the giver of life, there are consequences for this life and beyond it.

While sin is primarily a theological concept, evil is something that one can describe empirically as bad or noxious. Not all sinful deeds show immediately their evil or bad consequences. As limited beings we cannot always estimate the long-term consequences of individual actions. Sometimes something considered good eventuates bad results later on (e.g., the proliferation of nuclear energy to aid developing countries). Since often good and bad components are intertwined in a human action, it is difficult to designate an action as either good or evil (e.g., a dynamic leader who employs both peaceful and violent means to achieve the good in a community). Therefore it is important to consider each action before God and in its general applicability.

In rabbinic Judaism one distinguished between lethal sins, such as idolatry and the shedding of blood, and venial sins, which one committed unknowingly. For lethal sins one could achieve satisfaction only through one's own death, whereas for the latter one could obtain forgiveness through rites of purification and good works. This means that sin was largely understood as trespassing the divine law. In the New Testament we no longer find the distinction between different kinds of sin, and human sinfulness is directly related to God. For instance, in the Sermon on the Mount, Jesus shows how each human being is hopelessly entangled in sinfulness. But Jesus does not merely recognize this entanglement; he attacks sin in a totally new way. His whole life on earth was a continuous battle against the anti-godly powers. On the one hand, Jesus emphasized the thoroughgoing sinfulness of humanity, and on the other hand, he began to eliminate the cause of sin through his actions by pushing back the anti-godly powers that tempt humanity to sin.

Ushering in the kingdom of God, Jesus not only had table fellowship with sinners and forgave them for their sins (Mark 2:15–17), but he also, as one who stood in the place of God, established a new community with sinners. This shows the beginning and the anticipation of the end-time community of God with his people when he will no longer account their sins. In Jesus comes true what the servant of God had promised: "I, I am He who blots out your transgressions for my own sake, and I will not remember your sins" (Isa. 43:25). Neither the announcement of the kingdom of God nor the forgiveness of sin can be taken lightly, because they presuppose an answer, the acceptance of our forgiveness. Whoever refuses God's Holy Spirit, the Spirit that becomes visible in the life and destiny of Jesus, has forfeited the chance to return to God. That person pronounces judgment upon himself or herself and commits an unforgivable sin (Matt. 12:32).

Our Second Nature

In the context of the Noahic blessing we read the sobering words: "The inclination of the human heart is evil from youth" (Gen. 8:21). The statement that once brought the demise of humanity (Gen. 6:5) has now become the precondition for God's gracious covenant. Humans are sinful from birth to death, and therefore the psalmist exclaims, "Indeed, I was born guilty, a sinner when my mother conceived me" (Ps. 51:5). As Old Testament scholars affirm, the psalmist does not want to introduce here a traducianistic understanding of sin whereby sin is transferred by birth from mother to child. This idea was first introduced by Tertullian (ca. 160–ca. 212). The psalmist refers here to the sinful context into which a person was born and therefore talks about his "mother" Israel. This means that sin accompanies not only the history of individuals but also the history of the community. Similarly, when Paul affirms, "Just as sin came into the world through one man, and death came through sin, so death spread to all because all have sinned" (Rom. 5:12), he does not want to imply that it was Adam's fault that everybody sinned and died. Paul understands sin metaphorically, as a humanlike being whose destructive power found its ways into our world through the first human being. He does not talk about the age of death in a biological way. The age or eon of death has its beginning in Adam in the same way that the age or eon of life has its inception in Christ.

Theologians such as Augustine therefore affirm, "For the first man was able not to sin, was able not to die, was able not to forsake good."[4] Sorrow and suffering came into this world through human sinfulness. Yet already at Augustine's time some theologians contended that the first human being, since he was only human and not divine, had to die regardless of whether he sinned. Today one hardly speculates about conditions prior to the fall, because in the first chapters of the Bible the emphasis lies on God having created everything good. If the created is no longer good, one cannot attribute this to God but must attribute it to humans. Nevertheless, human death has a special quality, otherwise humans would not have concerned themselves from their earliest time onward with death and life beyond. Once humans distanced themselves from God, death was no longer natural but was considered something that

---

4. Augustine, *On Rebuke and Grace* 12.33, in *NPNF*[1] 5:485.

ought not to be. Against this fate of human finitude humanity has fought until today.

Paul emphasizes that nobody starts life in a neutral sphere; we always live in a sinful context that influences us. Sin is, so to speak, a heritage we carry around with us similar to other things that follow us from birth, such as our social status, a strong or weak memory, or a predisposition to being thin or heavy. At the same time Paul does not excuse us but calls us to personal responsibility since we know how we should lead our lives. Even the pagans, he says, have the law inscribed in their hearts, and their conscience attests against them (Rom. 2:14–15). Similarly, Luther explains, "The knowledge contained in the Law is known to reason."[5] We have already mentioned that the natural law as most clearly expressed in the Ten Commandments is known to all people. When Paul points out that humans have "served the creature rather than the Creator" (Rom. 1:25), he means that they no longer understand themselves as representing God. They have placed themselves in God's stead. They want to rule the world autonomously, being responsible only to themselves. In so doing, they must deny their human limits and surround themselves with the myth of being omnipotent, as we see most clearly with modern dictators. But even the average person today quite often understands himself or herself as the focal point of the world, which leads to serving only oneself rather than also being available to others. All this shows our sinfulness and idolatry.

Since humans are so deeply ensnared in sin, Paul can exclaim, "Wretched man that I am! Who will rescue me from this body of death?" But then he continues, "Thanks be to God through Jesus Christ our Lord!" (Rom. 7:24–25). Christ liberates us from the bondage to sin (cf. Rom. 5:21). If someone lives according to Christ and God's Spirit, this person does not live from himself or herself, but belongs to Christ and lives in and for Christ. Through this new relationship enabled by Christ, the basic estrangement from God has been overcome. This is accomplished only by God's grace and not through education or genetic manipulation. Sin no longer has power over us. Though we have to fight sin daily, we know that it has found its conqueror in Christ.

The Extent of Sinful Corruption

Through the ages the church has repeatedly pondered the issue of whether there is anything essentially good in humans upon which to build, or whether

5. Martin Luther, *Auslegungen des 1. und 2. Kapitels Johannes in Predigten* (1537/38), in WA 46:667.10–11.

humans are totally corrupted by sin. Shortly before 400, the ascetic monk Pelagius (ca. 360–420) arrived in Rome from the British Isles. He denounced the laxity of morals in urban Rome, admonished the people to lead decent lives, and reminded them of their own possibilities. If God had commanded us to do good, Pelagius argued, then we should be capable of doing good. God has given us a certain degree of freedom, and it depends on us whether we want to do the good or the bad. Pelagius understood freedom primarily as psychological freedom with which we can decide what we want to do. However, he equated this freedom of choice with moral freedom and forgot that a moral life is not the result of individual actions but consists of a whole life attitude, for instance, whether or not one wants to live in harmony with God. Pelagius was not so naive to assume that humans are without sin, but he insisted that they could be without sin. Since a newborn infant is without sin, it does not need baptism for the forgiveness of sin. One could easily call Pelagius' approach a self-redeeming moralism. One believes in human goodness and no longer needs Christ's salvific activity to be able to come back to God.

Just like today, in antiquity a fatalistic or deterministic attitude was widely spread among the people. Many thought that everything must happen just the way it does. To counteract this, most theologians emphasized personal responsibility instead of the unavoidability of sin. But this line of argument was problematic for Augustine. He pointed out that through unity with God the first human being could indeed have remained good. God would have then changed this possibility of humans not sinning and not dying to the impossibility to sin and to die. But Adam did not stay this way but became corrupted. According to Augustine, since Adam is the ancestor of all humans, all of us are corrupted. Sin does not spread by imitation but spreads by procreation. Sexual concupiscence, which accompanies the procreative act, makes the newborn child a victim of sin, even if the act itself is not a sin for the newborn. For a long time after Augustine sexuality was seen as something negative. Augustine agreed with Pelagius that a person can choose between virtue and vice, "but this will, which is free in evil things because it takes pleasure in evil, is not free in good things, for the reason that it has not been made free."[6] This means that once a person has turned away from God, that person cannot return to God. Individual actions may be morally good, but it is our life attitude that is decisive. If there is a plus sign (unity with God) in front of that life attitude, then God accepts its content. But if there is a minus sign (estrangement from God), then its content may be as good as it wants, but in the eyes of God it is not good. Augustine therefore says that the virtues a person may have "are

6. Augustine, *Against Two Letters of the Pelagians* 1.7, in NPNF[1] 5:379.

rather vices than virtues so long as there is no reference to God in the matter."[7] Because of the sinfulness that surrounds us, says Augustine, we deserve nothing but rejection by God, and we merit eternal death. If God accepts us, it is not because of our morally good lives but out of God's free grace. This reasoning made a deep impact on the former Augustinian monk Martin Luther. He writes in his exposition of the first article of the creed that God has provided for him everything "out of pure, fatherly, and divine goodness and mercy, without any merit or worthiness of mine at all! For all of this I owe it to God to thank and praise, serve and obey him."[8] The experience of the grace and goodness of God without any precondition should lead to a life of service to God and neighbor.

Nearly a thousand years after the controversy between Pelagius and Augustine, which was decided largely in Augustine's favor, a controversy erupted in 1524–25 between Luther and the learned Erasmus of Rotterdam (1462–1536). The arguments were almost the same as a millennium earlier because Erasmus emphasized in his treatise *On the Free Will* that God would not have given us his Ten Commandments if we could not keep them, and therefore we must cooperate with God toward our salvation. Luther, however, used the already mentioned metaphor of a human being as a beast of burden that goes in God's direction if it is guided by God or in the direction of the devil if it is ridden by the devil. According to Luther, it is not up to us to run either to God or to the devil since they fight with each other over our destiny. For Luther, free will with regard to our salvation is only an empty term, because if we had a free will with regard to salvation, we would not need Christ. We can entrust ourselves only to God's grace, remembering what God says in the words of the psalmist: "Call on me in the day of trouble; I will deliver you, and you shall glorify me" (Ps. 50:15). Of course, Luther was convinced that humans can act morally good, and should do so. But such activities do not contribute anything to our salvation. Moreover, good works are not a precondition for salvation but are a natural consequence of knowing Jesus Christ, to whom we owe our salvation.

The Broken Image of God

Genesis 1:26 uses two words to express that humans were created in the image of God. God says, "Let us make humankind in our *image*, according to our *likeness*." The second word rejects the conclusion that image means a

---

7. Augustine, *The City of God* 29.25, in NPNF[1] 2:418.
8. Martin Luther, *Small Catechism*, in *Evangelical Lutheran Worship*, 1162.

real depiction of God. Some have been tempted to draw theological conclusions from these two words. For instance, in the second century Irenaeus (ca. 130–ca. 200) claimed that through Adam's fall humanity lost its likeness to God, namely, its relationship to God, whereas its resemblance was maintained, suggesting that humans are reasonable and morally free creatures. This distinction between image and resemblance (Latin: *imago* and *similitudo*) could easily be understood to mean that only part of a human being fell prey to sinfulness, while the rest was preserved in original purity. Humanity need only improve to get rid of its sinfulness. In the late Middle Ages theologians even stated that humans had only a defect that could be perfected through supernatural grace. The image could be restored like a damaged picture. Luther, however, did not think much of such a distinction and asserted, "Humans must be an image either of God or of the devil, since they resemble the one according to whom they conduct their lives."[9] Luther understood a human being as a unity. Therefore, if any part of a human is sinful, then the whole being is sinful. The apostle Paul put the matter similarly when he said that a human lives either according to the flesh or according to the spirit, meaning either according to one's sinfulness or by focusing on God.

The Social Dimension of Sin

In the Gospel of John we read that the world is ruled by the prince of this world (John 14:30), that is, by the Evil One. It was only in Augustine's masterpiece *The City of God* that this topic was thematized again. Augustine says that there are two kinds of human societies or two cities in this world: "The one consists of those who wish to live after the flesh, the other of those who wish to live after the spirit; and when they severely achieve what they wish, they live in peace, each after their kind."[10] These two kinds of human society are not strictly separated from one another but are intertwined, whereby the one lives according to its own desires and the other according to God's will. Sin is described here as a social phenomenon that serves human self-glorification and is at least potentially destructive. Writing his book under the influence of the sack of Rome, Augustine perceived human history as a history of this world, which has its own judgment and which at the same time is God's judgment. For Augustine, it was because Rome was corrupted by sin that it was severely punished. The German theologian Albrecht Ritschl (1822–89) picked up on Augustine's thought in the second half of the nineteenth century, stating that

9. Martin Luther, *Über das 1. Buch Mose. Predigten* (1527), in WA 24:51.12–13, in his exegesis of Gen. 1:27.
10. Augustine, *The City of God* 14.1, in NPNF[1] 2:262.

sin has a societal structure (which, however, does not eliminate the responsibility of individuals). Therefore he talked about a kingdom of evil. The German American theologian Walter Rauschenbusch (1861–1918) drew upon Ritschl's ideas. He writes, "The evils of one generation are caused by the wrongs of the generations that preceded, and will in turn condition the sufferings and temptations of those who come after."[11] Rauschenbusch not only describes the societal dimension of evil; he also understands the kingdom of God, emphasizing that conversion from the kingdom of evil to the kingdom of God dare not be confined to the inner human being. It must also pertain to the sinful past of one's societal group. Rauschenbusch shows that sin is not only a matter of one's own decision, and that conversion does not just occur between oneself and God. Both have consequences for the whole human being. Sin as aversion from God influences our attitude toward ourselves, toward other people, and toward nature. In short, sin permeates our whole person.

11. Walter Rauschenbusch, *A Theology for the Social Gospel* (New York: Abingdon, 1945), 79.

PART 3

CHRIST THE REDEEMER

When we consider Christ as the redeemer, we can do this only under the presupposition that God acts in this world. Jesus Christ is the decisive action of God, as we are told in the first sentence of the Letter to the Hebrews: "Long ago God spoke to our ancestors in many and various ways by the prophets, but in these last days he has spoken to us by a Son" (Heb. 1:1–2). To understand Jesus appropriately, we must perceive him from the Jewish background out of which he emerged. To grasp his significance, we must also keep in mind the human situation that we described in the previous chapter.

Created in God's image, humanity continuously forfeits its task to be God's representative in this world. Therefore we can only expect that God will leave us to our own fate. Yet God does not act as we would expect. In unending patience and grace, God designs various ways in which humanity can get back on the right track. Since humanity brings to naught all these plans, God comes to us in a human guise to achieve what we are unable and unwilling to do. At the same time, this human figure serves as our source of inspiration and our goal. But who is this Jesus Christ? First of all, we must acknowledge that he was a human being who lived among us. Yet he must have been more than a human being, otherwise he could not have redeemed us. But first we must turn to Jesus' human dimension.

8

JESUS OF NAZARETH

None of the so-called founders of a world religion is as controversial as Jesus of Nazareth both with regard to his message and his person. There is hardly a debate about whether Muhammad ever lived or about what he taught. It is commonly assumed that he understood himself as Allah's prophet and made known to his followers Allah's revelation, which, as he claimed, he had received through an angel. Similarly, we know approximately when Buddha lived, who his parents were, and the main points of his doctrine. Yet with Jesus of Nazareth the situation is very different. There are still some people who occasionally doubt whether Jesus ever lived. This opinion was quite often voiced in the nineteenth century. Today the vast majority of New Testament scholars are convinced that Jesus was indeed a historical figure. Yet often they are far from unanimous on the significance of the person of Jesus and on the actual content of his teaching. The reason for this is twofold:

1. While Islam demands obedience and Buddhism emphasizes meditation, the Christian faith wants to be understood. With this, the danger arises that different people understand the person and message of Jesus in different ways.

2. Another reason is that Jesus is only in a very limited way the "founder" of the Christian faith. Of course, Jesus had followers during his lifetime. But only after his death (and his resurrection) was there a rapid increase in the number of people who understood him in some way as the Christ and designated him as such. The New Testament scholar Rudolf Bultmann

therefore wrote, "He who formerly had been the *bearer* of the message was drawn into it and became its essential *content. The proclaimer became the proclaimed*—but the central question is, in what sense?"[1] The important question is whether the earthly Jesus and his message are part of the Christian faith or whether they are its presupposition. Evidently, without Jesus' message there would be no New Testament. But the New Testament was written not just as a memory of Jesus' life and message.

The Gospels wanted to be more than a biography of Jesus' life and teaching. The Gospel of Mark, for instance, starts with the words, "The beginning of the good news of Jesus Christ, the Son of God" (Mark 1:1). Matthew starts by introducing the genealogy of Jesus with the words, "An account of the genealogy of Jesus the Messiah" (Matt. 1:1). John makes no reference to the historical Jesus. Instead, he starts with the words, "In the beginning was the Word, and the Word was with God, and the Word was God" (John 1:1). Only Luke is different because he wants to narrate everything as "an orderly account," not out of biographical or historical interest, but so that Theophilus, for whom he is writing his Gospel narrative, "may know the truth concerning the things about which you have been instructed" (Luke 1:3–4). It is not the purpose of any of the Gospel writers just to render the life and teaching of Jesus. The reason for this is not that they were ashamed that Jesus had died on the cross or, as some had claimed, that his mission had ended in a failure. To the contrary, they were convinced that Jesus was the Christ. They tried to show this and so were naturally less interested in just the human person of Jesus.

Since the Christian faith is not simply an obedient agreement to certain things, but rather a believing understanding, we cannot simply pass over Jesus of Nazareth who lived on this earth and focus only on Jesus Christ. Similar to the Gospel writers, we must attempt to understand how a faith in Christ came out of the life and activity of Jesus. This means that we must turn to the historical Jesus. We must ask if there is continuity between Jesus of Nazareth and the Christ as portrayed in the biblical documents. Furthermore, it is important to know how far there is continuity between the biblical Christ and the Christ of the faith of the church as, for instance, portrayed in the trinitarian and christological dogmas. We remember that the Jehovah's Witnesses argue that the Christian doctrine of the Trinity is nonbiblical and thus a superstition. Therefore the attempt to unearth the continuity between the

---

1. Rudolf Bultmann, *Theology of the New Testament*, trans. K. Grobel (New York: Scribner's, 1951), 1:33 (emphasis in the original).

historical Jesus and the Christ of the Christian faith is necessary to show the trustworthiness of the Christian faith.

Albert Schweitzer (1875–1965), the theologian, physician, and interpreter of Johann Sebastian Bach, stated in his famous 1906 investigation, *The Quest of the Historical Jesus*, that each age depicted Jesus in its own image. This is to some extent true. We need only think of the well-known portrayals of Jesus in the Nazarene style during the time of Romanticism, in which he was rendered with lightly curled, long blond hair, typical of northern Europeans. Or we could think here of liberation theology, which used Jesus for its own cause as a liberator from oppression and exploitation. Does this mean that we are stuck in a thoroughgoing relativism when we ask who this Jesus really was? Who was the resurrected Christ upon whom our faith is founded?

If we carefully read the Gospels, we obtain only a few bits of biographical information about Jesus. We do not know his height or the color of his eyes. Even the year of his birth cannot be determined with certainty. We do not obtain from Jesus those personal things that we usually find in a passport. Nevertheless, there are two details that are decisive for our understanding of Jesus and that we know beyond any doubt: (1) Jesus was a faithful Jew, and (2) his person and proclamation had an end-time significance. If we want to understand Jesus, we must perceive of him in the context of the Judaism of his time. Jesus grew up with the Hebrew Bible, which at that time consisted of the Pentateuch plus the prophetic books. He debated with the prevailing Jewish groups: the Pharisees, the Sadducees, and the scribes. The issue of whether he stood in continuity with the Jewish tradition led to his rejection by these groups, and finally to his conviction by the religious authorities of his time. Over the years the end-time significance of Jesus and of his message was pushed further and further into the background. Most people today regard him only as a moral authority from whom one can obtain certain help or advice for our present life. Yet the title "Christ," which means the anointed one and is the equivalent to the Hebrew "Messiah," shows that with Jesus' coming and with his message an end-time kingdom was expected. He was more than just a moral teacher.

Jesus as a Jew

The childhood narratives in Matthew and Luke show that Jesus was brought up as a faithful Jew. He was circumcised, instructed in the law, and obedient to his parents. He took notice of the religious movements of his time and insisted on being baptized by John the Baptist to be prepared for the immediate inbreaking of the end time. Since Jesus' public proclamation commenced without any preparations known to us, we may assume that his baptism by John had a catalytic influence similar to the prophets who experienced calls in the Old Testament. After his baptism Jesus began his public ministry. For a while, Jesus and John the Baptist conducted their missions alongside each other. But when John was put in prison and decapitated, his disciples buried him, and "then they went and told Jesus" (Matt. 14:12). This episode shows us that they felt so closely connected with Jesus that they shared with him the sad news. From that point on, Jesus' proclamation occurred independent of any other person or movement.

Since Jesus started his activities in close proximity to John the Baptist, we may ask ourselves whether there was much in Jesus' proclamation that was genuinely his own. John and Jesus agreed on many points. They were both unhappy with the present way of Jewish thinking and conduct (Matt. 3:10; 12:34), they intensely expected the end of the world (Matt. 3:10; 7:19), and they were convinced that one had to review one's conduct immediately and put oneself totally in God's service (Matt. 3:8; Mark 1:15). But there were also important differences between the two. While John was an ascetic, Jesus was not. In contrast to John, Jesus did not remain in the desert but traveled through the countryside and even entered houses of publicly known sinners (Luke 19:7). Jesus' message did not have the somber tone of the immediately impending judgment, because for him the time of salvation had already started, while for John this time was still to come. John pointed to a mightier one who would come after him and who would baptize with the Holy Spirit (Matt. 3:11). How different Jesus' message was from John's we can gather from Jesus' actions, which he interpreted in the light of the Old Testament metaphors of the time of salvation (Matt. 11:4–5; Isa. 35:5). At the same time, Jesus had high praises for John when he said, "Truly I tell you, among those born of women no one has arisen greater than John the Baptist" (Matt. 11:11). Yet with regard to John he did not lose the appropriate estimation when he added, "Yet the least in the kingdom of heaven is greater than he. . . . For all the prophets and the law prophesied until John came" (Matt. 11:11, 13). While John signified the conclusion of the Old Testament, with Jesus something new had begun. But what was new about it?

Until his death Jesus had been a faithful member of the Jewish community. In contrast to Muhammad and Buddha, he did not found a new religion. For many, he was just a Jewish rabbi or teacher. We hear at the beginning of his ministry, "When the sabbath came, he entered the synagogue and taught" (Mark 1:21). More than once Jesus was called "teacher" (Mark 5:35; 12:19), and his immediate followers were therefore called "disciples" (Mark 3:7). Jesus taught his disciples (Mark 8:31), who then taught others (Mark 6:30). It is not unimportant that the original New Testament designation for the tradition of the gospel was not "gospel" (Greek: *euangelion*) but "word" (Greek: *logos*) or "word of God" (Greek: *logos theou*), concepts that in Jewish terminology are synonymous with Holy Scripture.

In this way Jesus can be seen in close connection with the rabbinic tradition. This would also explain why in the New Testament the term *logos* is used to refer to the gospel, which tells us of Jesus and his activities. Similar to a rabbi, Jesus would not have taught indiscriminately, but he taught his disciples important things that they then learned by heart. But Jesus was not just one of the rabbis. In contrast to them, his teachings were illustrated with miracles (cf. Mark 2:9), something that was not usually done by rabbis. Therefore the people said about him, "He taught them as one having authority, and not as the scribes" (Mark 1:22), and they assumed that he was a prophet (Mark 8:28). Jesus' opponents, however, told the Romans that he was a Zealot opposing the Roman occupation of Palestine, and Pilate later convicted him as a resistance fighter.

When we look at the geographic areas in which Jesus lived and worked, again we receive the impression that he was a faithful Jew. If the few indications in the first three Gospels are reliable, Jesus stayed only in Jewish territory, except if he had to flee from his enemies (Mark 8:27). He dealt exclusively with Jews, and if he helped those of non-Jewish descent, he pointed this out as an exception (cf. Mark 7:24–30). Since the church was very much interested in mission work among non-Jewish people, it would have certainly emphasized Jesus' activity among them if there had been a historical basis for this. Even the rabbis in Jesus' time were not as conservative as he was, because, as we read in Matthew 23:15, they "cross sea and land to make a single convert" to the Jewish faith. Jesus understood himself to be sent only to Israel.

Yet Jesus was not narrow minded. He took notice of important people and events. His main dialogue partners, who eventually caused his death, were the Pharisees, the leading religious group of the time. Their main interest was to fulfill exactly the demands of the law as they saw it interpreted by tradition. Jesus did not reject the law either, but said, "Therefore, whoever breaks one of the least of these commandments, and teaches others to do the same, will be called least in the kingdom of heaven; but whoever does them and teaches them will be called great in the kingdom of heaven" (Matt. 5:19). With this attitude Jesus should have not encountered any problems from the Pharisees and the scribes, who with the rabbis largely emphasized the law. They could even have become friends with Jesus.

The situation, however, is somewhat different when we hear from Jesus: "Do not think that I have come to abolish the law or the prophets; I have come not to abolish, but to fulfill" (Matt. 5:17), and, "I tell you, unless your righteousness exceeds that of the scribes and Pharisees, you will never enter the kingdom of heaven" (Matt. 5:20). Such radicalism was not unknown in Judaism. The scribes and Pharisees could hear similar pronouncements from John the Baptist, who refused to proclaim any religious security, something that the scribes and Pharisees sought to achieve; instead, he called all people to repentance. We could even say that John himself could have preached the kind of radical interpretation of the law that is given in the Sermon on the Mount. Therefore such a call to repentance should have not caused any great problems for Jesus, even if that call hurt the self-understanding of the pious Pharisees and scribes since they endeavored to fulfill the demands of the law to the last iota.

But Jesus did not just radicalize the law and its demands. He claimed that with him the time of salvation had begun and the law had been fulfilled. This claim that he was the one who would bring about the kingdom of God and in whom the promissory history of Israel found its fulfillment started the controversy with the Jewish leaders, as we see in the trial of Jesus when the high priest asks, "Are you the Messiah, the Son of the Blessed One?" (Mark 14:61). If Jesus' message and actions had clearly shown messianic qualities, his claim to be the Messiah would not have been ultimately rejected. To understand this reaction, we must consider that the year 5,000, according to the Jewish calendar, had raised messianic hopes in many Jews, who believed that the Messiah would usher in the sixth millennium, the age of the kingdom of God. Therefore in the first quarter of the first century AD there were many messianic expectations. For instance, the prophet Theudas was sentenced to death in AD 46 by the Roman procurator, and a few years later an Egyptian prophet attempted with his followers to capture Jerusalem. But the Roman authorities acted swiftly and decisively. The Jewish writer Josephus (37/38–ca. 100) reported on another band of wicked men: "These were such men as deceived and deluded the people under pretense of Divine inspiration, but were for procuring innovations and changes of the government; and these prevailed with the multitude to act like madmen, and went before them into the wilderness, as pretending that God would there show them the signals of liberty."[2] Messianic hopes were always directed toward the abolition of the Roman occupation in Palestine. One expected that the Messiah would rescue Israel from exile and slavery and the whole world from oppression, suffering, war, and especially heathenism. The salvation of humanity also included the salvation of nature. The messianic age would bring great material riches, and

2. Flavius Josephus, *Wars of the Jews* 2.13.4.

the earth would yield an abundance of grain and fruit, which humanity could enjoy without much toil.

In comparison to these expectations, Jesus' life and mission cannot be regarded as having messianic characteristics. Jesus never affirmed the political hopes that were associated with the Messiah. Some of his followers thought that this might change once Jesus entered Jerusalem to celebrate the Last Supper with them. Again, however, he did not occupy the city and did not proclaim himself as Messiah (cf. Luke 24:21). He most likely refused the title Messiah when someone wanted to confer it on him. Even Peter's confession that Jesus is the Messiah was not affirmed by Jesus (cf. Mark 8:29–30). Jesus did not show any interest in the political and nationalistic aspirations connected to the coming of the Messiah. He did not want to be misunderstood as a political liberator. We do not read that he conspired against the Roman occupying army or that he called for resistance against them. Though his indictment ultimately was of a political nature, he clearly rejected it. "My kingdom is not from this world" (John 18:36) was his answer to Pilate. How then should we describe his life and mission?

Here the trial before the high priest contains some clues. The high priest concluded from Jesus' answer to the question "Are you the Messiah, the Son of the Blessed One?" that Jesus had committed blasphemy. How could Jesus' answer be understood in that way? It seems that Jesus was referring to commonly held Jewish end-time expectations when he said, "I am; and 'you will see the Son of Man seated at the right hand of the Power,' and 'coming with the clouds of heaven'" (Mark 14:62). But when we consider the Old Testament usage of the phrase "I am" (Greek: *ego eimi*), the situation looks completely different. In Hebrew "I am he" (*ani hu*) is used only with regard to Yahweh, the Old Testament name for God, and is an abbreviation of the longer formula of divine self-disclosure, "I am Yahweh." At important points in the Gospels, Jesus used the Greek phrase *ego eimi* in analogy to this Old Testament self-disclosure of God. For instance, in Mark 13:6 he says, "Many will come in my name and say, 'I am he!' and they will lead many astray." The answer that Jesus gave to the high priest was not a simple affirmation of the question. Rather, Jesus identified himself with God. This means that he had lifted his messianic secret and had come to understand that he was identical with God. The reaction of the high priest is very understandable. Since Jesus did not agree with the ideas one generally held about the Messiah, the high priest and many others concluded that Jesus had committed blasphemy. It was evident that he must be sentenced to death, and for this they needed the help of the Romans because the Jewish people themselves were not allowed to carry out capital punishment.

EXCURSUS: LUTHER AND THE JEWS

Since we have emphasized that the human person Jesus of Nazareth was born a Jew and died as one, it is important from a Lutheran perspective to explain how Martin Luther dealt with this historical fact. The claim has often been made that there is a straight line from Luther to the persecution of the Jews during the German Third Reich. But this is simply wrong. As with anyone who wrote as much as Luther did, it is easy to find quotations revealing a person's opinion or prejudices. To do justice to Luther, however, we must see him in the context of his time. Even with his most outlandish remarks with regard to the Jews, Luther "was taking up suggestions long made from another side. They are neither original nor harsher than those that others at the time had made, and across all ecclesiastical and spiritual persuasions."[3]

On the eve of the Reformation, the Jews in Europe had a very hard time. Already in 1290 the Jews had been expelled from England by King Edward I (1239–1307). In 1492 they had been evicted from Spain, and in 1506 approximately two thousand Jews were killed in Lisbon, Portugal. The learned Erasmus of Rotterdam lauds France in 1570 that in contrast to other countries it "remains not infected with heretics . . . with Jews, with half-Jewish marraños [i.e., converted Spanish Jews]."[4] The fifteenth century saw an increase in the expulsion of Jews from cities or districts in the German empire. By the time of the Reformation the urban expulsion was nearly completed. "After 1520 the Jews were only expelled from a relatively small number of cities, while in the preceding period from 1388 (Strasbourg) until 1519 (Regensburg, Rothenburg ob der Tauber) nearly 90 expulsions had been conducted."[5] For instance, in Regensburg the former member of the cathedral chapter and later Anabaptist Balthasar Hubmaier (1485–1528) was instrumental in having the Jews expelled from the city in February 1519. The Jewish ghetto, including the synagogue, was destroyed, and in its stead a pilgrimage church was erected for "The Beautiful Mary." Luther lived in this milieu that was so antagonistic to the Jews. In 1523 he composed a pamphlet with the title *That Jesus Christ Was*

3. Bernhard Lohse, *Martin Luther's Theology: Its Historical and Systematic Development*, trans. and ed. Roy A. Harrisville (Minneapolis: Fortress, 1999), 344.

4. Erasmus of Rotterdam, "Letter to Riccardo Bartolini" (no. 549, March 10, 1517), in *The Correspondence of Erasmus: Letters 446 to 593; 1516 to 1517*, trans. R. A. B. Mynors and D. F. S. Thomson (Toronto: University of Toronto Press, 1977), 279.

5. Heiko A. Oberman, "Luthers Beziehungen zu den Juden: Ahnen und Geahndete," in *Leben und Werk Martin Luthers von 1526–1546. Festgabe zu seinem 500. Geburtstag*, ed. Helmar Junghans (Göttingen: Vandenhoeck & Ruprecht, 1983), 1:520.

Born a Jew. After defending the Jews against various slanderous accusations, he then writes:

> If the apostles, who were also Jews, had dealt with us Gentiles as we Gentiles deal with the Jews, there would have never been a Christian among the Gentiles. Since they dealt with us Gentiles in such brotherly fashion, we in our turn ought to treat the Jews in a brotherly manner in order that we might convert some of them. For even we ourselves are not yet all very far along, not to speak of having arrived.
>
> When we are inclined to boast of our position we should remember that we are but Gentiles, while the Jews are the lineage of Christ. We are aliens and in-laws, they are blood relatives, cousins, and brothers of our Lord. Therefore, if one is to boast of flesh and blood, the Jews are actually nearer to Christ than we are, as St. Paul says in Romans 9.[6]

Three observations are important for us here: (1) Luther agrees with Paul that the Jews are closer to Jesus according to their descent than gentiles are because we come from paganism. Therefore they merit our special attention. (2) Luther concedes that we can hope for the Jews' conversion only if we treat them in a brotherly manner and in humility. (3) Luther hopes that at least some of the Jews will convert to Christianity. Conversion, however, cannot be conducted by force but must occur by the power of the gospel and the love of the Christians. In addition, Luther contends that the Jews unjustly wait for the Messiah, because he has come already as Jesus Christ.

In 1536 the Saxon elector John Frederick (1503–54) issued an edict forbidding the Jews to take up residence in his territory or to work there. They were also not allowed to traverse his territory. Josel of Rosheim (1476–1554) from Lower Alsace, a well-known representative of Judaism, intervened. Luther responded to Josel that he himself had done much for Judaism. "Yet because your people misuse my service in such a bad way and also do things which we Christians cannot tolerate from them, they themselves have deprived me of all support which I could have had with regard to the princes and lords."[7] It had been his hope, Luther further wrote, that through this friendly treatment God would bring them "to their Messiah." Yet this friendliness only strengthened them in their error. Therefore he said he could not do anything for them.

In 1543 Luther's pamphlet *The Jews and Their Lies* appeared. This treatise is often regarded as typical for Luther and his attitude toward the Jews. But again, one must read it in its historical context. The first sentence reads, "I

---

6. Martin Luther, *That Jesus Christ Was Born a Jew* (1523), in *LW* 45:200–201.
7. Martin Luther, "An den Juden Josel" (no. 3157, June 11, 1537), in *WA BR* 8:89.4–8.

had made up my mind to write no more either about the Jews or against them. But since I learned that these miserable and accursed people do not cease to lure to themselves even us, that is, the Christians, I have published this little book, so that I might be found among those who opposed such poisonous activities of the Jews and who warned the Christians to be on their guard against them."[8] Luther had heard that the Jews were trying to convert Christians, and it made no sense to him to wait for the conversion of the Jews to Christ. Luther's only hope was that "they reach the point where their misery finally makes them pliable and they are forced to confess that the Messiah has come, and he is our Jesus. Until such a time it is much too early, yes, even it is useless to argue with them about how God is triune, how he became man, and how Mary is the mother of God."[9] Luther then concludes, "Thus we cannot extinguish the unquenchable fire of divine wrath, of which the prophets speak, nor can we convert the Jews. With prayer and the fear of God we must practice a sharp mercy to see whether we might save at least a few from the glowing flames. We dare not avenge ourselves. Vengeance a thousand times worse than we could wish them already has them by the throat. I shall give you my sincere advice."[10] Luther still has not abandoned the hope that the Jews would recognize Christ as their Messiah. He wants to take no vengeance on account of their stubbornness and their boasting that they have the true faith, because vengeance is God's business alone. But then comes his advice:

> First set fire to their synagogues or schools and to bury and cover with dirt whatever will not burn, so that no man will ever again see a stone or cinder of them. . . . Second, I advise that their houses also be razed and destroyed. . . . Third, I advise that all their prayer books and Talmudic writings, in which such idolatry, lies, cursing, and blasphemy are taught, be taken from them. . . . Fourth, I advise that their rabbis be forbidden to teach henceforth on pain of loss of life and limb. For they have justly forfeited the right to such an office by holding the poor Jews captive with the saying of Moses (Deut. 17[:10 ff]) in which he commands them to obey their teachers on penalty of death, although Moses clearly adds: "what they teach you in accord with the law of the Lord." Those villains ignore that. They wantonly employ the poor people's obedience contrary to the law of the Lord and infuse them with this poison, cursing, and blasphemy. . . . Fifth, I advise that safe conduct on the highways be abolished completely for the Jews. . . . Sixth, I advise that usury be prohibited to them. . . . Seventh, I commend putting a flail, an ax, a hoe, a spade, a distaff, or a spindle into the

8. Martin Luther, *The Jews and Their Lies* (1543), in *LW* 47:137.
9. Luther, *Jews and Their Lies*, in *LW* 47:139.
10. Ibid., 268.

hands of young, strong Jews and Jewesses and letting them earn their bread in the sweat of their brow, as was imposed on the children of Adam (Gen. 3[:19]).”[11]

As noted above, this advice is not new for the time of Luther. The advice he gives is not an appeal to people in the street to attack the Jews. Even if heresy drew capital punishment—we remember that Luther as a heretic was declared to be an outlaw—Luther did not demand this for the Jews, but still hoped for their conversion. Moreover, he thought that their rabbis had misled them. He wrote, “Even when one persuades them out of Scripture, they retreat from the Scripture to rabbis and declare that they must believe them, just as you Christians (they say) believe your pope and your decretals. That is the answer they gave me.”[12] According to Luther, the Jews were misled by the teachers. Therefore one should prohibit the rabbis from teaching because they spread wrong doctrines. Even the expulsion of the Jews was understandable at that time because in a given territory, such as the Holy Roman Empire of the German nation, there could be only one religion. The legal safety of Jews was always in jeopardy and could be granted only by the Emperor or a prince who then demanded a special tax for that privilege. It was not until 1555 at the Diet at Augsburg that the estates (i.e., the princes), but not the people, were given free choice to decide between the old religion and the Augsburg Confession. This possibility of choice for the estates was an unheard of innovation. Before that the respective religion had to be uniform in the whole empire. This means that up to 1555 even those territories in which the Reformation had taken root were actually outside the law. Religious tolerance came very gradually, and in many countries today, even in Europe, it is far from being accepted. Furthermore, Luther was of the opinion that Christians would be held accountable on Judgment Day if they permitted the Jews to publicly blaspheme Christ by stubbornly rejecting Jesus as the Messiah and also if they “protect[ed] and shield[ed] them.”[13] Blasphemy cannot be permitted. This was a commonly held opinion at the time of Martin Luther.

Today we can neither repeat Luther’s advice and reference to judgment day nor approve of it. These words are from a different time, and in our view they can only be regarded as regrettable. Therefore it was appropriate that in 1994 the Church Council of the Evangelical Lutheran Church in America rejected Luther’s anti-Semitic writings. We can be thankful that we live in a different time, and we should do everything possible so as not to digress back to this way of thinking from an earlier era. Yet there are two

11. Ibid., 268–72.
12. Martin Luther, “Against the Sabbatarians: Letter to a Good Friend” (1538), in *LW* 47:66.
13. Luther, *Jews and Their Lies*, in *LW* 47:279.

points in Luther's thinking to which we must pay heed: Jesus is the Messiah for all people, even for the Jews. This obliges us not to withhold the gospel from the Jews. Luther, however, emphasized in this respect that we always maintain a brotherly way of conduct with the Jews. This kind of conduct is more pressing than ever, especially in Germany in light of the "final solution of the Jewish issue" proposed during the Third Reich. And yet we should not overlook the fact that the National Socialism of the Third Reich was a religious, neo-pagan ideology. Not only Jews ended up in the concentration camps, but so did many confessing Christians. So when church administrations today are hesitant about baptizing Jews, even if they wish to be baptized, this can only be equated with the denial of the gospel.[14] One denies not only Luther and the church that has learned from his essential insights, but even the gospel itself. In this regard, we read in the *Bethel Confession* (*Betheler Bekenntnis*) of 1933: "The church cannot be exempted from its duty to call Israel to repentance and to baptism disregarding any cultural and political considerations. Neither can Christians stemming from heathenism separate themselves from Christians coming from the people of Israel."[15] We cannot deny the gospel to anybody. But now back to Jesus of Nazareth who is the focal point of the Protestant faith.

Jesus as an End-Time Figure

If Jesus is God's self-disclosure in human form, then God has come to God's people and the end-time has commenced. The kingdom of God is in our midst. Since Jesus was conscious of his role as Messiah, his message and his actions coincided with this role. As an end-time figure, he proclaimed an end-time gospel in an end-time era.

14. We want to refer here to an "Announcement concerning the Development of the Christian-Jewish Relationship" of the Fall Synod of the Evangelical Lutheran Church in Bavaria (November 26–27, 2008). It states: "Activities which have as their goal a conversion of Jews to Christianity are unthinkable for the Evangelical Lutheran Church in Bavaria." In the discussion that ensued from this statement, the presiding bishop Johannes Friedrich and the president of the Synod Dorothea Deneke-Stoll jointly declared that "the comprehensive mission of the church remains without doubt. . . . The issue concerning the statement of the Synod in the city of Straubing is the way of this mission. An active missionary approach towards the Jews is unthinkable for the Evangelical Lutheran Church in Bavaria because of historical reasons" (*Korrespondenzblatt* 124 [March 3, 2009]: 48–50).

15. *Das Bekenntnis der Väter und die bekennende Gemeinde (Das sog. Betheler Bekenntnis)*, in *Die Bekenntnisse und grundsätzlichen Äußerungen zur Kirchenfrage des Jahres 1933*, ed. Kurt Dietrich Schmidt (Göttingen: Vandenhoeck & Ruprecht, 1934), 128.

Jesus did not provide his audience with a timetable or inform them in detail about the things to come. Rather, he confronted them in such a way that he demanded an immediate decision from them. This means he did not pronounce any esoteric end-time doctrines but confronted the people with the radical decision for or against God. This was at the same time a decision for or against Jesus and his actions. His proclamation, person, and actions formed a unity that challenged people to a decision. "Follow me, and let the dead bury their own dead" (Matt. 8:22); "no one who puts a hand to the plough and looks back is fit for the kingdom of God" (Luke 9:62); "and blessed is anyone who takes no offense at me" (Matt. 11:6). These and many other assertions show in an exemplary way the necessity of an immediate decision in the here and now. The now is the decisive point of history and no longer the future as it was in the apocalyptic time of early Judaism or in the promissory history of the Old Testament.

The necessity to make a decision in the present is exemplified by Jesus' actions. When John the Baptist sent two of his disciples to Jesus to ask him whether he was the promised one or whether they should wait for someone else, he did not refer to any titles that had been conferred on him. In his answer he related to himself the Old Testament metaphors connected with the time of salvation. When Jesus changed water into wine at the wedding at Cana (John 2:11), this epiphanic miracle referred to the Old Testament understanding of wine as a symbol of the time of salvation. In Jesus salvation had become visible. Therefore Jesus talked of new wine, which should not be poured into old wineskins (Matt. 9:17). The time of old has passed, the time of salvation has commenced. Jesus announced this very clearly when he said, "But if it is by the finger of God that I cast out the demons, then the kingdom of God has come to you" (Luke 11:20). The kingdom of God has commenced with Jesus of Nazareth. What had been expected for centuries and what had been projected for so long into the future or into the present had now begun. "The kingdom of God is among you," Jesus said (Luke 17:21). He did not call for an immediate decision because he was such an important preacher, or because his message contained important words of wisdom. The decisive point was that with Jesus the kingdom of God had commenced, and therefore it was the time of decision. The goal of history had been fulfilled in him.

The announcement of the kingdom of God is at the center of Jesus' proclamation. But what did Jesus mean? He always used the concept "kingdom of God" in an end-time context. For instance, he taught his disciples to pray, "Your kingdom come. Your will be done, on earth as it is in heaven" (Matt. 6:10). It is no surprise that Jesus talked about an end-time kingdom. If the present is the time of decision, then the implication is that the time of salvation must be imminent. The unity between God and humanity that had been destroyed is restored and salvation commences. But the kingdom of God is not only the realization of a future end-time age in which we can live with God and with each other without fear and anxiety. As the Beatitudes (Matt. 5:3–12) show, the acceptance of those who are despised and rejected was essential for Jesus and his proclamation of the kingdom. By calling the poor "blessed" (Matt. 5:3; cf. Luke 6:20), Jesus revealed the revolutionary character of the kingdom. He announced salvation not only to those who could be expected to enter the kingdom, those who were religiously faithful and morally upright, but especially to the despised and those who according to prevailing opinion never had the opportunity to enter the kingdom. When Jesus had table fellowship with the despised of his time, the tax collectors and other public sinners, this was a gesture of communion. It showed that he offered them peace, trust, and forgiveness and that he accepted them into the coming kingdom. This was no idiosyncrasy of Jesus since he represented God and announced that God loves those who are despised and lost. He exemplified the identification of God with those who came from lowliness (cf. Luke 1:52).

Jesus not only pardoned sinners, but he also announced that those who live according to a different way of conduct belong to the kingdom of God. Love toward neighbor, which springs from God's love to us, becomes the main criterion for the people of the kingdom (Mark 12:28–34). In reminding his audience of this, Jesus said nothing new. They could recognize from Scripture that love is the criterion for any pious Jew (cf. Lev. 19:18; Deut. 6:4). But in Jesus the commandment of love became an active power and did not remain an abstract principle. Jesus showed this in his own conduct with his preference for the poor (Luke 14:12–14), who in the eyes of most religious people were unacceptable. As the parable of the good Samaritan (Luke 10:30–37) shows, love knows no boundaries. It is more than a pious duty, because it is the giving of one's own self as an answer to God's self-giving in Jesus and God's call for humanity to return and be reconciled to him.

Though Jesus emphasized the decisive character of his own person and of the present time, he was no doomsday prophet who conjured the immediate end of the world, except to affirm the necessity of an immediate decision for or against God. Neither his Jewish contemporaries nor the Jewish polemicists after his resurrection accused him of announcing the immediate end of the world, which never occurred. One could hardly think that such a false prophecy would not have been exploited by his opponents if Jesus had actually announced it. But he was not interested in such prophecies. The Gospels show us that in that fact he distinguished himself from John the Baptist, who in glowing terms announced the immediate coming of the end. But why did

Jesus have no interest in this? Perhaps we can understand this better if we consider his self-understanding.

Though Jesus did not put himself into the focus of his teaching—as we noted just at the trial before the high priest did he publicly confess his real identity—it would be unrealistic to assume that he never said a word about himself. But how can we distinguish clearly between how the people experienced him and talked about him after his resurrection, and what he indeed said about himself? This problem comes to the fore when we look at the titles of Jesus.

Without doubt most Christians would claim that Jesus was the Christ and designated himself as such. A careful reading of the New Testament shows that the title "Messiah," or in Greek "Christ," occurs only fifty-three times in the Gospels and 280 times in other New Testament writings. The presumably oldest Gospel, the Gospel according to Mark, gives no clear indication that Jesus used the title for himself. The Gospel according to John, in which this title occurs more frequently, never uses it as if Jesus applied it to himself. This means the title Messiah did not play an important role in the life of Jesus. In contrast, for instance, to Judas Maccabeus or Bar Kokhba, Jesus did not want to be considered a political or religious Messiah.

Yet there was another title less politically and nationalistically tinged that Jesus most likely used, that of "Son of Man." It occurs eighty times in the Gospels but only four times in the rest of the New Testament. It is used in all four Gospels and almost exclusively in the sayings of Jesus, not in those about Jesus. Indirect support for the thesis that Jesus used this title lies in the fact that it was rarely used in the Jewish apocalyptic literature after Jesus. We find it only in 4 Ezra and in 1 Enoch. Rabbi Abbahu (ca. 300) writes in the Jerusalem Talmud, "If a man says to you 'I am God,' then he lies; if 'I am the son of man,' he will finally regret it" (J Ta'an 2.1).

Jesus and the first Christian community did not invent the concept "Son of Man." In early Jewish apocalyptic Judaism, it already had a definite connotation. The end-time function of the Son of Man was primarily to be the judge of the people of God. Yet Jesus changed the image of the coming Son of Man in such a way as to suggest that he will judge all nations. But the Son of Man is for him not only a title of exaltation but also one of humiliation. He connects this image with that of the suffering servant of God who judges the world in the name of the Lord, suffers substitutively for the people, and reconciles them with God. This is most clearly expressed in Mark 10:45 where Jesus says, "For the Son of Man came not to be served but to serve, and to give his life a ransom for many."

With this pronouncement of Jesus we have already touched on the first group of the Son of Man sayings, those that speak about him who is going to die and be resurrected. The second group of Son of Man sayings deals with one who has come to judge and to save. The third refers to the earthly activity of the Son of Man. All three groups have eminent end-time significance but are not colored by popular nationalistic overtones. Jesus is the Son of Man who lives unknown among the people. Only at the end of time will he appear openly to judge and to redeem. Though he does not yet live as the Son of Man in glory, his actions already reveal who he is. He is the master of the law (Matt. 5:21–22); he can judge and forgive sins (Mark 2:10–28); he can condemn and provide salvation (John 5:25–27). According to the Gospel of John he even permits the man who was born blind and who had been healed by Jesus to fall down before him and adore him (John 9:35–37). This kind of adoration was reserved strictly for God, but Jesus as the Son of Man, as God's representative, permits his own adoration and is eligible for such cultic devotion.

The deepest self-understanding of Jesus, however, cannot be condensed to a title. It is a strictly singular phenomenon that Jesus is the final self-disclosure of God. Thus the end of all history is anticipated in him in a proleptic way. We remember here that Jesus' confession that he was the ultimate self-disclosure of God led to his conviction as a heretic. This is not surprising. The Gospel of John tells us, for instance, how Jesus attempted to show who he was, but to no avail. Here the crucial term "I am" (*ego eimi*) is used in a way that parallels its use in the Synoptic Gospels. When Jesus was talking with the Samaritan woman, she said to him with the traditional messianic expectation, "I know that Messiah is coming. . . . When he comes, he will proclaim all things to us." Jesus corrected her by saying, "I am he, the one who is speaking to you" (John 4:25–26). Jesus revealed himself as the full self-disclosure of God, but the woman did not understand him. She was too much entangled in the traditional pattern of messianic thinking.

Although Jesus designated himself as the full self-disclosure of God and emphasized that with him the kingdom had commenced, nobody—not even the disciples—believed him until after Easter. They were all caught up in the traditional thinking that the Messiah and the end were close at hand but still outstanding. They closed their eyes to the realities of the present and expected everything to happen in the near future. But this emphasis of Jesus on the present raised new questions. Just what does this mean? Is there nothing else to come? Did everything already happen in the life and death of Jesus of Nazareth?

Jesus refused to make any predictions about when the end of the world would occur. "About that day or hour no one knows . . . but only the Father" (Mark 13:32). Since God entered this world in a visible way in Jesus, we cannot postpone preparing for our encounter with God. We cannot wait until we assume that the time of the end of the world will soon come. We must always be ready because Jesus is the decisive event in history. He did not comfort the one criminal on the cross with some future expectation, but assured him that "today you will be with me in Paradise" (Luke 23:43). Jesus' person, his proclamation, and his activity demand an immediate decision, and this decision implies an immediate reward. This does not mean that the future will be insignificant. Quite the opposite! Only because of Jesus' presence will our future make any sense.

Symbolically speaking, Jesus and his destiny are the lens through which the different lines of history since the creation of the world are focused and projected into the future. The future has become predictable because it receives its future-directedness from Jesus Christ. Jesus told his followers that they should not be worried about the future, because in him and their attitude toward him the future has already been irreversibly decided. Of course, Jesus' claim that he determines and shapes the future ran contrary to most popular messianic hopes and expectations. Most of the people expected the total fulfillment of history in the present, just as many still do today. They wanted Jesus to be a political messianic leader who would once and for all liberate Israel from its enemies. Even some of his disciples confessed after Jesus' death with bitter resignation, "But we had hoped that he was the one to redeem Israel" (Luke 24:21). Not until they recognized Jesus as the resurrected Christ did their mood and their opinions change.

Even the resurrection did not provide a foolproof answer to Jesus' life and destiny. Now the question had to be decided whether his resurrection should be interpreted in a strictly apocalyptic way as the first act of the final end-time drama, or whether it was the ultimate event of the proleptic anticipatory history of Jesus. Many contemporaries of Jesus seem to have interpreted it as the first act of the end-time drama, after which the other events of the last days were to follow in rapid succession. This hope, that the end should come soon, is traceable in many places in the New Testament. Most books of the New Testament were written in awareness of this expectation. But the answer that the writers of the New Testament gave did not promote an intensification of the hopes for an immediate end. Instead, the writers emphasized that something new had dawned with Jesus, especially with his resurrection as the Christ. History, as we know it, has found its end and goal in Jesus.

9

JESUS AS THE CHRIST

Jesus of Nazareth was a historical person who walked on this earth. Jesus as the Christ did not live on this earth, nor was he a historical figure—judged by the usual historical criteria. He cannot be confined to our history because he was and is the originator of history. Jesus of Nazareth had proclaimed a definite message. Jesus as the Christ is the content of the Christian proclamation. Though we must carefully distinguish Jesus of Nazareth from Jesus as the Christ, it is the Christian conviction that they are one and the same person. Therefore the decisive question is how and in what way the proclaimer became the proclaimed, or how and in what way Jesus of Nazareth became Jesus the Christ. This coincides with the question, who is Christ?

The reason that Jesus of Nazareth became the Christ was not primarily because of his life but because of something that had happened to him at Easter. The Easter event allowed the disciples to see Jesus in a totally new light, and they also understood themselves completely anew. We see this most clearly with Peter. Before Easter Peter was the leader of the Twelve; after Easter he became the leader of the Christian community. This was not just a change in position. Before Easter Peter declared boastingly that he would never betray Jesus, even if all others would abandon him (Matt. 26:33). A few hours later, just to save his own skin, the same Peter denied that he had anything to do with Jesus (Matt. 26:69–75). After Easter this coward with the big mouth had become a totally different person. Peter preached about Jesus as the Christ everywhere, and when he was summoned by the Jewish authorities to desist from that proclamation, he answered, "We must obey God rather than any human authority" (Acts 5:29), and went on to tell these authorities about Christ and his significance.

Something similar happened to the other disciples. Before Easter they were people who had joined the Jesus movement for various personal or ideological reasons, and they even let their leader die alone. With the exception of some women—one of whom was Jesus' own mother—and perhaps John, none of his followers were at Golgotha. But after Easter we encounter the same disciples as confessing evangelists. They became astoundingly unanimous in their understanding of Jesus as the Christ, and they were ready to die for their faith in him. If we explained the Easter events as mere psychological events within the disciples, we would be at a loss to show how they became confessing Christians, which led to the rapid spread of the Christian faith. The only clue is the turning point of the resurrection of Christ.

The Turning Point of the Resurrection of Christ

For the first Christians, the resurrection of Christ was the foundation of their faith and their hope in a new future. This was expressed especially in the title *kyrios* (Lord), which was conferred on Jesus Christ by the post-Easter Christian community. This title was also used for the emperor in the official Roman cult and also for pagan gods. They were all *kyrioi* (lords). The title also served in the Septuagint, the Greek translation of the Old Testament, to render the Hebrew name *Yahweh*. In the hymn in Philippians 2:5–11, which describes the salvific missionary activity of Jesus, the term *kyrios* is used for Jesus at the end of his earthly activity and implies equality with God: every knee shall bow to Jesus, and he shall be proclaimed *kyrios*. This new status does not threaten God's sovereignty but rather increases God's glory.

The Newness of Christ's Resurrection

The new status that Jesus obtained is unthinkable without the resurrection. In the oldest creedal confession in the New Testament (Rom. 10:9), the statement "Jesus is Lord" is equated with faith in his resurrection from the dead. Both have a salvific quality. Jesus' equality with God establishes his cosmic rule, including his rule over all Christians. Therefore it was important for Paul's call to the apostolate that Jesus was the Lord (Rom. 1:3-4). Jesus is no superhuman mediator between God and us. At times Paul does not strictly distinguish between Jesus Christ and God; instead, the term *kyrios* suggests how God acts with this world. All other powers and lords (*kyrioi*) are second-ary, while Jesus Christ's rule is original and all-encompassing.

Through the resurrection the hidden Messiah becomes the revealed one. Jesus of Nazareth was not just a human being like we are; he was God himself. He is not a fact of the past but the decisive factor who determines the present and the future. In Jesus' resurrection something new occurred. This is exempli-fied by the parallel between God's salvific activity in Jesus with God's creative activity at the beginning. For instance, in its opening chapter the Gospel of John sets the coming of Christ in parallel with the creation in the beginning. Paul, too, shows a clear correspondence between the first Adam and Christ as the new Adam (Rom. 5).

The resurrection does not mean a return to an ideal state of the past. If this were the case, we would fall prey to a cyclic view of history as represented by most of the religions and philosophies. Yet the Christian faith asserts the exact opposite, as we read in the Letter to the Colossians: "For in him all things in heaven and on earth were created, things visible and invisible, whether thrones or dominions or rulers or powers—all things have been created through him and for him" (Col. 1:16). When Christ is called "the firstborn of all creation" (Col. 1:15), this signifies that Christ who is equal with God does not just stand at the beginning of creation, but through his resurrection is the goal toward which creation moves. Creation is not static but dynamic, and the "very good" that God pronounced at the beginning of the creation (Gen. 1:31) does not imply that it cannot be perfected. Therefore the fall of humanity should not be understood as a descent to a lower level of continuous sinfulness, but as the original "no" of humanity to live in harmonious unity with God, a "no" that continues to tinge creation until this day. Each of our independent and thus sinful actions attests to this original denial and rejection of God's plan, which aims at salvation and completion in Jesus Christ.

Yet God remains with God's creation even in its estranged or fallen state. When the evangelist Luke praises the ancestry of Jesus, which extends to Adam and finally to God's own self (Luke 3:38), he indicates that God's activity at the beginning and his action in Jesus Christ must be understood as a unity. Death will not be replaced by life, so that we may return to our original condition. If that were so, a new fall could follow. But for the resurrected Christ, death is no longer a possibility. Jesus' resurrection is no restoration, but the first point of a new creation, a creation in completion. This is shown by Paul in his let-ter to the congregation in Rome: first he introduces Christ as the new Adam (Rom. 5), then he mentions baptism as the beginning of our participation in the new creation (Rom. 6), then he shows the tension within us since we are citizens of the new world but still living in the old one (Rom. 7), and finally he draws out the conclusion of God's creative activity in Christ's resurrection for all creation (Rom. 8).

God's creative activity in Christ's resurrection points to a new creation that at some point will replace the old one. Here the empty tomb is important, not as a proof for the trustworthiness of Jesus Christ's resurrection, but as an indication that the present creation will not continue forever. The earthly body of Jesus was transformed and replaced by something totally new. Therefore the first Christians did not use the narrative of the empty tomb as a proof of Christ's resurrection.

The Existential Quality of Christ's Resurrection

The Christian faith in the resurrection did not emerge from a gradual development of an idea of the resurrection in the Jewish tradition. The concept of a future resurrection of humanity was part of Jesus' worldview and that of the first Christians. But the resurrection of Jesus did not just validate this apocalyptic idea of the resurrection. For instance, when we follow Paul's line of argument in 1 Corinthians 15, he does not start with the already understood idea of resurrection but refers to the Christian tradition of the resurrection of Christ and explains its significance. Christ was not just the first one who had been resurrected as one might think following apocalyptic thought. But Paul does not get tired of emphasizing that Christ's resurrection is the presupposition for our own resurrection. Therefore he asserts, "If Christ has not been raised, then our proclamation has been in vain and your faith has been in vain" (1 Cor. 15:14). The resurrection of Jesus Christ cannot be separated from the rest of world history and rejected as irrelevant. It is the presupposition for the Christian existence as a community of people who, in a proleptic way, already participate in a new life. It is also the foundation of the Christian hope for a final realization of this new life.

The significance of Christ's resurrection becomes evident only when we consider it in the context of apocalyptic hopes. Within this context the disciples realized that God affirmed the authority of Jesus, which he already assumed during his life on earth. They also realized that in the destiny of Jesus the end of history had occurred in proleptic anticipation and that God had completely disclosed God's self in Jesus as Lord. On the basis of the resurrection of Jesus Christ, the apocalyptic idea of a general resurrection could be transformed into the Christian hope of the resurrection. Therefore the New Testament announces Jesus not just as "the first to rise from the dead" (Acts 26:23) and as the beginning, the firstborn from the dead (cf. Col. 1:18), but as the one who "was raised from the dead by the glory of the Father, so we too might walk in newness of life" because "we will certainly be united with him in a resurrection like his" (Rom. 6:4–5). We trust in God who "raised the Lord and will also raise us by his power" (1 Cor. 6:14). While the apocalyptic concepts provide the background material for understanding the total implication of Christ's resurrection, our hope is founded not on those ideas but on Christ's resurrection alone.

In contrast to the historical fact of the crucifixion of Jesus of Nazareth, the resurrection of Jesus as the Christ transcends strictly empirical verification. Since the resurrection contains a claim that goes beyond our earthly reality, meaning that Jesus is actually the Messiah, an empirical proof of this is just as impossible as proving the existence of God. The New Testament sources were cognizant of this, otherwise they would not have reported that a rumor was started that "his disciples came by night and stole him away while we were asleep" (Matt. 28:13). We also read that when Jesus appeared to his disciples for the first time as the resurrected Christ, "they were startled and terrified, and thought that they were seeing a ghost" (Luke 24:37). Such a reaction by the disciples excludes the possibility for a strictly empirical proof of the actuality of the resurrection.

Though there is no possible empirical proof for the resurrection, we are confronted with the fact that in the self-understanding of the disciples a drastic change occurred that is difficult to explain by strictly innerworldly causes. Something seems to have occurred that goes beyond the normal conceptual possibilities of humans and is an immediate activity of God. But a strict test of proof for this cannot be conducted because whenever God is involved, such occurrences cannot be verified by science. At the same time, the possibility of such a divine action cannot be precluded. This line of reasoning was pursued by the authors of the New Testament. Yet the narratives of the resurrection also show that a resurrection is not a matter of course. To show the true situation with regard to the resurrected One, or the empty tomb, God explained what had happened either through the interpretative words of the resurrected One or through God's messengers (angels). The language of facts pertains to things within our space-time continuum. Anything beyond that can only be disclosed to us by God.

Stations of Christological Clarification

The clarification of who Christ was and what he affected for us starts with the New Testament witnesses but goes far beyond them and practically continues through the whole history of Christendom. Yet already in the New Testament and in the early church the decisive conclusions were reached.

God's Decisive Activity in Jesus Christ

The New Testament writers show convincingly that God acted in Jesus Christ decisively for us and for the whole world. In him the complete self-disclosure of God has occurred. Mark, who composed the oldest Gospel, wanted to put an end to all speculation about Jesus by emphasizing that Jesus made known the secret of the kingdom of God just to his disciples, albeit after the Easter event. The interval between the resurrection of Jesus Christ and his parousia, meaning his return, is the time of world mission.

The Gospel of Matthew points out very strongly that all of the Old Testament promises have found their fulfillment in Jesus. There are no promises that point beyond Jesus Christ. He is the fulfillment of the Old Testament hopes and expectations. Therefore many Old Testament end-time titles are conferred on Jesus, such as Messiah, Son of David, and King of Israel. This shows that he stands in true continuity with the Old Testament. The church retains this continuity, though it is only a temporary phenomenon existing until the return of Christ. The church is not yet a pure community of true believers, and in the final judgment the just are separated from the unjust (Matt. 13:30). Therefore the topic of the coming judgment is important for Matthew and for the self-understanding of the Christian community.

In the Gospel according to Luke the present time is no longer understood as an interim only, but is part of salvation history. At the beginning of the Gospel, Jesus is placed into the context of world history since he is the focal point through whom history receives its significance. There are three important stages of history: first the time of Israel, then the time of Jesus as the center of history, and finally the time of the church. It is interesting that John the Baptist is considered not as a precursor of Jesus but as the last prophet of the old time (Luke 16:16). Jesus' coming is without any preparations. For Luke, the decisive event has occurred with the coming of Jesus, and one day Jesus will return to bring about the final end of all history. Nothing essentially new will occur then, because the same Jesus Christ who has gone back to his Father will come again as the Lord of the whole world. Those who labor to spread the Christian faith are not left alone; the exalted Christ is present with them, and they work in his name and in his Spirit. This is shown especially well in the second volume of Luke, his Acts of the Apostles.

In the Gospel according to John we again encounter a different situation because for John salvation is already a present reality for the faithful. This does not mean that the future is unimportant, because already now it can be drawn into the present. This is shown in Jesus, who is God's Word incarnate (John 1:14), so that God is present in Jesus' actions and words. Through this "real presence of God" in Jesus, the oppositions are overcome between the present and the future life as well as between life and death, and time and eternity. The main point of history has already been reached because the prince of this world has already been judged (John 16:11). But it is not evident to everyone that the opposition between God and world is overcome. Therefore the Gospel of John is the gospel of great misunderstandings. The unbelievers just cannot grasp who Jesus is, and they exclude themselves from participating in the real future.

Finally, we must turn to Paul, whose writings are the earliest in the New Testament. Though he was not a disciple of Jesus during Jesus' life on earth, Paul became the most influential theologian of New Testament times. He, too, emphasizes the continuity between the Old Testament promises and that which has occurred in Jesus Christ. One can gather from these promises that the events which pertain to the end of the world have already started with Jesus' coming, death, and resurrection. Paul is convinced that we live in the end-time. The old eon has passed, and the Messiah has come. This new eon is not yet fully here, because the Messiah has not yet returned in power. This not-yet, this end-time proviso, does not worry Paul, because the end will come and a new world and new eon will emerge according to God's plan. Decisive is the resurrection of Jesus, which makes possible the resurrection of the dead. Christ is the end of the law (Rom. 10:4) and the end of history. The old covenant no longer pertains to us because a new covenant has been established (2 Cor. 3:6). We live in a transitional phase, a period of faith (2 Cor. 5:7) and of waiting (Rom. 8:23). Yet this transitional existence is already shaped by the future. In baptism—made possible through Christ's death and resurrection—we are new people even while we live under the conditions of the present world. Paul, and with him the other New Testament writers, understood Jesus as the Christ in the light of his resurrection. They emphasized that in this interim we are called to a faithful and active time of waiting in order to participate in the fulfillment of the new creation, which has been foreshadowed in Jesus Christ's resurrection. For the New Testament writers the Christ event has become the decisive turning point of history.

Equality with God

When it became evident to the Christian community that God had acted in a decisive way in Jesus Christ for the future of the world and humanity, the question emerged concerning the relationship between Jesus Christ and God. How is Jesus Christ as the bringer of salvation related to God as the sender of salvation? For us this question may sound strange because it is clear to us that

Jesus is the Messiah. But in the Greek language, which was used to propagate the Christian faith, the New Testament titles for Jesus such as Son of God and Son of Man had little meaning. Even the Greek word *Christos* (the Anointed One) was just a translation of the Hebrew word *Mashiach* (Messiah).

In the second century the word *Christ* was originally translated by using the word *logos*, which means "the word" or "the world order." In the opening of the Gospel of John we read, for instance, that "in the beginning was the Word, and the Word was with God, and the Word was God" (John 1:1). In analogy to Stoic conceptuality, the Word was understood as the reason of the world and as the expression of the cosmic world order. Whoever agrees with this order is in congruence with God. Such a person knows how to conduct himself or herself before God and how to obey God's ordinances. Through the *logos* conceptuality, Christians could accept what was agreeable with their faith from other religions because through his seminal *logos* (*logos spermatikos*) the one God was present in the whole world. God had also shown God's self in the Word that became flesh (*logos ensarkos*) in Jesus of Nazareth. If one understood Christ only as the *logos*, as God's world reason, Christ could easily be understood only as a derivative of God, meaning that he was of secondary significance.

After a long debate that erupted into literal battles over the issue of whether Christ was similar to God, equal to God, or different from God, it was decided in 325 at the First Ecumenical Council at Nicaea that Christ was of one being with the Father. Nicaea was a city east of present-day Istanbul, Turkey, and was the winter residence of Emperor Constantine. In the summer of 325 Constantine summoned approximately three hundred bishops to attend a council at his residence to discuss the issue of Christ's relationship to God. There was a rather strong wing under the leadership of the presbyter Arius (ca. 280–336) from Alexandria, Egypt, that hesitated to concede to Christ's equality with God. They were afraid that this doctrine would move the Christians too close to the pagans who worshiped more than one god. At the time of the council Athanasius, a deacon of bishop Alexander of Alexandria, insisted, however, that Christ has equality with God. He was convinced that Christ could only accomplish salvation if he was equal with God. For Athanasius, too, there loomed the fear of analogies of the Christian faith with other religions. If Christ had not really been God, then similar to the many demigods or divine figures of Greek mythology, Christ would have had only limited influence and could not have really affected salvation. At the Nicene Council the bishops agreed that Christ is equal with God. The result was the so-called Nicene Creed. This statement of belief was expanded somewhat in 381 at the First Council of Constantinople, although it is still referred to today as simply the

Nicene Creed. Since the Council of Nicaea was convened by the emperor, the decisions of the council became law in the empire, and those who deviated from the decisions were exiled unless they changed their minds. Since some did not agree with the decisions of the council, this unfortunately led to the first split in Christendom.

Indeed, the decision of the council is difficult to understand. This is especially the case because Greek language and thought, unlike Latin in the western part of the empire, could not easily describe how two beings (God the Father and Jesus Christ) could be one in being if they were not identical. The basic thought behind the council's decision was indeed Latin, in which two persons could participate in the same substance and remain distinct persons. Yet in Greek conceptuality, if two are of one being, then it is much more difficult to understand why they are actually two persons and not just one.

Even more difficult were the discussions in 381 at the Council of Constantinople. There the Holy Spirit entered into the theological considerations concerning God the Father and Jesus Christ. When speaking of the Holy Spirit, the bishops confessed that the Spirit is "the Lord and Giver-of-life, who proceedeth from the Father, who with the Father and the Son together is worshiped and glorified."[1] Though the Holy Spirit is seen here on the same level as Father and Son, the council did not want to accord the Spirit equality in being with the Father and the Son. The expression familiar to us in the West that the Spirit "proceeds from the Father and the Son" is not contained in this creed but is of Western origin. The council initially emphasized that Christ is on the same level as the Father, and in the West this was achieved by saying that the Spirit proceeds in the same way from the Father and the Son. Yet the East always maintained that the Spirit proceeds from the Father through the Son and is present in all of creation. This West's unilateral change of the Nicene Creed, the so-called *filioque* (meaning "and from the Son" in Latin), led to a continuous conflict between East and West and finally, together with other problems, caused the split between the church of the West and that of the East in 1054.

Truly Human and Truly Divine

Once the church had recognized the essential equality of God and Christ, the next issue arose as to how the divinity and the humanity of Jesus Christ were related in that one person Jesus. Was Jesus Christ a divine being encased in a human body, or was he sometimes divine (for instance, when he performed miracles) and sometimes human (for instance, when he slept)? What

1. "The Second Ecumenical Council: The First Council of Constantinople," in *NPNF*[2] 14:163.

tormented the theologians was not only the issue of the unity of the person of Jesus Christ but also the much more existential question of whether Christ could provide our salvation. If he was not completely God, then he could not save us, because his divinity was defective, and if he was not completely human, then he could not fully identify with us. In either case, salvation was in jeopardy. Gregory Nazianzen (also called Gregory of Nazianzus and Gregory the Theologian) addressed this concern when he stated, "For that which He [Christ] has not assumed He has not healed; but that which is united to His Godhead is also saved."[2]

After many suggestions and many un-Christian controversies in which one theological party usually condemned the other as heretical and vice versa, the Council of Chalcedon in 451 finally provided clarification. It was the Western church under Pope Leo that helped to find a solution. In an earlier controversy the pope had been asked to voice his opinion. In a letter of 449, the famous Tome of St. Leo, the pope emphasized the divine and the human nature of Christ, whereby "each of the natures retains its proper character without defect."[3] At this council the following confession was decided upon: Our Lord Jesus Christ "is perfect in Godhead and perfect in manhood, very God and very man, of a reasonable soul and [human] body consisting, consubstantial with the Father as touching his Godhead, and consubstantial with us as touching his manhood. . . . He must be confessed to be in two natures, unconfusedly, immutably, indivisibly, inseparably."[4] Though some still think today that the decision of Chalcedon was not clear enough, something astounding had happened. After many centuries of heated debates, church leaders concluded that the church could not answer these questions. The church admitted that it did not know how in Jesus Christ the divine nature relates to his human nature. It could emphasize only *that* in Jesus Christ the full humanity and the full divinity were present, but not *how*. It could explain only that these two natures of Christ were neither mixed together nor changed, neither torn apart nor separated from each other. This decision became imperial law since the church had by now become the official church of the Roman Empire. In official theology the belief in the two natures of Christ inseparably connected with each other had prevailed.

But many simple Christians, especially in Asia Minor, Syria, Palestine, and Egypt, preferred to believe in one nature of Christ, namely, the divine nature. In contrast to the official theology of the church, they were interested

2. Gregory of Nazianzen, Epistle 101.7, in *NPNF*[2] 7:440.
3. "The Tome of St. Leo," in *The Seven Ecumenical Councils of the Undivided Church*, in *NPNF*[2] 14:255.
4. "The Definitions of the Faith of the Council of Chalcedon," in *NPNF*[2] 14:264.

in Christ's godhead, not in his humanity. Since the Council of Chalcedon, however, had decided differently, the Monophysite (one nature) church split off and is still prevalent in present-day Armenia. Mention must also be made of the Nestorian churches, which prevailed for a long time in Persia and extended all the way to China. Nestorius (ca. 381–ca. 451), who for a few years had been the patriarch of Constantinople, went the opposite direction to the Monophysites. He declared that Mary had given birth to Christ and not to God, and therefore tried to emphasize the unity of the person of Christ. Since the rejection of Chalcedon implied the rejection of an imperial law, in less than two hundred years the "heretical" parts of the church found protection under the expanding religion of Islam. The "heretics" hoped that Islam would grant them more religious freedom than their "orthodox" brothers and sisters. Initially their hopes became true since they could exercise their faith without being exiled. Yet they were second-class citizens with many restrictions and in the long run they dwindled down to a minority.

Christological deliberations did not cease with Chalcedon. Yet the main point had been decided. After becoming human, the Son of God was still totally divine in the unity of the one person Jesus. Yet he was never forced to deny his total humanity. From then on the conviction that Jesus is truly human and truly divine became the starting point of all christological reflections.

Our Savior

Christological considerations still kept theologians busy. We need only think of Anselm of Canterbury, who in the summer of 1098 presented to the public his small book *Why God Became Man*. As previously mentioned, Anselm introduced a thesis as to how Christ saved us. Anselm's view has been regarded with favor by the Roman Catholic Church especially since the Council of Trent (1545–63). Even Protestants have been impressed by Anselm's argument. In the early church, however, a different idea of atonement prevailed. It was held that salvation had been achieved by deceiving the devil: Through the fall the devil had taken hold of all humans. When Jesus came onto this earth, the devil wanted to subjugate him under his authority. Yet in contrast to us, Jesus was without sin. Since Jesus was totally human and since the devil attempted to take hold of this sinless person, the devil forfeited his authority over humanity. He attempted to triumph over Christ by nailing him to the cross, but he was deceived concerning the true nature of Christ. As Origen thought, he could not destroy the pure soul of Christ. When Christ was resurrected from the tomb, he overcame death, and through this victory the devil had to cede humanity to Christ.

For Anselm the thesis of a deception was unintelligible. Why should God rescue humanity from the devil through a deception? This sounded more like a fairy tale. Anselm emphasized that human sinfulness was of such magnitude that only God could eliminate it. Even the smallest sin is an attempt to dethrone God. If sin is of such magnitude, how can we come back to God? This can be accomplished only by Jesus Christ, who is one with God. Though human, Jesus lived in full unity with God, which means he did not have to die. When he voluntarily died, he did more than what could have been expected from him. Because of Christ's divinity, this excessive sacrifice has unlimited significance and allowed others to participate in it. If we cling to Christ, we can benefit from his merits. In arguing this, Anselm believed that God's honor was reinstated because God's justice demands that our deficits be equalized by something that exceeds that which can be expected from us. We could say that this kind of argumentation is typically Western and Latin in its attempt to explain salvation in legal terms.

Yet classical Christology was not forgotten, as we see with Thomas Aquinas. In his *Summa Theologica* Thomas asserted that the incarnation brought to us "the full participation of the divinity, which is the true bliss of man and end of human life."[5] At the same time he picked up Anselm's theory of atonement and explained that through the unity of God and humanity there occurred a multitude of activities in which salvation is mediated to us, including Christ's voluntary suffering[6] and the exemplary development of his virtues.

Looking at the first articles of the Augsburg Confession of 1530, one immediately recognizes that the Lutheran Reformers adopted the ancient trinitarian and christological dogmatic decisions. In understanding God as triune, Luther perceived a decisive difference from other religions. Luther explained in a sermon: "Augustine and other ancient teachers have said: the external work of the Trinity is undivided. Father, Son, and Holy Spirit are one creator, not three, over against the created. This is how far the Turks and the Jews and the Pagans get. But we shall not only look at God from outside in his works, but God wants that we also recognize him from inside. But how is he inside? There is Father, Son, and Holy Spirit. That is not to adore three Gods. Inside he is one united being and three persons."[7]

When we encounter God as Father, Son, and Holy Spirit, we do not have just an outside view of God as in other religions, but we can, so to speak, look into God's heart. Luther did not attempt to explain in a speculative way

5. Thomas Aquinas, *Summa Theologica* III.2.r
6. Cf. Thomas Aquinas, *Summa Theologica* III.4.r2–3.
7. Luther, *Die Promotionsdisputation*, in WA 39/2:305.23.

the mystery of the Trinity. He was reminded here of Philipp Melanchthon's assertion at the beginning of his *Loci Communes* (1521), the first Lutheran dogmatics: "The mysteries of divinity we have the more rightly adored than investigated."[8] If we reject the Triune God, then we have access only to a natural knowledge of God that comes from the outside. But when we follow the Triune God, then we understand God in the way that God disclosed God's own self. Christ is, so to speak, the window through which we can look at God's heart.

Luther said in one of his table talks, "True theology is practical, and its foundation is Christ, whose death is appropriated through faith."[9] Three aspects of this statement are important: (1) The foundation of theology is Christ. We can talk about God correctly only when we perceive of God through the Christ event. (2) True theology is the doctrine of salvation, which is practical theology. What God has done for us, not God's or Christ's being, interests us most. (3) The work of Christ (his death) can be perceived only through faith and not through reason. With this dictum Luther rejected all theological and christological speculations unless they were important for our understanding of salvation. Luther took very seriously Christ's incarnation and emphasized that God's self-disclosure in Jesus Christ must be in the center of theology. God has shown God's own self in Jesus Christ, and therefore Christ is our only access to God. But it cannot be empirically proven that God meets us in Christ. We can grasp God only in his humanity, and for Luther this means in the crucified Christ. Therefore Luther contends in the *Heidelberg Disputation*, "True theology and recognition of God are in the crucified Christ."[10]

Here we encounter some important implications of Luther's emphasis on the cross: (1) The cross makes it impossible that we approach God from our side. If we attempt to work our way through nature to God, as occurs today in the intelligent design movement, which assumes that through science it can recognize a creator behind the creation, then we only adore a construct of our own ideas. (2) The cross of Christ and God's suffering are so astounding that they cannot be the result of our own fantasy. Either they are complete nonsense or they really are what they assert to be. Therefore a theology of the cross always contradicts speculation. The cross is not good because it logically connects us with God, but because God has used it to show God's own self to us. (3) The cross is so shocking and unusual that God must explain its significance to us so that we can properly grasp it. This means God's revelation

---

8. Philipp Melanchthon, *Loci Communes*, trans. Charles Leander Hill (Boston: Meador, 1944), 67.

9. Martin Luther, *Table Talk* (no. 153), in *LW* 54:22.

10. Martin Luther, in his explanation of thesis 20 of the *Heidelberg Disputation* (1518), in *LW* 31:53.

is always self-disclosure in which, from beginning to end, God maintains the initiative. (4) Finally, the cross shows us how God acts. God's decisive action always has the appearance of the opposite, it looks like an apparent defeat but is the exact opposite. This means it is closely connected with a creation out of nothingness. God acts in a surprising way that we would not expect, and does so without any precondition from our side. But we must refrain from always associating God with negativity. The cross means rather that God acts in unexpected ways. It was Luther's deepest conviction that we can never fathom God's ways. God must first open our eyes so that we can understand his miraculous activity, for instance, his redemptive action on the cross.

Luther emphasized the incarnation of Christ and maintained the strict unity of both natures in Christ, the human and the divine. This was his point of contention against other groups of the Reformation, such as the Reformed and the Spiritualists. In his *Confession concerning Christ's Supper* (1528) Luther declared, "The humanity is more closely united with God than our skin to our flesh—yes, more closely than body and soul."[11] Since Christ is truly human and truly divine, there is no God except in the human being Jesus Christ. This unity of God and Christ led Luther to speak of Christ's omnipresence. While Huldrych Zwingli (1484–1531) emphasized God's omnipresence, he wanted to restrict Christ's presence after his ascension to his celestial abode, since Christ is still in heaven. Luther, however, argued that since Christ participates in God's being, he is just as omnipresent as God, in both his divine and his human natures. Luther affirmed the so-called *communicatio idiomatum*, meaning that one nature participates in the respective properties of the other nature. What can be said about the human being Jesus must also be said of the divine Jesus and vice versa. In this way the unity of Christ's person can be properly maintained. This means that God is not present in nature as God is present in Christ, because in Christ God is present in a personal way. Similar to the Eastern Church, Luther could confess that Mary had given birth to God. Through the *communicatio idiomatum* it was clear for Luther that the body of Christ can be present everywhere. This was especially important for his affirmation of the "real presence" of Christ in the Lord's Supper. Zwingli, however, would only admit a spiritual presence.

Though some items are speculative in Luther's christological assertions, they are always associated with God's salvific activity. We see this especially clearly at two central points of the Christian faith. Expounding the second article of the Apostles' Creed in his *Small Catechism*, Luther emphasizes the two natures of Christ and then immediately focuses on Christ's salvific

11. Martin Luther, *Confession concerning Christ's Supper* (1528), in *LW* 37:219.

activity as it was enabled by the two natures. He confesses, "I believe that Jesus Christ, true God, begotten of the Father in eternity, and also a true human being, born of the virgin Mary, is my Lord. He has redeemed me, a lost and condemned human being."[12] In a similar way, Luther writes in the *Smalcald Articles* (1537) "that Jesus Christ, our God and Lord, 'was handed over to death for our trespasses and was raised for our justification' (Rom. 4[:25]); . . . Nothing in this article can be conceded or given up, even if heaven and earth or whatever is transitory passed away."[13] Here Christ's death and resurrection are connected with our justification by God. Christology and the doctrine of salvation belong together because Christ is God's gift for us. Therefore Christ must be understood primarily under the aspect of salvation.

Because salvation is God's doing alone, we can rely only on God and not on ourselves. Luther concluded, "We confess that good works must follow faith, not only must, but follow voluntarily just as a good tree not only must produce good fruits, but does so freely."[14] Human activity is no precondition but is a necessary answer to God's activity in Jesus Christ. Therefore Luther rejected any works righteousness, in which someone attempts to be justified before God through his or her own effort. It is the other way around: by recognizing that we are accepted by God for Christ's sake, good works follow out of thankfulness. Luther writes in his exegesis of the Psalms, "Faith is the beginning of all good works."[15] Faith is the reliance on God's salvific activity, and that recognition results in our gratitude. "It belongs to a Christian heart that it proves to be thankful, above all not only to God, but also to all people."[16] If this thankfulness is not activated, then God's activity is not understood in its existential relevance. Luther was here following the apostolic precept: "For we cannot keep from speaking about what we have seen and heard" (Acts 4:20).

The Two Aspects of Christ

We now ask in conclusion, what is Christ's significance for us today? In answering this we need to follow the basic decision of the ancient church, reiterated through the centuries, to regard Christ as truly human and truly divine. This leads first to the acknowledgment that Jesus Christ is the human face of God.

12. Martin Luther, *The Small Catechism*, in *The Book of Concord*, 354.
13. Martin Luther, *The Smalcald Articles* (pt. 2, art. 1), in *The Book of Concord*, 301.
14. Martin Luther, *Theses Concerning Faith and Law* (1535), in *LW* 34:111 (thesis 34).
15. Martin Luther, *Operationes in Psalmos* (1519–21), in *WA* 5:119.14–15.
16. Martin Luther, *Predigt am 22. Sonntag nach Trinitatis* (October 28, 1537), in *WA* 45:195.1–2.

The Human Face of God

Jesus Christ is the human face of God who comes to us and who lived among us. In talking this way about Jesus, we must first reflect on the history of Jesus of Nazareth. Though it is sometimes still doubted whether Jesus actually lived, such extreme skepticism has become rare today. Much more often the question is posed whether Jesus as the Christ can still have significance for our faith in God. Many people admit that Jesus lived and even that he had good insights. Yet they question whether he was really more than an especially gifted person. We can counter such a skeptical attitude only by looking carefully at history, because whatever is claimed about Jesus as the Christ must be found in the history of Jesus of Nazareth. Otherwise our assertions are pure speculation.

When we search for the historical Jesus, as far as he is accessible in the New Testament, we gain the impression that from the life and destiny of Jesus certain conclusions can be drawn that transcend empirical verification and observation. Rudolf Bultmann expressed this appropriately when he wrote, "Jesus' call for a decision implies a Christology."[17] Jesus confronted his audience in such a way that it raised the possibility of his messianic character. Yet this is not a proof that Jesus was indeed the Messiah. The messianic character of Jesus cannot be empirically verified. Jesus of Nazareth leaves, historically speaking, an impression that can be ascertained by means of historical research. Yet the Christ remains hidden in the human person of Jesus of Nazareth. We must be mindful of this when Jesus of Nazareth and the extraordinary events that occurred throughout his lifetime are explained strictly in a this-worldly context. For instance, the virgin birth can be depicted as a narrative derived from the virgin births reported in other religions. Jesus' death can be explained as intentional suicide after an unsuccessful mission, and the empty tomb as the result of his disciples stealing his corpse (Matt. 28:13). The appearances of the resurrected One can be shown to be the visions of a spirit (Luke 24:37), and the announcement of Jesus concerning his impending death and resurrection as later additions by the evangelists. Taken by itself, the human side of Jesus does not necessarily imply salvific qualities. Whatever goes beyond the usual destiny of a human being can be explained without abandoning a this-worldly frame of reference. This becomes evident with the many misunderstandings of Jesus as they are reported by the writer of the Gospel of John. When Jesus, for instance, says that somebody must be born anew (John 3:3), Nicodemus immediately misunderstands this to mean that an old person must be born again in a biological manner (John 3:4). We must conclude that Jesus as the

17. Rudolf Bultmann, *Theology of the New Testament*, trans. K. Grobel (New York: Scribner's, 1951), 1:43.

Christ cannot be ascertained or proven through historical research or rational deductions. The New Testament affirms this. Jesus, for instance, reacts to the confession of Peter, "You are the Messiah, the Son of the living God," with the words, "Flesh and blood has not revealed this to you" (Matt. 16:16–17).

While the so-called historical Jesus does not allow a proof that Jesus is indeed the Christ, we dare not neglect the human side of Jesus, because only through that side do we know something about Christ. But how can we make the transition from the human figure of Jesus of Nazareth to Christ the Redeemer? Already Jesus confronted his audience with the call for decision that they either accept him as the Son of Man sent by God or reject his claim. Our situation is no longer that of Jesus' contemporaries so that we must decide between an either/or. The Easter event separates us from Jesus' contemporaries. In the eyes of the original followers of Jesus and of all those who have followed him since then, the resurrection event showed that Jesus was indeed the one who he claimed to be. He was and is the Messiah. Therefore our decision for Christ is founded both on Jesus of Nazareth and on that which occurred with him at Easter. Our faith is founded not just on our decision to accept Jesus as the Messiah, but this decision is strengthened and affirmed through the present Lord Jesus Christ. We do not believe in Jesus, but we believe in Jesus as the Christ. We dare not separate Jesus as the human face of God from Jesus as the Christ, because only as the Christ does Jesus have salvific significance. In a similar way we dare not consider only the cross of Christ, but must grasp this in the context of the resurrection to perceive its actual significance. For Christians, Holy Week does not end on Good Friday but finds its culmination at Easter. This means that two very opposed facts (death and resurrection) meet there. This is without analogy in human history and therefore indicates an activity of God that transcends our usual experience. Martin Luther expressed this in his Christmas hymn "From Heaven Above," where we read, "The blessing that the Father planned, / The Son holds in his infant hand" and, "In manger-bed in swaddling clothes / The child who all the earth upholds."[18]

The finite is enabled to hold the infinite or, as the Gospel of John says, "the Word became flesh" (John 1:14). The theologian Paul Tillich expressed the same concept that under the conditions of existence (i.e., our world) the essence (i.e., Christ) has appeared.

This coincidence of opposites, of the divine and the human in Jesus, was so exceptional that not even his family understood the presence of the divine. When Jesus started his mission, we read with regard to his family, "They went out to restrain him, for people were saying, 'He has gone out of his mind'"

18. *Evangelical Lutheran Worship*, hymn 268, stanzas 4 and 5.

(Mark 3:21). This means they wanted to declare him insane so that he could not be punished for his conduct. It is not surprising therefore that besides his mother, Mary, none of his immediate relatives played an important role among his disciples during his life on earth. At the crucifixion, too, only his mother was present, but no other relatives. Even after Easter this did not change significantly. We hear not one word about Jesus' mother in the early church. Only his brother James assumed a leading role among the Christians in Jerusalem. Even the disciples did not give much credence to reports about Jesus' resurrection (Luke 24:10–11). We have a similar situation at Pentecost with people outside the circle of his disciples. When the disciples proclaimed to them the resurrection of Christ, some people simply said they were drunk (Acts 2:13). Others were afraid and had no explanation for the disciples' actions (Acts 2:12).

God is present in Christ in a way that reason would not expect. This presence that transcends reason is also affirmed by Paul when he declares to the Christians in Corinth, "For Jews demand signs and Greeks desire wisdom, but we proclaim Christ crucified, a stumbling block to Jews and foolishness to Gentiles" (1 Cor. 1:22–23). This does not mean that the cross is simply nonsensical. God does not act in a nonsensical way, but in a way that reason would not expect. This is made clear by Paul when he writes, "None of the rulers of this age understood this; for if they had, they would not have crucified the Lord of glory" (1 Cor. 2:8). Those who were in authority in the world did not recognize God's wisdom and thereby did not perceive who Jesus actually was. Otherwise they would not have crucified him. But how can we understand God's activity if it transcends our own reason? Again, Paul explains, "No one comprehends what is truly God's except the Spirit of God. Now we have received not the spirit of the world, but the Spirit that is from God, so that we may understand the gifts bestowed on us by God" (1 Cor. 2:11–12). God must open our eyes through the Spirit so that we can acknowledge that Jesus is not just a human being but God in a human body. This again affirms the priority of God's activity in the salvific process and makes certain that we are not misled by our own ideas.

The Way to a New Dimension

When we consider the divine aspect of Jesus, we encounter a new world that is not accessible to us from our side. This new dimension makes us realize that Jesus is God and implies God, and therefore is involved in our salvation and even in the transformation of the cosmos. To this we add, from Colossians 2:9, "For in him the whole fullness of the deity dwells bodily." This full godhead of Jesus is not a historical fact, as for instance the events of the second World War, but it is in history and at the same time beyond history. Just as with the existence of God, Jesus' godhead is inaccessible as a historical or philosophical proof. We can only perceive of it once it has been pointed out to us. When Paul affirms, for instance, in Romans 10:10, "For one believes with the heart and so is justified, and one confesses with the mouth and so is saved," he admits that the acknowledgment of the godhead of Christ can come only through faith and not through rational research.

While the humanity of Jesus is the presupposition for perceiving the divinity of Christ, the latter is not just the consequence of the former; but by acknowledging the godhead of Christ, we affirm that the human being Jesus did indeed tell the truth about himself. Consequently, we can trust the human person of Jesus as God. He is the foundation and the source of faith, out of which comes faith in Jesus as the Christ. But Jesus is not the object matter of the Christian faith, because Christians always believe only in Jesus *as the Christ*. If the fullness of the Godhead is in Jesus, then he is equal to God. This is shown in a very interesting way in the biblical documents.

In the Old Testament "Yahweh" is the proper name for God. This proper name is rendered in the Septuagint, the Greek translation of the Old Testament, as "Lord" (*kyrios*). In the New Testament Jesus is called *kyrios*, which implies that he is God. Again, we must be mindful of the creedal confession quoted by Paul: "If you confess with your lips that Jesus is Lord, and believe in your heart that God raised him from the dead, you will be saved" (Rom. 10:9). The fact that Jesus is the Lord, meaning God, maintains a strict monotheism in the Christian faith. It shows that as Jesus of Nazareth God has entered humanity in a personal way or, as we said, that Jesus is the human face of God. God's entering humanity did not occur after Jesus' baptism or resurrection, but occurred from the very moment God assumed a human form. Therefore Mary is rightly called "mother of God," or *theotokos* in Greek. She is not a co-redeemer, because she did not effect God's becoming a human being, but she was the means by which God came into the world.

Since Jesus was of divine nature, his divinity pertains to his whole life. This means that we must talk about the suffering and death of God in Jesus. While in philosophy God is usually considered impassible (incapable of suffering or feeling), according to the Judeo-Christian understanding God acts and is involved in all of history, including the suffering in history. Therefore we must assert that in Jesus' death the God who became human ceased to be, in both his human nature and his divine nature. But this does not mean that God died altogether on Good Friday. We must distinguish here between God in God's self and God for us. Were it otherwise, the dialogue between Jesus and his

Father would make no sense. Similarly, when we talk about God's weakness and God's suffering, we mean the God who became flesh and who revealed God's self to us. We are not talking about God as God is in God's self.

The human formed a personal unity with the divine in Jesus of Nazareth. This does not mean that through the divine the human was simply lifted up to a higher plane. Nor did the divine help the humanity of Jesus of Nazareth during his earthly life. If this were so, we could think, for instance, that Jesus did miracles with the help of his divine nature, but that when Jesus ate, slept, and took care of other human necessities, the divine receded and only the human came to the fore. Jesus did not live on earth as a superhuman being, but in the way that God intended humans to live, in complete union with God. Jesus was the exemplary human being, the pioneer and perfecter of our faith (cf. Heb. 12:2). He showed in his life the purpose for which humanity had been created, not for estrangement from God, but for harmony and unity with God. For Jesus, God was not a distant God but was so close that Jesus could address God as his Father. Naturally, Jesus was tempted by sin, as is indicated, for instance, at the beginning of his ministry, but he did not yield to it. Jesus showed in his life that the goal of humanity, union with God, was again attainable. Therefore he pointed us to a new humanity, which he himself represented.

But how could Jesus achieve salvation for us? One way of answering this question was to say that God's wrath toward our sinfulness had been transformed into love. Paul writes in 2 Corinthians 5:18, "God . . . reconciled us to himself through Christ." Similarly, he says in Colossians 2:13, "God made you alive together with him, when he forgave us all our trespasses, erasing the record that stood against us with its legal demands. He set this aside, nailing it to the cross." Satisfaction for our sins occurred on the cross when Jesus died for our sins and fulfilled God's demands for justice. Jesus freed us from the condemnation that we had brought upon ourselves through our sinful conduct. He atoned for our sins on the cross. Today some theologians have raised questions about whether God really had to see blood in order for humans to be saved.

But there is another way in which God's salvific history can be described, namely, in the dramatic dualism that we hear, for instance, in Martin Luther's well-known hymn "A Mighty Fortress Is Our God." There Luther writes:

> If we in our strength confide,
> Our striving turns to losing;
> The righteous one fights by our side,
> The one of God's own choosing.

> You ask who this may be:
> Christ Jesus, it is he,
> The Lord of hosts by name.
> No other God we claim!
> None else can win the battle.[19]

Against the powers of darkness and sin we cannot be victorious. For this reason God has sent to us Jesus Christ, who fights in our place against them and, as it says in the next stanza of the hymn, who also can overcome them. In the Gospel according to Luke, Jesus says, "But if it is by the finger of God that I cast out the demons, then the kingdom of God has come to you" (Luke 11:20). The whole ministry of Jesus is described in the Gospels as a battle against the anti-godly powers, from his temptation at the beginning to his struggle and prayer in Gethsemane at the end. Jesus did not succumb to these powers but was victorious, and he liberated us from them. Therefore Paul could exclaim, "'Where, O death, is your victory? Where, O death is your sting?' The sting of death is sin, and the power of sin is the law. But thanks be to God who gives us the victory through our Lord Jesus Christ" (1 Cor. 15:55–57). While in the first view of salvation one looks more to God, who accomplished it, the second perspective shows more clearly from whom we were saved, from the tempting anti-godly powers. Therefore, the first view should not be held exclusively, otherwise we may forget what it is from which we have been saved. But neither should we limit ourselves to the second view, because we may forget the one who has saved us.

In his work *Christus Victor*, the Swedish Lutheran scholar Gustav Aulén (1879–1977) discusses three models or types of the doctrine of reconciliation. He juxtaposes the classical model, which he finds in the Greek and Latin theologians of the early church and in Luther, with the Latin model, which he discerns primarily in Anselm of Canterbury, Lutheran orthodoxy, and Albrecht Ritschl. Aulén attributes a third model to the Enlightenment and liberal Protestant theology. In the classical view God reconciled the world to God's self. Aulén writes, "He Himself reconciles the world with Himself and Himself with the world."[20] The classical type is essentially dualistic in its outlook, particularly because "of the Divine warfare against the evil that holds mankind in bondage, and the triumph of Christ."[21] For the Latin type Aulén introduces a legal theory of satisfaction through which "God is the object of Christ's

---

19. Ibid., hymn 505, stanza 2.
20. Gustaf Aulén, *Christus Victor: An Historical Study of the Three Main Types of the Idea of Atonement*, trans. A. G. Herbert (London: SPCK, 1970), 146.
21. Ibid.

atoning work."[22] He says of the third type that "the Atonement is no longer regarded as in any true sense carried out by God. Rather, the Reconciliation is the result of some process that takes place in man, such as conversion and amendment."[23] In writing *Christus Victor* Aulén wanted to demonstrate that from beginning to end atonement is God's own work. Therefore the classical type agrees with the Christian proclamation: God loves the world so much that he gave God's only Son. But we must also consider that these three models and our preference for one in particular are only human attempts to put into words what God did in Jesus Christ for our salvation.

The Cosmic Christ

So far we have dealt primarily with the individual aspect of salvation. This must now be broadened in a twofold way to include all of humanity and all of creation. Sometimes Christians are charged with salvation egotism, the notion that they think only of their own salvation. Yet every Sunday Christians confess in the words of the Apostles' Creed that salvation extends also to those who lived on earth before Jesus came into the world. We mean here the expression "He descended into hell," or as we now say in a more appropriate translation, "He descended to the dead." Though this descent of Christ into the realm of the dead is nowhere expressly mentioned in the New Testament, it is presupposed in several passages. For instance, in Matthew 12:40 a passive stay of Jesus in the realm of the dead is implied ("for three days and three nights the Son of Man will be in the heart of the earth"), while other places point to an active stay. Revelation 1:18 says, "I was dead, and see, I am alive forever and ever; and I have the keys of Death and of Hades," indicating that Jesus has won the victory over the powers of the realm of death. Finally, there are some references where this descent is understood as the time of proclamation to some or to all in the realm of the dead. We read in 1 Peter 3:19, "He went and made a proclamation to the spirits in prison, who in former times did not obey." And in 1 Peter 4:6 we read that "the gospel was proclaimed even to the dead."

For the first Christians it was of existential significance whether only they would be accepted into God's kingdom or whether those people who had lived in an earlier time, who had had no opportunity to hear and accept the gospel of Jesus Christ, would be given that opportunity. From what the Christians

22. Ibid., 2.
23. Ibid., 146.

knew about Jesus, they could not imagine that he or God would punish those people for not accepting the gospel if they had never been able to hear it. The dead could not be guilty in a personal or direct way. From this reasoning, the idea of a descent of Christ into the abode of the dead emerged. Since Jesus was truly human and truly divine, when he rested in the tomb, at least according to his godhead, he would have had the ability to remain active. Therefore the early Christians believed that Christ had preached the gospel to the dead between Good Friday and Easter Sunday, and had confronted them with the decision to accept him as the savior.

In Western ecclesial art the resurrection of Christ is usually depicted as if Christ emerged from the tomb, so to speak, as a genie rushing out of a bottle. The focus is on Christ and his resurrection alone. But in Eastern Orthodox ecclesial art this is very different. There the resurrection has salvational significance for all humanity. Christ is depicted as pulling Adam out of Hades, the realm of death. Then Eve clings to Adam. Further down we see that the hinges and locks with which the abode of the dead had been locked are broken. Further above we discern David and Solomon. All of this shows that Christ was resurrected not just for himself but for the salvation of all humanity. In a similar way Luther described how we preach that Christ has broken the gates of the realm of death and has guided the dead out of this realm with a flag in his hand.[24] Luther also emphasized that Christ had not been resurrected for him alone but we and our resurrection hang together with his destiny. Luther proclaimed in a sermon that Christ "has not been resurrected alone for his person, but that things cling so together that it [i.e., his resurrection] pertains to us and we are standing with him who has been resurrected and are grasped since our resurrection and life, as Paul says, has started in Christ."[25]

It is interesting that the church never dogmatically decided who could have been saved through Christ's activity in the realm of the dead. Was it only a few Old Testament patriarchs or all the dead except for some really evil people? The church has emphasized only that there is a possibility of salvation for those who, during their life on earth, had no opportunity to accept Christ as their savior. With this it left the answer to the question of who will ultimately be saved to God. God alone can decide.

We could ask now whether Christ's "descent into hell" is an inappropriate speculation substantiated by only a few marginal New Testament passages or whether we should not simply concede that Christ went to the dead as everybody else who dies. Yet theologians of the early church who considered

24. Cf. Martin Luther, *Predigten des Jahres 1533*, in WA 37:65.
25. Luther, *Predigten des Jahres 1533*, in WA 37:68.7–12.

this assertion of the Apostles' Creed and the relevant New Testament passages were not just interested in speculation. They, like theologians today, had an existential interest in those who were separated by geography or time from the Christ event. These theologians recognized, from what Jesus told us about God, that God is not a merciless God but gives every person a chance. They found a possibility for such a chance in the so-called descent of Christ into hell.

Yet the church affirmed, at the same time, that one can only be saved through God's mercy in Jesus Christ. Therefore it never condoned a general pardon as did, for instance, the German poet Heinrich Heine (1779–1856), who in a frivolous way quipped shortly before his death, "God will forgive because that is his métier."[26] To the contrary, forgiveness is only received if it is really accepted, whether in this life or in the life beyond. Therefore the church today prays in every service for all people and for their salvation. Yet the church has rightly not dared to describe how God will save most or all of the people, or who exactly is included in God's plan of salvation. We can only entrust all people to God's mercy and do our best throughout our lives to witness and pray that they will be convinced of the truthfulness of the Christian faith. Everything else must be left to God.

We can now move on from the assertion in the Apostles' Creed that Christ "descended into hell" to the assertion that he "ascended into heaven and is seated at the right hand of the Father." Though Christ's ascension has been celebrated as a special day since the fourth century, for many people, including many Christians, it is hard to understand. Some exegetes claim that in the earliest tradition the resurrection of Christ was simultaneously understood as his exaltation to God (cf. Rom. 8:34), and that Luke later put an interval between the resurrection and the ascension as the time when Christ could still be seen on this earth. Regardless of the exact moment of the ascension, we may wonder about the sphere into which Christ ascended.

Luther rejected Zwingli's interpretation that Christ sat in a certain place at the right hand of the Father. According to Luther, this would mean that Christ could not sit still for one moment, since at this time it was believed that the heavens were continuously moving. Therefore he objected to Zwingli and others: "They speak childishly and foolishly, assigning to Christ a special spot in heaven like a stork with its nest in a tree."[27] Christ's sitting at the right hand of God should not be understood in a spatial way. If I say that somebody is my right hand, I do not mean this literally. It signifies rather that he

26. Quoted in Wolfgang Hädecke, *Heinrich Heine. Eine Biographie* (Munich: Hanser, 1985), 531. Hädecke concedes that this quotation contains "the whole Heine" though its authenticity "cannot be verified."

27. Luther, *Confession concerning Christ's Supper*, in LW 37:281.

or she does everything in my name and therefore is indispensable for me. In a similar way, in sitting at God's right hand, Christ becomes the agent of God's activities and is elevated to equality with God so that he is as omnipresent and almighty as God the Father. This has for us the consequence that Christ's salvific activity is acceptable to God. Therefore we hear the exalted Christ say, "All authority in heaven and on earth has been given to me" (Matt. 28:18). Christ's participation in God's power is the final point of his salvational activity until the still outstanding parousia (Christ's return) and the universal transformation of this world.

We have now arrived at the point where we must consider Christ's relevance for the whole world. Christ not only achieved our salvation and transformation into a new bodily existence, but he did the same for the whole world. Paul writes, "The creation waits with eager longing for the revealing of the children of God; for the creation was subjected to futility, not of its own will but by the will of the one who subjected it, in hope that the creation itself will be set free from its bondage to decay and will obtain the freedom of the glory of the children of God" (Rom. 8:19–21). What was begun in Christ, and in which we already participate proleptically, still needs completion. As scientists tell us, the whole cosmos will come to an end because of its space-time limitation. We cannot find imperishableness and eternity in our space-time existence. The cosmos, or at least part of it, must be changed in such a way that it can participate in God's eternity. How this will occur goes beyond our imagination. Scientific assertions do not help, because science only does research within space and time. Speculative assertions are also of no help, because they attempt to discover what is reserved for God alone. Yet we know in which direction everything is going because ultimately God will be all in all. As Paul writes, "When all things are subjected to him, then the Son himself will also be subjected to the one who put all things in subjection under him, so that God may be all in all" (1 Cor. 15:28). This means that Christology issues again into the unity of God.

PART 4

THE HOLY SPIRIT AS GOD'S EFFICACIOUS POWER

Apart from Pentecostal churches, the Holy Spirit has never achieved the same eminent significance in the Christian church as God the Father and Jesus Christ. This also holds true in Christian theology. Nevertheless, God's Spirit is the power to whom the first Christians witnessed as the one that encouraged and strengthened them. Before we consider how the Holy Spirit is efficacious in the church, an institution that makes up the communal structure of Christian life, we should first reflect on the Holy Spirit itself.

10

THE HOLY SPIRIT

The presence of the Spirit of God is not confined to the church but extends throughout all of creation. We recognize this at once when we consider the biblical significance of God's Spirit.

The Biblical Testimony

In the Old Testament, "spirit" (Hebrew: *ruah*) signifies the natural phenomenon of the wind, of the breath, and generally that which gives life to the body (cf. Gen. 6:17). In Job 32:8 we find the interesting remark, "But truly it is the spirit in a mortal, the breath of the Almighty, that makes for understanding." It is God's Spirit and not one's education that endows a human being with wisdom. Connected to this is the possibility for biological life, because this too is given by God. *Ruah* is the "whiff" that comes from Yahweh and will return to him. It is what makes us alive. We read in Job 34:14–15, "If he should take back his spirit to himself, and gather to himself his breath, all flesh would perish together, and all mortals return to dust." Often this human breath is considered to be inseparable from Yahweh's Spirit. This Spirit is also creative, as we gather from Psalm 33:6: "By the word of the LORD the heavens were made, and all their host by the breath of his mouth." *Ruah* is used here synonymously with "word" (Hebrew: *dabar*), the same word with which, according to Genesis 1:1, the world was created. Yahweh's Spirit or breath is the creative power of life that determines the duration of our lives and directs all natural powers.

While now only individuals are gifted with God's Spirit, in the end-time Yahweh will pour out his spirit "on all flesh." Then, as Yahweh promised to Israel, "your sons and your daughters shall prophecy, your old men shall dream dreams, and your young men shall see visions" (Joel 2:28). Similarly, we read in Ezekiel 36:26–27: "A new heart I will give you, and a new spirit I will put within you; and I will remove from your body the heart of stone and give you a heart of flesh. I will put my spirit within you, and make you follow my statutes and be careful to observe my ordinances." Though humanity cannot exist without the spirit, only God's Spirit can direct humans to right living and to fulfilling God's will. Therefore the psalmist prays, "Create in me a clean heart, O God, and put a new and right spirit within me. Do not cast me away from your presence, and do not take your holy spirit from me. Restore to me the joy of your salvation, and sustain in me a willing spirit" (Ps. 51:10–12). Life, energy, and freedom are not to be taken for granted, for they are God's gifts. God gives the Spirit and we are vivacious, wise, and renewed. But when God takes away the Spirit, we are confused, sick, and like those in the pit, that is, like those in the grave. At some time God will pour out the Spirit in such measure that we will live in complete union with God, so that we can participate in God's immortality (cf. Ezek. 37:1–14). While the fulfillment of this prospect will take place in the eschaton in an all-encompassing way, already now in a partial way it can be proleptically anticipated, for instance, in the Israelite covenant community, or even outside of it, since God's activity upholds all of creation.

Early Judaism increasingly recognized that the Spirit has a certain degree of independence. This can be seen in the writings between the Old and the New Testaments, for instance, in the writings of Qumran. In the *Rule of the Community* (1QS 3.13–4.26) "a spirit of meekness, of patience" whom "God loved" is juxtaposed to "the spirit of deceit."[1] Some scholars point out that in the Bible the Holy Spirit is often considered in a personified way when it speaks, calls, or proclaims.[2] This is shown especially clearly when one source of Scripture is used to explain another source. The Holy Spirit seems to become

---

1. *The Rule of the Community*, in Florentino García Martínez, *The Dead Sea Scrolls Translated: The Qumran Texts in English*, 2nd ed., trans. Wilfred G. E. Watson (Grand Rapids: Eerdmans, 1996), 6–7. Cf. also John L. Levison, "The Two Spirits in Qumran Theology," in James H. Charlesworth, ed., *The Bible and the Dead Sea Scrolls: The Princeton Symposium on the Dead Sea Scrolls* (Waco, TX: Baylor University Press, 2006), 169, for further information.

2. Cf. Hermann L. Strack and Paul Billerbeck, *Kommentar zum Neuen Testament aus Talmud und Midrasch* (Munich: C. H. Beck, 1924), 2:134.

God's partner in fulfilling the same functions that earlier were ascribed only to God's justice and compassion. Yet the Spirit is no independent actor. Rather, the divine reality reaches humanity through the Spirit and thereby causes humanity's reaction.

At the time of early Christianity there was a religious movement called *gnosis*, which advocated a syncretistic doctrine of salvation stemming from late antiquity. Especially among the educated, this *gnosis* (knowledge) was a serious competitor with the Christian faith for influence. In Gnosticism, as it is referred to today, God is strictly separated from the world, and the creator god of the world is another god. The spirit as the life-giving power of God is often understood as a substance that is imprisoned in the body. Humans do not have a twofold relationship as advocated by the Christian faith, one with God and the other with the world, but a twofold nature, one material and one spiritual. Yet for the Gnostics only the spiritual nature is significant. Through some kind of primal fall, this spiritual nature became entangled in the material world, from which it wants to be set free. Since God is spirit, this spirit is not the actual creator of the material, but only its life-empowering source. Therefore the material cannot be redeemed. Redemption is only achieved when humans are released from their material bodies to return to their original spiritual existence, that is, to God. Yet when we listen to Paul, he says the exact opposite. We are not redeemed from our bodies, but "this perishable body puts on imperishability, and this mortal body puts on immortality" (1 Cor. 15:54). Gnosticism as a serious rival movement to early Christianity was highly dualistic in its understanding of humans and of the world. It had no regard for the material and the bodily aspect of a person. Only the inner self, the spiritual, was deemed worthy of salvation.

When Jesus says, according to Matthew 12:28, "But if it is by the Spirit of God that I cast out demons, then the kingdom of God has come to you," he uses the Old Testament understanding of the Spirit. God's Spirit empowers Jesus to achieve unusual deeds. In the Gospels the endowing of humanity with the Spirit (Greek: *pneuma*) is mentioned as an end-time event (Mark 1:8). The most important example of this is Jesus, because at his baptism the Spirit descended on him (Mark 1:10). Just as God created the world in the beginning through the Spirit, now God creates the firstborn of the new creation through the Spirit (Matt. 1:18; Luke 1:35). While in Matthew and Mark the Spirit of God is mentioned relatively seldom, in Luke-Acts the presence of the Spirit is characteristic of the church. At Pentecost the apostles are filled with the Holy Spirit (Acts 2:4), and whoever is baptized into the Christian community receives the Holy Spirit.

In John the Spirit takes on a more cosmological function. The Spirit is now understood as the sphere that is in opposition to everything carnal. We read, on the one hand, about the Spirit who comes from above and, on the other hand, about the flesh, the devil, and the present cosmos that is from below. Jesus says, "God is spirit, and those who worship him must worship in spirit and truth" (John 4:24). The Spirit who is identified with the life-empowering force of God and of Christ is the Spirit "that gives life; the flesh is useless. The words that I have spoken to you are spirit and life" (John 6:63). True life can only be found in the sphere of the Spirit, that is, with God. As the passages on the Advocate show, the Spirit is also "the Spirit of truth, whom the world cannot receive" (John 14:17). Nevertheless, we hear emphatically in John that "the Word became flesh" (John 1:14), because humanity lives in the world and not in a godless vacuum. Through the coming of Christ everyone has the opportunity to be born again (John 3:7), and therefore everyone has an opportunity to live according to the Spirit.

Similar to John, Paul identifies the Lord Jesus Christ with the Spirit when he writes, "Now the Lord is the Spirit, and where the Spirit of the Lord is, there is freedom" (2 Cor. 3:17). In opposition to Gnosticism, the spiritual and the bodily dimensions are not opposed to each other. Rather, Paul says of the body, "It is sown a physical body, it is raised a spiritual body" (1 Cor. 15:44). Paul can be confident that the bodily will be transformed into the spiritual because the first Adam was a living being while Christ as the final Adam "became a life-giving spirit" (1 Cor. 15:45). The bodily receives its direction and transformation from the spiritual, since Christ received that transformation too through his resurrection. This transformation toward the Spirit and toward Christ is not only wishful thinking. Already now God has given us the Spirit as a pointer and as a first step toward that future. Therefore Paul can remind the Christians to "walk not according to the flesh but according to the Spirit" (Rom. 8:4). If Christians must be reminded of their new life in Christ, then it is not surprising that non-Christians understand their connection with God even less clearly. Yet according to Paul this is no excuse for their behavior: "For what can be known about God is plain to them, because God has shown it to them. Ever since the creation of the world his eternal power and divine nature, invisible though they are, have been understood and seen through the things he has made. So they are without excuse" (Rom. 1:19–20). Though God and the Spirit are present in the whole world, they can be properly recognized only where they make themselves recognizable, which means in the historical configuration of Jesus Christ. This is the reference point from which the life-sustaining power of the Spirit can be properly understood and clarified. This was acknowledged by the early church.

The Early Church

In the Old Testament the Holy Spirit is not understood as being independent from God but is always God's Spirit. The same is true in the New Testament. Yet there the relationship between God and the Spirit has been complicated through Jesus Christ. Since Jesus as the Son (of the Father) is connected with God, the issue had to be clarified as to how Jesus Christ and the Spirit are related to each other. The church first understood that through God's Spirit, God caused God's Son to become human, and also through the power of the Spirit the Son was resurrected. But the relationship between the Spirit and Jesus goes even further. For instance, in 2 Clement 9:5, a homily that was most likely written in the second century, we read, "If Christ the Lord who saved us, being first spirit, then became flesh, and so called us." This means that Jesus was spirit before he became flesh. Similarly, we read in the Pastor of Hermas, a very popular book of the Christian church from the second to the fourth century, "The Holy, pre-existent Spirit that created every creature, God made to dwell in flesh, which He chose. This flesh, accordingly, in which the Holy Spirit dwelled, was nobly subject to that Spirit, walking religiously and chastely, in no respect defiling the Spirit."[3] We notice here the strict unity of Son and Spirit, and we also read that the Holy Spirit was preexistent and that through the Spirit the divine power was present. Bishop Theophilus of Antioch (ca. 180) continued these deliberations:

> God, then, having His own Word internal within His own bowels, begat Him, emitting Him along with His own wisdom before all things. He had this Word as a helper in the things that were created by Him, and by Him He made all things. He is called "governing principle" [*arke*], because He rules, and is Lord of all things fashioned by Him. He, then, being Spirit of God, and governing principle, and wisdom, and power of the highest, came down upon the prophets, and through them spoke of the creation of the world and of all other things.[4]

Two points are noteworthy here: (1) God is present as God through the *logos* (Word), through which God discloses God's self. (2) The connection between Proverbs 8:22 and John 1:2 shows that the essence of the *logos* is the *pneuma*, or the Spirit. *Pneuma* and *logos* are inseparably united in God. But *pneuma* and *sophia* (wisdom) are also interchangeable. With this, however, nothing is said about the internal relationship of the Godhead. The main emphasis is on

---

3. The Pastor of Hermas, *Similitude* 5.6, in *ANF* 2:35–36 (also called the Shepherd of Hermas).
4. Theophilus of Antioch, *To Autolycus* 2.10, http://www.ewtn.com/library/patristc/anf2–3.txt.

God's self-disclosure in God's external work. Since the mediation of creation through the *pneuma* is not denied, Theophilus attempts to show that God becomes active in the *pneuma*. Therefore in the historical reality of Jesus, the *pneuma*, the life-creating power of creation, becomes flesh.

Irenaeus of Lyon also emphasizes the close union of God the Father, Son, and Spirit, especially in opposition to Gnostic systems. In those systems there were extended speculations about the powers and authorities by which differentiations and distinctions in the Godhead were created. Irenaeus, however, stresses the inseparable unity of God. From Scripture he learned that there are no differences in God. "Since God is all mind, all reason, all active spirit, all light, and always exists one and the same, as it is both beneficial for us to think of God, and as we learn regarding Him from the Scriptures, such feelings and divisions [of operation] cannot fittingly be ascribed to Him."[5] God is not a composite being but exists in the unity of Father, Son, and Spirit. In contrast to the Gnostics, Irenaeus has no need to assume some intermediate being who created the world, because God creates everything through God's own self. Though Son and Spirit must be seen as a unity, they are also to be distinguished from each other. In opposition to Jewish thinking, Irenaeus emphasizes that the Father cannot be recognized without the Word, meaning without the Son. This shows that the activity of the Spirit outside the church cannot be perceived without reference to God's self-disclosure in the Son. Irenaeus also points out that perishable, earthly, and composite things cannot render an image of the spiritual "unless these very things themselves be allowed to be compound, limited in space, and of the definite shape, and thus no longer spiritual, and diffused, and spreading into vast extent, and incomprehensible."[6] This means there is no natural knowledge of God unless God takes the initiative and makes God's self known in space and time.

Athanasius of Alexandria, too, describes the close relationship between Father, Son, and Spirit: "As the Son is in the Spirit as in his own image, so also the Father is in the Son."[7] When he refers the salvific process to all three, he declares, "For as the Son, who is in the Father and the Father in him, is not a creature but pertains to the essence of the Father . . . so also it is not lawful to rank with the creatures the Spirit who is in the Son, and the Son in him."[8] For Athanasius there is a clear progression: the Father sends the Son, and the Son in turn sends the Spirit. Since the Son belongs to the being

5. Irenaeus, *Against Heresies* 2.28.4, in *ANF* 1:400.

6. Irenaeus, *Against Heresies* 2.7.6, in *ANF* 1:368.

7. Athanasius, *Epistle I (To Serapion)* 1.20, in *The Letters of Saint Athanasius concerning the Holy Spirit*, trans. C. R. B. Shapland (London: Epworth, 1951), 115.

8. Athanasius, *Epistle I (To Serapion)* 1.21.

of the Father, and the Spirit to the being of the Son, there is no difference in perfection because all three are one. In harmony with Scripture, Athanasius emphasizes that the Spirit participates in the incarnational process. Similarly, God has created everything through the Word. The Spirit is active in the creation as well as in the incarnation. The Spirit is continuously active in creation because "the Father, through the Word, in the Holy Spirit, creates and renews all things."[9] Athanasius understands creation and sanctification as one work. The creative activity of the Spirit is seen in the context of God's sanctifying activity.

These assertions find their concluding codification at the Council of Constantinople (381), when the Creed of Nicaea was amended especially to emphasize the function of the Spirit. The council affirmed that the Holy Spirit participated in the incarnational process, and acknowledged that Jesus Christ "was incarnate by the Holy Spirit and the Virgin Mary and became human."[10] Then we read that the Holy Spirit is "the Lord and life-giver, Who proceeds from the Father, Who is worshipped and glorified together with the Father and the Son, Who spoke through the prophets." Most of these assertions have scriptural precedents, such as Luke 1:35 ("The Holy Spirit will come upon you"); 2 Corinthians 3:17 ("The Lord is the Spirit"); John 6:63 ("It is the spirit that gives life"); and John 15:26 ("The Spirit of truth who comes from the Father, he will testify on my behalf"). Yet nowhere in Scripture do we find a reference to the Spirit "Who is worshipped and glorified together with the Father and the Son." Even when Basil the Great writes that "the Son is confessed to be of one substance with the Father, and the Holy Ghost is ranked and worshipped as of equal honor,"[11] we hear nothing in this confession that the Holy Spirit is of one being with the Father and the Son. Some council fathers may have been hesitant to attribute to the Holy Spirit the same status as the Father and Son.

The Reformers and Present-Day Theology

So far we have noticed that the Holy Spirit has prime importance with respect to three points: (1) as God's life-giving power of creation, (2) in God's incarnational process in Jesus Christ, and (3) as God's life-empowering and sanctifying activity in the church. While the last two points can be seen as the

9. Athanasius, *Epistle I (To Serapion)* 1.24.

10. John H. Leith, *Creeds of the Churches: A Reader in Christian Doctrine from the Bible to the Present*, rev. ed. (Atlanta: John Knox, 1977), 33, for this and the following quote.

11. Basil the Great, *Letter* 90.2, in NPNF[2] 8:176.

work of the Spirit in the church, the first one goes beyond any ecclesial activity. This becomes most clear in the statements of the Reformers.

It was a matter of fact for Martin Luther that God is active in history. Yet how could God be active there except through the Spirit? What occurs in conformity with God is enabled through the guiding power of the Holy Spirit. Therefore Luther states, "If a prince governs well, it is not innate nor is it learned only through books, but it is learned through the inspiration of the Holy Spirit with experience."[12] From the Old Testament Luther recognized that God's activity is not limited to Israel. That God is active outside of salvation history becomes clear in Luther's idea of "miracle-working men," whom, according to Luther, God sends at critical points in history to change the course of history and to avoid evil. The Holy Spirit is active in the history of salvation as well as in the political history, in the church as well as in the "godless" world. In the world everything occurs through the power of the Holy Spirit. "Therefore all the duties of Christians—such as loving one's wife, rearing one's children, governing one's family, honoring one's parents, obeying the magistrate, etc., which they regard as secular and fleshly—are fruits of the Spirit."[13] Luther shows here that the Spirit is the power in all of life that incites and enables us to live in harmony and in peace. What we so often take for granted and assume comes from our own ingenuity, the natural law, human reason, or other natural sources, Luther understands as the work of the Holy Spirit. Since in Scripture, and in the witness of the early church, the Spirit is God's creative and life-giving Spirit, Luther's conclusions are not surprising. He knew that without the Spirit the world would be threatened by chaos and destruction. But it was clear to him that not everybody automatically accepts the working of the Spirit. Some people are immune to it. The Reformer John Calvin also recognized the Spirit as life giving and life sustaining, yet he did not see this function of the Spirit as being independent of the soteriological activity of the Spirit. With the Reformers, creation and new creation are seen as interconnected, because the main work of the Spirit is the salvific process.

The Lutheran confessional writings hardly reflect on the working of the Spirit in and through creation. In article 18 of the Augsburg Confession we read concerning free will that humans have "no power, without the Holy Ghost, to work the righteousness of God, that is, spiritual righteousness." This assertion is certainly true. Yet it becomes one sided if it is isolated from the activity of the Holy Spirit in the world. The Holy Spirit does not just

---

12. Martin Luther, *In XV Psalmos graduum (1532–33)*, in *WA* 40/3:209.5–6, in his comments on Ps. 127:1.

13. Martin Luther, *Lectures on Galatians (1535)*, chaps. 1–4, in *LW* 26:217, in his comments on Gal. 3:3.

make it possible for humans to obtain righteousness before God; the Spirit also preserves creation and sustains it. Here the danger arises that the world is perceived as autonomous, not as part of God's good creation in which God is active through the Spirit. It is not surprising then that in the confessional writings the Holy Spirit is almost exclusively seen in connection with special gifts and that the world is wrongly left to the anti-godly destructive powers. Present-day theology has in part overcome this dangerous narrowing of the Spirit's activity.

The German American systematic theologian Paul Tillich offers an extensive treatment of the Holy Spirit in the third volume of his *Systematic Theology*.[14] First he illuminates the presence of the divine Spirit in the human spirit and in the history of humanity. The divine Spirit manifests itself in the human spirit predominantly through faith and love. The Spirit creates a spiritual community through the New Being in Christ. This spiritual community has an impact on culture by opening the avenue of the spiritual presence. While the secular culture as such is not spiritual, the divine Spirit "is not bound to the media it has created, the churches," and the profane, though having no sanctifying character, "is open to the impact of the Spirit even without the mediation of a church."[15] This means that the Holy Spirit is present in the profane world, both in religions and in culture and morals. Because of the ambiguity of the world, the presence of the Spirit is not always directly discernible. Tillich writes: "The [divine] Spirit grasps the [human] spirit, and only indirectly the *psyche* and the *physis*. The universe is not yet transformed; it 'waits' for transformation. But the Spirit transforms actually in the dimension of the spirit. Men are the first fruits of the New Being."[16] The world is not simply without salvation, but the prince of this world is still active in it and raises his awful head in a destructive way against God's good creation.

The French Jesuit and paleontologist Pierre Teilhard de Chardin (1881–1955) starts with an evolutionary understanding of life and is convinced that through God's incarnation in Jesus Christ a process has been initiated by which all matter will be more and more permeated by God's Spirit. "One day the whole divinizable substance of matter will have passed into the souls of men; all the chosen dynamisms will have been recovered: then our world will be ready for the Parousia."[17] One is reminded here of the Gnostic idea that what can be

14. Paul Tillich, *Systematic Theology*, vol. 3, *Life and the Spirit: History and the Kingdom of God* (Chicago: University of Chicago Press, 1963), 11–314.

15. Ibid., 262.

16. Ibid., 295.

17. Pierre Teilhard de Chardin, *The Divine Milieu: An Essay on the Interior Life* (New York: Harper & Row, 1965), 110.

redeemed will be torn away from the world and ushered toward the divine presence. Yet in contrast to Gnosticism, Teilhard does not advocate a separation between spirit and matter. The goal of the whole creative process, in which the Holy Spirit is the creative principle, is the spiritualization and divinization of matter and humanity. Through the divine activity the world will one day be transformed into Christ's sphere. The Spirit is thereby the creative and life-giving power of God. It is present in all of life and all of being and ushers humanity irresistibly toward God. Yet the Roman Catholic Church noted, Teilhard says, almost nothing about the anti-godly powers that resist such a final transformation of the world. Creation is the starting point for the process of divinization, which God effects through the all-creative Spirit.

The theologian Wolfhart Pannenberg states on a biblical basis, "God as Spirit is the miraculous depth of life out of which all life originates. In the Old Testament 'spirit' is the creative origin of life."[18] As the breath of life given to humans by God, the Spirit is also the source of truth and freedom. The Spirit enlivens us and sets us free to recognize the true dimension of life. The basic activity of the Spirit, according to Pannenberg, is "the creative activity of bringing forth life and movement."[19] Pannenberg shows that the Holy Spirit is involved in a vast area of activity that comprises both nature and humanity as well as the whole of salvation. According to Pannenberg, there is a close connection "between the soteriological activity of the Spirit in the believer and the Spirit's activity as creator of all life, as well as its eschatological new creation and completion."[20] Since humans continuously interact with their environment to adapt to it and live in it, they need a foundation beyond themselves to assess appropriately their own conduct. Pannenberg asserts that such a foundation can only be found in the reality that holds everything together, meaning God's Spirit. Confronted with the ambiguity of life, Pannenberg says:

> The Christian message, with its assurance of a new life that will no longer be subject to death, provides a new and unshakable confidence, a new presence of the Spirit. . . . The Spirit of this new life, lived in the community of faith, is none other than that which animates and quickens all living things. Only because it is the same Spirit that by the inspiration of life's overwhelmingly rich self-transcendence is the source of all life, the Spirit active in the Christian community is no escapist opiate or piety, but is the Power which enables the

18. Wolfhart Pannenberg, *Gegenwart Gottes: Predigten* (Munich: Claudius, 1973), 106, in a sermon on John 4:19–24.

19. Wolfhart Pannenberg, *Systematic Theology*, trans. Geoffrey W. Bromiley (Grand Rapids: Eerdmans, 1998), 3:19.

20. Ibid., 14.

faithful to bear and finally vanquish the absurdities and disappointments of the world as it is.[21]

With this assertion we have returned to the biblical affirmation that the Spirit of God gives humans power and insight to withstand the problems of life, and beyond that it opens for them hope that through the power of the Spirit a kingdom of everlasting peace and communion with God can be established. We have noticed that the Spirit of God in its efficacy is not limited to the ecclesial sphere or to individual Christians, but is effective throughout the whole world for the well-being of humans and the realization of the kingdom of God.

21. Wolfhart Pannenberg, "The Spirit of Life," in *Faith and Reality*, trans. John Maxwell (Philadelphia: Westminster, 1977), 38.

11

THE CHURCH

Since its inauguration at Pentecost with the outpouring of the Holy Spirit on the disciples, the church has been closely connected with the activity of the Spirit. But the church cannot be thought of without Jesus Christ, whose name it bears. Yet it is strange, on the one hand, that Jesus of Nazareth announced the nearness and even the presence of the kingdom of God, and, on the other hand, that he would have founded the church. In the Gospels we find the term "church" (*ecclesia*) only three times, and there only in the Gospel according to Matthew. Most important is Matthew 16:13–20, where we find the famous confession of Peter. We notice that this passage consists of two episodes. In the first, Jesus asks his disciples who they think he is, and Peter answers with the messianic confession, "You are the Messiah, the Son of the living God" (Matt. 16:16). Without directly referring to this confession, Jesus says in the second episode, "I tell you, you are Peter, and on this rock I will build my church, and the gates of Hades will not prevail against it. I will give you the keys of the kingdom of heaven, and whatever you bind on earth will be bound in heaven, and whatever you loose on earth will be loosed in heaven" (Matt. 16:18–19). The word "Peter" (*kephas*) is derived from the Aramaic word "rock" (*kepha*), showing that the term is very old. The assumption that Jesus endowed Peter with the task to be the cornerstone of the church makes sense only if Jesus knew himself to be the Messiah. If Jesus was the Messiah, then the circle of the disciples was not only a group of people who followed their leader but the core of the end-time community who reacted to the presence of the Messiah. This community was not a holy remnant, a notion mentioned by the Old

Testament prophets (Isa. 10:20–21), but the community of the new people of God. That they depicted the new Israel is attested to by the fact that Jesus did not limit his activity to a few elected ones but extended his ministry to all of Israel. Since Peter was the speaker of the disciples, the task and the promise given to him appeared to have public sanction by Jesus. Because we cannot discern any other reason from the Gospels that Peter should be designated to such a position, the selection must have been founded on Jesus' will alone.

Yet on the basis of these texts one should not equate the church with the kingdom of God. The first Christian community recognized Jesus' proclamation of the kingdom of God not only as a present reality but also as an end-time goal. The kingdom of God will be fully realized in the eschaton, while the present time is a proleptic anticipation of this eschaton. This means that the church is an end-time phenomenon as it waits for the full realization of the kingdom, and yet it lives in proleptic anticipation of this kingdom.

The Formative Era

During the short time covered by the New Testament documents, the church grew in an astounding way. At the beginning of his activity, Jesus called twelve apostles, in analogy to the twelve tribes of Israel, and sent them out as his emissaries (Mark 3:14). Forty years later there were Christian communities in Rome, Athens, Corinth, and many other places in Asia Minor and Palestine. Since the Christian church had expanded beyond the boundaries of Israel, it was no longer seen as an obligation to maintain the circle of the Twelve. When James the son of Zebedee was killed, his place among the Twelve remained empty. Yet earlier, when Judas had been eliminated, Matthias filled his place after the casting of lots to complete the number twelve (Acts 1:15–26). During that time those who were called apostles had the most influence. Originally, they were identical with the Twelve. The prerequisite for an apostle was that one had been called and sent by Jesus. This means the apostles were the carriers of the New Testament message and the first Christian missionaries.

At first the apostles were chosen from among the disciples of Jesus. Not every disciple became an apostle. As we see especially in the last chapters of the Gospel of John, not just the encounter with the resurrected Christ was foundational for the mission of Peter, but also the explicit charge given through Christ. In a similar way Paul emphasizes that he had been called to be an apostle when he introduced himself to the Christian community in Rome (Rom. 1:1). An apostle had an authoritative position within the Christian community because together with the other apostles he represented the risen

Lord and was entrusted with a mission. He also had the task to proclaim the one by whose authority he was sent. This is true for the whole time between Christ's resurrection and his parousia, when he will return in power (cf. Acts 1:6). Christ is present through an apostle, and that apostle is endowed with the Holy Spirit. Pentecost, then, was the beginning of the missionary activity and at the same time the starting point of the Christian church. There and then the apostles were endowed with the Spirit. They did not become superhuman beings through the Spirit, but the Spirit took them as they were and used them as tools (cf. Acts 10:35). We may assume that in the beginning only the Twelve and a few others, such as James the brother of Jesus and also Paul, were counted as apostles.

When Peter gave his address at Pentecost, it was evident that his audience had ties to Judaism. Therefore they understood Peter when he called them to repent and to follow the Messiah. Christians were not separatists but understood themselves in true continuity with the messianic expectations of the Jewish faith, which they now saw as fulfilled. They followed the call of the apostles and "devoted themselves to the apostles' teaching and fellowship, to the breaking of bread and the prayers" (Acts 2:42). Initially, they did not separate themselves from other Jews and had no special initiation rituals, because Christian baptism can be understood in analogy to the Jewish baptism of repentance. Yet it was decisive that the Christians claimed Jesus as their Lord (Rom. 10:9). Jesus' resurrection and the outpouring of the Holy Spirit gave them the conviction that Jesus was the Messiah and that they formed the messianic community. As we can see especially in the Gospel according to Matthew, the whole history of Jesus could be understood as a history of the fulfillment of the Old Testament promises.

Though the Christians are often called "saints" in the New Testament (cf. Acts 9:13; Rom. 1:7), they did not think of themselves as being better than other Jews. It was in analogy to the Old Testament covenant community (Exod. 19:6) that they called themselves "a chosen race, a royal priesthood, a holy nation" (1 Pet. 2:9). But they did not see themselves in unbroken continuity with the Old Testament community, because they confronted Israel with the message of Jesus as the Messiah (Acts 2:36). Yet even Paul as the missionary to the gentiles, who came mainly out of Hellenism, was not indifferent to the destiny of his own Jewish people (Rom. 11:1). He even thought that the mission to the gentiles was a means by which all of Israel would accept Jesus as their Messiah and would also be saved (Rom. 11:13–26).

With the mission to the gentiles, the issue arose whether one first had to become a Jew, which for a man meant being circumcised, before one could become a Christian. After a long and heated discussion, the apostles decided that missionaries to the gentiles did not have to bring their newly converted people first to Judaism before they could become Christians. Of course, the Jewish Christians were much more conservative on this issue than those who worked on the mission field of the gentiles. When it became evident that Israel as a whole would not accept Jesus as the Messiah, and when in AD 70 Jerusalem as the focal point of Jewish messianic hopes was destroyed, the way was opened for an all-embracing church with a predominantly Hellenistic background. Writing from this perspective, the evangelist Luke divided the history of salvation into three epochs: first, the history of Israel leading up to John the Baptist (Luke 16:16), then the history of the activity of Jesus (Luke 4:16–19), and finally, the time of the church and its exalted Lord.

At the beginning of the Acts of the Apostles, we read that the church has a mission to the ends of the earth (Acts 1:8). The presence of the Holy Spirit, which is foundational for the Christian community, is understood as the counterpart to the dispersion of humanity at the Tower of Babel, when humans sought to reach God through their own power (Gen. 11:1–9). Now God has come down to us and has poured out God's Spirit as announced by the prophet Joel (Joel 2:28–29). This means the church exists not just in a messianic but also in an end-time epoch. Though there will be temptations and persecutions for the church and its members, these trials will not last forever (Acts 14:22). Christians should not withdraw from the world or become pessimistic, because they know that they are a light for the gentiles (the nations) and should carry the message of salvation to the ends of the earth (Acts 13:47). The church, as a tool of its exalted Lord, is an interim institution in this world and will not remain forever. Jesus has fulfilled the first part of his promises, and the church has believed that he will return soon. Yet more than two thousand years have passed, and the Lord of the church has still not returned. In many ways the church has absorbed the world into itself and has often forgotten that it is only an interim institution and not part of the world order. When we look at the history of the church, we notice that next to high points are many dark places. Besides maintaining fidelity to its Lord, the church has often betrayed him. Nevertheless, the church has endured through the centuries because its structure, which is confessed in the Nicene Creed as one, holy, catholic (all-embracing), and apostolic, has in itself the means to reform.

The Present Structure

Empirically viewed, the four structural aspects of the church—unity, holiness, catholicity, and apostolicity—are in stark contrast to the church's appearance.

In Africa alone there are more than six thousand ecclesial communities. There has been a rift between the Protestants and the Catholics since the sixteenth century, and between the Orthodox Church and the churches of the West since 1054. Unity was never a strong point of the church. We see in Luke-Acts that from the very beginning the church had no monolithic structure. The church shows itself as one church in different ways and in different locations (cf. 1 Cor. 1:2).

Far into the twentieth century, there were almost endless divisions in the church on the Protestant side. Since the middle of the twentieth century, however, the tendency has gone in the opposite direction. Disregarding all diversities, the church has become more and more cognizant that a unity somehow still exists since all Christians belong together. For instance, the sixteen hundredth anniversary of the Nicene-Constantinopolitan Creed (381) was celebrated by all churches together. The unilateral addition by the Western churches that the Holy Spirit proceeds from the Father *and* the Son was relativized by the Roman Catholic Church by making it into an option. This means that the so-called *filioque* ("and from the Son") need no longer be the symbol of separation between East and West. At the Second Vatican Council (1962–65), Protestant and Orthodox faithful, who were once called heretics and schismatics, were invited as official guests and observers. In the *Decree on Ecumenism* the council even declared: "Promoting the restoration of unity among all Christians is one of the chief concerns of the Second Sacred Ecumenical Synod of the Vatican."[1] While during the First Vatican Council (1869–70) there was still the mentality of demarcation over against the Protestants, this had largely been overcome at the Second. It became obvious to observers that the Second Vatican Council had learned from the First. The Roman Catholic Church did not suddenly deny its past but put the accent on something different. For instance, concerning the laity we now read: "They are in their own way made sharers in the priestly, prophetic, and kingly functions of Christ. They carry out their own part in the mission of the whole Christian people with respect to the Church and the world."[2] Or we hear in a citation of the church father Jerome (347–419): "Ignorance of the Scriptures is ignorance of Christ."[3] This statement almost sounds like the Lutheran emphasis on "Scripture alone." On the other side, Protestants began to see that they were not allergic to everything Roman Catholic, but realized that the two had much more in common than was initially thought.

1. *Decree on Ecumenism* 1, in *The Documents of Vatican II*, ed. Walter M. Abbott (New York: Guild Press, 1966), 341.
2. *Dogmatic Constitution on the Church* 31, in *Documents of Vatican II*, 57.
3. *Dogmatic Constitution on Divine Revelation* 25, in *Documents of Vatican II*, 127.

This readiness to learn from each other is also true for the Protestants themselves. For instance, the World Council of Churches, with its seat in Geneva, Switzerland, was founded in 1948 in Amsterdam. At its fifth plenary assembly in Nairobi (1975), the assembly recommended to the churches "to provide opportunities for a careful study and evaluation of the concept of conciliar fellowship as a way of describing the unity of the Church."[4] Since then, many documents of growing agreement have ensued from bilateral and multilateral discussions between various denominations. This is evidenced by the 640-page volume of the complete reports and consensus texts of interconfessional dialogues on a global level from 1998 to 2005.[5] And not only documents emerged, but many churches actually merged—for instance, the Church of South India, the Church of North India, and the Evangelical Lutheran Church in America. Naturally, on the road to unity there have been setbacks, including the unfortunate documents of *Dominus Iesus* (2000), in which the Roman Catholic Church emphasized that "the Church of Christ, despite the divisions which exist among Christians, continues to exist fully only in the Catholic church."[6] Then we read further on: "The ecclesial communities which have not preserved the valid Episcopate and the genuine and integral substance of the Eucharistic mystery are not Churches in the proper sense."[7] This statement means that the only true church is the Roman Catholic Church. Protestant churches are not churches in the truest sense because they have no valid episcopacy, meaning they are not under Rome. But such documents cannot stop the road toward unity. If churches preach reconciliation and are irreconcilable, they are no longer trustworthy. Moreover, the doctrinal boundaries no longer coincide with the boundaries between the churches, but they cut through the various churches themselves. For instance, liberal Protestants have more in common with liberal Roman Catholics than with their conservative Protestant brothers and sisters in Christ. Today individuals and groups can be together in one denomination and have little in common with each other. Furthermore, many of the theological differences that allegedly exist between denominations are very difficult for lay people to understand. Therefore the segregation in

4. Breaking Barriers, *Nairobi 1975: The Official Report of the Fifth Assembly of the World Council of Churches, Nairobi, November 23–December 10, 1975*, ed. David M. Patton (Grand Rapids: Eerdmans, 1976), 69.

5. Jeffrey Gros, Thomas F. Best, and Lorelei F. Fuchs, eds., *Growth in Agreement III: International Dialogue Texts and Agreed Statements; 1998–2005* (Grand Rapids: Eerdmans, 2007).

6. Congregation for the Doctrine of the Faith, *Declaration "Dominus Iesus" on the Unicity and Salvific Universality of Jesus Christ and the Church* 16, http://www.vatican.va/roman_curia/congregations/cfaith/documents/rc_con_cfaith_doc_20000806_dominus-iesus_en.html.

7. *Declaration "Dominus Iesus"* 17.

different churches is more the result of institutional inertia than of actual theological differences.

The Whole People of God

When we perceive the church as the whole people of God, we should not draw boundaries too narrowly or too widely. In the people's churches of Germany (*Volkskirchen*), everybody belongs to the church who has not officially left it. This means that one can be a member of the church without having ever participated in a worship service. In the United States, church membership is usually determined by whether a person has taken Holy Communion at least once a year, or whether a person financially supports the church. This is very different from what we see in Acts 2:42–46 regarding church membership. The Christians came together daily in the temple, listened to the teaching of the apostles, prayed together, participated in the Lord's Supper, and had communion with each other. But regular attendance at a worship service and generous donations are not infallible marks of being a Christian. These traits might be engendered by social pressure or tradition. Therefore the church father Augustine equated the visible church with the institutional church. At the same time, he distinguished the visible church from the invisible church, which may be larger or smaller than the visible one. In medieval Europe the last judgment was often depicted in the tympanum, the triangular space above church portals. In such depictions, to the left of the judgment seat are the condemned. Among the condemned are always some with insignia indicating that they are members of the ecclesial office. This shows that church membership alone, even if one exercises an ecclesiastical function, is not a sign of true faithfulness, nor is it an indication of whether a person belongs to the "true church."

When we talk about the people of God, we are not talking about an institution, a church, or a denomination, but first of all of those who assemble and sanctify God, the God who has shown God's self in Jesus Christ. This does not make the institutional church irrelevant, because it is the place where the Christian tradition is maintained and the gospel is proclaimed. Yet it must be continuously measured by the intention of its founder, Jesus Christ.

The church is not a club that furthers the interests of it members, like a soccer club for instance. Rather, the church furthers exclusively the interests of its founder. When the church is described in the Apostles' Creed as one, holy, catholic community of saints, these attributes are derived not from the church itself or its members but from Jesus Christ, its founder, who sanctifies it and asks for a pledge of allegiance, and who guarantees its all-encompassing or catholic aspect. As the shepherd of the flock, Jesus Christ also signifies the church's communal character. All essential aspects of the church point to Jesus because there would be no Christian church without the Easter event, the event that made it possible for Jesus as the Christ to gather his followers after his death and resurrection. The Lord's Supper is not a privilege of the church but is celebrated upon the command of Jesus Christ. Similarly, baptism is not an entrance ritual into the church. In baptism we are related to the dying and rising of Christ. Even the proclamation occurs in the name of Christ and has its center in Christ. Christ is the wellspring and the content of the Christian church. The church is founded by him, proclaims salvation in his name, and celebrates the sacraments, which can be traced back to him and his activity.

Pentecost, the day when the Holy Spirit was poured out on the followers of Christ, is traditionally regarded as the birthday of the church. While the gift of the Holy Spirit is often regarded as something that enables one to speak in tongues, the promise of the prophet Ezekiel to Israel sounds very different: "I will give them one heart, and put a new spirit within them; I will remove the heart of stone from their flesh and give them a heart of flesh, so that they may follow my statutes and keep my ordinances and obey them. Then they shall be my people, and I will be their God" (Ezek. 11:19–20). Of course, the Spirit can enable one to experience ecstatic phenomena, but the most important function of the Spirit is the empowerment to lead a life in harmony with God. This harmony issues into a harmony among people, so that through the power of the Holy Spirit the people of God can rediscover their original unity. Though at Pentecost the creation of a new humanity commenced as an all-encompassing community, there immediately arose disunity. The reason for this is that human sinfulness is still active in individual Christians and leads to a denial of their common ground and their common goal. When we continuously keep the power of the Spirit in the forefront, then the church can be a true community. The Spirit unites us with Christ just as Jesus told his disciples: "I am the vine, you are the branches. Those who abide in me and I in them bear much fruit, because apart from me you can do nothing" (John 15:5).

As self-assured as an ecclesial community may be, only in communion with the Lord of the church can there be true community. This becomes especially evident in the concept of the "body of Christ," which Paul quite often uses to describe the church. He writes, for instance, "Now you are the body of Christ and individually members of it" (1 Cor. 12:27). Later, Christ is considered the head of the church, his body, in which he is totally present (Eph. 1:23). Church exists whenever the Christian community coincides in word and deed with Jesus Christ, its head and founder. The church cannot found itself, but similar to its unity, its foundation is a given. The church can only rediscover this given unity anew. Through its tight connection with Christ, the church represents him and symbolizes his rule over the whole world.

Since Christ has given the church the charge and the privilege to represent him, it is endowed with saving power. This power is shown in the fact that the church administers Word and sacrament in Christ's place and hands them on to the faithful. Then there is the charge of mission in Matthew 28:19: "Go therefore and make disciples of all nations, baptizing them in the name of the Father and of the Son and of the Holy Spirit." It is not surprising that Cyprian (200/210–258) declared in the third century that "there is no salvation out of [i.e., apart from] the Church."[8] This does not mean that the church itself, as an institution, can offer a means of salvation, because Christ instituted the church as a means of salvation. Only when the church represents Christ is it really the church and the bringer of salvation for all people. Without the church there would be no proclamation of the gospel, because it is the church that preserved the gospel through the centuries. In this way, the church represents Christ in mediating his message, handing on his offer of salvation, and providing the context for the Christian faith and life.

The Priestly Office

Over against the elevated office of the priest prevailing in the Roman Catholic and the Orthodox traditions, the churches of the Reformation emphasize the priesthood of all believers. In so doing the churches of the Reformation follow the original Greek meaning of the word *laos*, from which our word *lay* (layperson or laity) comes. In the Greek translation of the Old Testament, *laos* stands for the people of God, or Israel. In the New Testament it signifies the Christian community. Paul, for instance, writes (quoting God's statement as rendered by the prophet Hosea), "Those who were not my people I will call 'my people,' and her who was not beloved I will call 'beloved'" (Rom. 9:25). Everyone who belongs to the people of God is a layperson, a part of the people of God. Soon, however, *laos* was understood to mean the Christian community as distinct from its leaders, especially those who presided in the worship service. (This was no absolute novelty, because already in the New Testament this was the case with the service in the synagogue.) Now the term *laos* stands no longer for the whole people of God but for the people in contradistinction to their leaders. Martin Luther emphasizes this difference when he writes:

8. Cyprian, *Epistles* 72.21, in *ANF* 5:384.

For although we are all priests, this does not mean that all of us can preach, teach, and rule. Certain ones of the multitude must be selected and separated for such office. And he who has such an office is not a priest because of his office but a servant of all the others, who are priests. When he is no longer able to preach and serve, or if he no longer wants to do so, he once more becomes a part of the common multitude of Christians. His office is conveyed to someone else, and he becomes a Christian like any other. This is the way to distinguish between the office of preaching, or the ministry, and the general priesthood of all baptized Christians.[9]

We can gather the following from Luther's statement: (1) According to his understanding there are not two classes of Christians, one class that occupies the priestly office and another that comprises the laypersons. All Christians are entrusted with the priestly office and should conduct themselves in a priestly manner both in their way of life and in the proclamation of God's word. (2) For the sake of good order some are called to the governing office because not all of them can preach, teach, and preside. This is not an office of authority, but one of service for the community and for Word and sacrament. (3) The special office of governance, or rather of preaching, does not give the person a special status. Instead, it must be considered to be purely functional. Once this service can no longer be executed, the person steps back into the prior state of the common priesthood.

The Roman Catholic Church, too, emphasizes the one priestly office in which both clerics and laypersons participate. We read in the documents of the Second Vatican Council: "The lay apostolate, however, is a participation in the saving mission of the Church itself. Through their baptism and confirmation, all are commissioned to that apostolate by the Lord Himself. . . . Besides this apostolate, which pertains to absolutely every Christian, the laity can also be called in various ways to a more direct form of cooperation in the apostolate of the hierarchy."[10] This means that the laity is in principle not excluded from involvement in the church on every level. But Vatican II also talks about a special office that differs "in essence and not only in degree" from the common priesthood of the faithful.[11] Yet how can one reconcile this difference "in essence" between the priestly office and the common priesthood with the more egalitarian understanding of the office in the Lutheran church? Moreover, one must consider that we are no longer in the Middle Ages, a time when there were only priests and laypeople in the church. Now

---

9. Martin Luther, *Sixth Sermon on Psalm 110* (June 9, 1535), in *LW* 13:332.
10. *Dogmatic Constitution on the Church* 33, in *Documents of Vatican II*, 59–60.
11. *Dogmatic Constitution on the Church* 10, in *Documents of Vatican II*, 27.

we have a multitude of voluntary and semivoluntary coworkers in the church who in some way or other participate in this one office. The Lutheran theologian Ulrich Kühn (1932–2012) points correctly to the concept of governance:

> A service of governance does not just appear in the lists of the special gifts in Paul, but is also executed primarily by the apostle himself in his Pauline congregations. One can only grasp sufficiently the coordination of these services and offices in the Pauline congregations when one considers the function of governance executed by the apostle himself. . . . Sociological insights contribute to perceiving a special service of governance which has ultimate responsibility as indispensable for a congregation. Not just the proclamation of the gospel would be reserved for the bearer of such a special office . . . but his task would be better described to be one of stimulating, coordinating, and integrating the various services for the sake of what happens in the proclamation. Such service of governance is a spiritual service, a service which occurs in proclaiming the word and not primarily in a technological management function. . . . The service of the spiritual governance of a congregation is in its center always also a service for the unity. This holds true both for the respective local congregation as well as for the regional and total ecclesial community of all local congregations.[12]

The reference to the office of governance would allow us to reconcile the Lutheran emphasis on the functional aspect of the office with the Roman Catholic emphasis on the essential difference of this office from that of the common priesthood. A special office of governance has precedents in the New Testament and is necessary unless the church dissipates in a multitude of independent or only loosely interconnected congregations. This danger looms large especially in Christian communities, such as Baptists and Pentecostals, who emphasize almost exclusively the immediate connection to Christ, but much less the earthly manifestation of Christ's undivided body (cf. 1 Cor. 12:12–20). One should also not overlook that Philipp Melanchthon in his *Apology of the Augsburg Confession* rejected a priesthood that made sacrifices for the people, but he did not reject the ordering function of that office. He wrote, "But if ordination is understood with reference to the ministry of the Word, we have no objection to calling ordination a sacrament."[13] Consequently, in the Roman Catholic–Lutheran dialogue the justifying statement was made that "even though Lutherans do not speak of ordination as a sacrament, there is yet 'substantial convergence' between the Catholic and

---

12. Ulrich Kühn, *Kirche: Handbuch Systematische Theologie* (Gütersloh: Gerd Mohn, 1980), 10:193.

13. Philipp Melanchthon, *Apology of the Augsburg Confession* (art. 13: "Of the Number and Use of the Sacraments," 11), in *The Book of Concord*, 220.

Lutheran understanding and practice."[14] In the Lutheran tradition ordination is not considered a sacrament in the strict sense of the term, but to call ordination a sacrament is not in principle rejected. On the one hand, this priestly office is instituted by God, and on the other hand, one is delegated to this office by the community. Therefore article 5 of the Augsburg Confession says that "the ministry of teaching the gospel and administering the sacraments was instituted" by God. The office of the proclamation of the gospel and the administration of the sacraments, which means the governance of a congregation or of the whole church, in some ways has a special status among all other offices and services in the church.

But the ordination to this special office of governance is not an additional or separate rite, but must be seen in analogy to the commissioning of certain people for special tasks that arise within the Christian community. This means that the laity should not be seen in opposition to the clerics or vice versa. Paul therefore writes: "For as in one body we have many members, and not all the members have the same function, so we, who are many, are one body in Christ, and individually we are members of one another. We have gifts that differ according to the grace given to us" (Rom. 12:4–6). All Christians are tied together as one community. But they are endowed with different gifts and are responsible for using these gifts in their proper way. The laity is not in competition with the clerics, nor are laypersons substitute clerics if clerics are missing. They cooperate with the clerics, and both support each other. Since most laypeople have secular professions and have no particular theological education, their time and their theological expertise are limited. Therefore they should not be confronted with demands that call for fully educated clerics or clerics who work full time. Laypeople are not "subclerics" but Christians whose main task is to witness to their faith through their life in a non-Christian world. They are often more effective in this witness than are clerics because they usually do not get paid for their Christian service. One could, however, surmise that clerics execute their service only because they get paid for it. This becomes even more critical if clerics are present in the worship service only when they have a leadership function. Intentionally or unintentionally, they imply that they attend and serve only when they get paid for it.

We must reject the notion that priests or pastors are employed by their respective congregations for services that no one else was willing to do. Though they are called to a special office in a congregation and usually also by that congregation, they are ultimately neither responsible to that congregation nor

14. *Facing Unity: Models, Forms and Phases of Catholic-Lutheran Church Fellowship* (1984; par.78), http://www.pro.urbe.it/dia-int/l-rc/doc/e_l-rc_facing.html.

even called by it, but are responsible to and called by their Lord Jesus Christ, whom they ultimately serve. Therefore, we read in article 5 of the Augsburg Confession: "So that we may obtain this faith, the ministry of teaching the gospel and administering the sacraments was instituted. For through the Word and sacraments as through instruments the Holy Spirit is given, who effects faith where and when it pleases God in them that hear the gospel." The main task of the preacher is the proclamation of the gospel and the administration of the sacraments. In contrast to this assertion of the Augsburg Confession, in many Protestant churches the office of proclamation can also be assumed by others who have no appropriate theological education, while the administration of the sacraments, especially the Lord's Supper, is always carried out by an ordained pastor. Word and sacrament are of equal value and should be administered by the one office instituted by God. It is irrelevant whether a preacher fills the office full time and is paid by the congregation, or only part-time and has another profession to manage the finances of the congregation. This latter situation is often the case in the so-called diaspora (from Greek *diaspora*, meaning scattering or dispersion of Christians) and in younger churches that cannot afford to pay a fully educated theologian in every congregation. Here one should heed article 14 of the Augsburg Confession, where it states, "Concerning church order they teach that no one should teach publicly in the church or administer the sacraments unless properly called." If one separates Word and sacrament, the danger arises that the sacrament is given an elevated status, so that only special people can administer a sacrament, while the Word is accessible to everyone. The proclamation of the Word, however, is as important as the administration of the sacraments.

According to biblical understanding, the Word of God is of no lesser significance than a sacrament. Therefore, the *Dogmatic Constitution of the Church* of the Second Vatican Council rightly says: "Among the principal duties of bishops, the preaching of the gospel occupies an eminent place. For bishops are preachers of the faith who lead new disciples to Christ. They are authentic teachers, that is, teachers endowed with the authority of Christ."[15] Similar to Protestant churches, the Roman Catholic Church puts the teaching function, not the administrative function or any other function, in first place. Yet it is strange that in practical application the Roman Catholic Church allows the teaching and preaching function to be delegated to deacons and laypersons, while the celebrative function of administering the sacraments, for which an exact wording is prescribed, can be administered only by priests and bishops. Such a distinction cannot be derived from the New Testament.

15. *Dogmatic Constitution of the Church* 25, in *Documents of Vatican II*, 47.

Though governing functions are mentioned there, one cannot deduce who can administer the sacraments and who can proclaim the gospel. According to Paul, it is only important that everything is done in an orderly way and that the tradition is maintained which has been received from the Lord. It also cannot be deduced from the New Testament that the governing function is imprinted for life on the bearer of the function according to the motto "Once a priest, always a priest." Recently, the Roman Catholic Church allowed not only priests but also bishops to be relieved of the duties of their office to retire, yet their status as priests remains untouched by this change.

The special priestly office should further the essence of the church and not hinder it. Often this office was so focused on the pastor that laypersons had little opportunity to participate meaningfully and actively in the life of the congregation. This led to a lamentable inactivity of the laity, especially in the traditionally Lutheran countries of Scandinavia and in Germany. Only recently has there been a change, albeit for the wrong reason, meaning a shortage of pastors. Since this office is not exhausted in the administration of the sacraments and in proclamation, it should be a matter of fact that pastors can appropriately conduct their work only when they do so in communion with the laity.

Especially in the United States, larger congregations sometimes have a specialization of full-time coworkers. Whether and how such specialization is needed depends on the needs of a congregation. Conversely, the scarcity of priests in Roman Catholic churches has often led to the use of deacons and pastoral assistants who practically take over the work of a priest without having a special priestly ordination. This dangerous scarcity of priests occurs when we strictly hold to the traditional concept that certain tasks can be conducted only by priests. We must not overlook the fact that all of the faithful can participate in the one office and that in cases of need no task need only be reserved for a priest.

EXCURSUS: UNBRIDGEABLE DISSENSION IN UNDERSTANDING THE OFFICE?

In the past fifty years a far-reaching theological consensus has been achieved between the Lutheran churches and the Roman Catholic Church except in the understanding of the priestly office. The study document of the

Lutheran–Roman Catholic Commission for Unity on *The Apostolicity of the Church* (2005) arrives at the sobering conclusion: "At present the relationship is asymmetrical insofar as Lutherans recognize the ministry of the Catholic Church as apostolic, while the reverse is not the case from the Catholic side."[16] According to Roman Catholic understanding, one of the four attributes of the church (one, holy, all-encompassing, and apostolic) is missing in the Lutheran church. It has a deficiency in its office because it is not truly apostolic. Therefore, the Lutheran church is no church in the true sense, and the functions of the pastor, especially with regard to the Lord's Supper, are not fully valid. Because of this, it is the rule that a member of the Roman Catholic Church is not allowed to participate in a Lutheran Eucharist, and there is also no eucharistic communion which means that neither priests nor laypersons can participate in the Eucharist of the other denomination. How should Lutherans react to these conclusions?

In 2008 the Lutheran World Federation released a document titled *Episcopal Ministry within the Apostolicity of the Church*, a declaration that goes back to a consultation of 2002 and is the result of ecumenical dialogues. In contradistinction to the argument, especially adduced by the Roman Catholic Church, that "apostolic" means an uninterrupted chain of carriers of tradition, the Lutheran declaration puts the main emphasis on continuity in content.

> Apostolic tradition in the church means continuity in the permanent characteristics of the church of the apostles: witness to the apostolic faith, proclamation of the Gospel and faithful interpretation of the Scriptures, celebration of baptism and the eucharist, the exercise and transmission of ministerial responsibilities, communion in prayer, love, joy, and suffering, service to the sick and needy, unity among the local churches and sharing the gifts which the Lord has given to each. Continuity in this tradition is apostolic succession.[17]

This statement anticipated what was expressed in the common study document *The Apostolicity of the Church*: "This study reveals a fundamental agreement between Lutherans and Catholics that the gospel is central and decisive in the apostolic heritage. Thus we agree that the church in every age continues to be 'apostolic' by reason of its faith in and witness to the gospel of Jesus Christ."[18] It was discovered through biblical and historical studies that

---

16. *The Apostolicity of the Church* (2005), 270, http://www.pro.urbe.it/dia-int/l-rc/doc/e_l-rc_ap-04.html.

17. *Episcopal Ministry within the Apostolicity of the Church: The Lund Statement by the Lutheran World Federation—A Communion of Churches* (Lund, Sweden, March 26, 2007), 29, http://ecumenism.net/archive/docu/2007_lwf_lund_episcopal_ministry_apostolicity_church_en.pdf.

18. Ibid., 150.

many things presented by the Roman Catholic Church as a matter of fact had actually been developed over the course of history, for instance, the apostolic leadership office and the three-part order of the office of deacons, priests, and bishops. Therefore, the following insight was reached:

> No human authority is able to guarantee the truth of the gospel since its authenticity and its power to evoke faith is inherent to the gospel itself (its *extra nos*). On the other hand, however, the faithfulness of the church requires certain forms of traditioning and a particular ecclesial ministry of proclamation, reconciliation, and teaching in order to ensure the orderly transmission of the apostolic teachings.[19]

In view of the complicated historical developments, it was concluded that more care must be taken when certain truth claims are made. Nevertheless, a special office tied to the ordination is considered indispensible. This office has the special responsibility to witness the apostolic tradition and to proclaim it anew to each generation in the authority given by Christ. For geographical areas larger than a local congregation, this office is usually executed by a bishop who generally ordains pastors and supervises them in their pastoral duties to document the unity of the church. Therefore, the above mentioned study document arrives at the insight: "There are now many individuals at many locations in Christendom who exercise the office of supervision which in the Roman Catholic Church is performed by a bishop."[20] The amazing conclusion is then drawn: "But if the consensus of bishops is the definitive sign of apostolicity of their doctrine, then Catholics cannot exclude these other episkopoi from the circle of those whose consensus is according to the Catholic view the sign of apostolicity of doctrine." If this insight gained the upper hand in the Roman Catholic Church, there would be no reason for it not to acknowledge as valid the office as it is executed in the Lutheran church. Then the unity of the church in its historical diversity would move considerably further ahead.

The Threefold Direction

When we ask why the church exists, we must look in three directions: past, present, and future. The church preserves the memory of that which gave it

19. Ibid., 64.
20. Ibid., 291, for this and the following quotation.

existence, it plays an important role in the present, and it gives hope for the future.

Preserving the Past

Since the church should not abandon the memory of what gave it existence, it cannot be separated from its origin. Especially in Europe many churches have almost become museums of art history. While the church is not a museum, similar to a museum it has a preserving character. It preserves that which contributed to its origin. Yet one must continually ask in a critical way what should be preserved and what should not. The church dare not hold on to ideas or traditions just because they are old. Since from a historical perspective the origin of the church lies in the past, the present direction of the church must be aligned with that past so that one can discern whether it has remained true to its origin. In critically reflecting on this continuity, one cannot naively appeal to the New Testament because already in the New Testament we encounter different traditions. Next to the Twelve (apostles) we have Paul and Barnabas who are also called apostles (Acts 14:14) and Paul appointed elders (*presbyteroi*) in each church (Acts 14:23) and he mentions elders and bishops almost in one breath as if there were synonymous (Titus 1:5–7). The Reformation insight of "Scripture alone" necessitates that tradition should be viewed critically. As a church we are not obliged to one tradition or any tradition, but to the person Jesus Christ who is the content of the gospel. All traditions must be measured by the gospel of Jesus Christ and by the tradition that has brought about this gospel. Tradition is necessary because God's Word comes to us by means of tradition. Even Scripture is the result of a process of tradition (cf. Luke 1:1–4; John 20:30) and is always understood within the tradition in which its reader lives. Even within the same confessional family, different cultural traditions can influence the reading of the gospel tradition. For instance, a Roman Catholic from Italy will understand Scripture differently from one in Argentina. Liberation theology, which originated in the predominantly Roman Catholic environment of Latin America, was opposed by the Roman Catholic authorities in Europe. This shows that the Word of God always speaks to different situations. If one absolutizes one particular tradition, the dangers of provincialism and division arise. We should always be mindful of the fact that each individual tradition is part of the one tradition that goes back to the Lord and is embedded in the Judeo-Christian heritage.

The handing-on of the tradition of the gospel is the presupposition for the existence of the church and the Christian faith. All churches have their own point of view from which they see the gospel tradition. For the Lutheran, it is the Pauline insight of justification by grace alone; for the enthusiasts at the time of the Reformation, it was the conscience of the individual under the guidance of the Holy Spirit; and for John Calvin, it was the glory of God and God's kingdom. These different viewpoints can enrich our own access to the gospel tradition. They show that catholicity or general validity of the church cannot be fully achieved by one single tradition. Ultimately, it is a gift of God that necessitates continuous ascertainment and acceptance. Only the one tradition of the gospel to which the churches witness in different ways can be called truly catholic. If we close ourselves off from the insights of other churches, the danger of heresy arises, which means that we pursue our separate way and are no longer interested in the unity of the Christian tradition. Since heresy is a deviation from the whole truth appreciated by the church, it often concentrates on one aspect of tradition and neglects others. Therefore, it is important to observe heresies very carefully and to ask whether they perhaps point to important aspects of tradition that themselves have been neglected. Just turning our back to heresies is the wrong way to deal with them. Heresies must be dealt with and must be carefully and critically considered.

The church is a communion of people that extends beyond the visible boundaries of their peculiar institutions. These people do not transcend these boundaries because they are driven by a common cause, but because they are called together by Christ. Therefore, belonging to the church means belonging to the Lord who has been active in it in the past, who is active in it now, and who will be active in it in the future. Jesus Christ does not belong to one single church but is beyond all churches and ecclesial communities.

When we remember that we belong to the communion of saints, we become aware that we are not the first Christians but are part of a community in and through which Christ has acted in the past. A church that has no regard for the communion of saints is forgetful of God's activity in the past and therefore neglects the impetus for its activity in the present. Even if the church has problems understanding itself as a communion of saints, it implicitly agrees to that communion by using the Old Testament Psalms and other parts of worship that tie the church to the past. Of course, the church has overcome its national restriction to Judaism. It no longer hopes for a national restoration of Israel and for assembling all nations at Mount Zion (cf. Isa. 2:3). Yet the church stands in continuity with Israel and witnesses the fulfillment of the promises given to Israel. Since Israel is, so to speak, the spiritual forebear of the church, the church must also always deal with Israel. The presence of the Jewish people serves as a reminder that the gospel has not been preached and lived in love in a way that would entice this nation to accept Jesus as the

Messiah. As mentioned, Luther had always considered it shameful that we have not met the Jews with the necessary love, but he himself then advocated very unkind and totally unapprovable actions in order that the Jews would finally acknowledge Jesus as their Messiah. The presence of the Jewish people reminds us also of the still unresolved tension within God's salvation history. With all the faithful, including the Jewish people, we await the coming of God and the public establishment of God's kingdom. As those whose foundations have been laid in the past and who consider themselves members of God's people, we approach the future with hope and expect the end-time fulfillment.

The Heart of the Present

The church is the heart of the present in proleptically anticipating the future. In contradistinction even to Judaism, for Christians the ecclesial community is no longer identical with the political community. In the past two hundred years, almost everywhere a separation of state and church has occurred. Even in countries that still have a state church, such as Great Britain with the Anglican Church, a high percentage of people do not belong to any church. While usually the sacraments are given only to church members, the Word in the form of law and gospel is principally directed to everybody. Therefore, in every country the church has the task to be a guardian by reminding society of God's directions for life, meaning God's commandments, and pointing out to society that the present life is not everything that is in store for them. This means that the church stands in opposition to the prevailing trends in society. This does not mean that it turns itself against society. Yet to be relevant to the world, the church dare not imitate the world, but it must offer something to the world that the world does not have. The church is vital for society because without the church or some other religious organization, the world is in danger of forgetting what humanity ultimately is: a community that comes from God and that should be oriented toward God. To be able to remind society of that which is truly human, the church must have a hearing in society. It is not by accident that in countries where human rights are severely threatened, the activities of the church are usually also endangered. There is a certain tension between church and society. On the one hand, the church has attempted to dominate society (as it did over and over again in the Middle Ages), and on the other hand, the state has tried to assume religious traits (as in state ideologies such as Marxism). To counter these temptations the Lutheran tradition has introduced the so-called doctrine of the two kingdoms, or rather the teaching of two reigns of God.

EXCURSUS: THE TWO REIGNS THEORY

The medieval church held the theory of two swords, according to which the pope as the successor to Christ had two swords or two kingdoms. He gave the emperor the worldly one as a fief, while he himself held on to the spiritual one. In the late Middle Ages, William of Ockham (ca. 1285–1347) and Marsilius of Padua (ca. 1290–1342/43) pointed out that this doctrine rested on a problematic allegorical interpretation of Luke 22:38. At the time of Luther, criticism of this doctrine continued. Luther already doubted in 1518, in the *Disputation on the Merit of the Indulgences*, whether the pope could have a spiritual and a worldly kingdom. In Luther's view, the Bible talks about only one sword, "the sword of the Spirit" (Eph. 6:17).[21] While Augustine distinguished two kingdoms, the world kingdom (*civitas terrena*) and the spiritual kingdom (*civitas dei*), which have opposing goals, Luther sees these as the two ways in which God reigns over the world.

> God has established two kinds of government among men. The one is spiritual; it has no sword, but it has the word, by means of which people are to become good and righteous, so that with this righteousness they may attain eternal life. God administers this righteousness through the word, which he has committed to the preachers. The other kind is worldly government, which works through the sword so that those who do not want to be good and righteous to eternal life may be forced to become good and righteous in the eyes of the world. God administers this righteousness through the sword. And although God will not reward this kind of righteousness with eternal life, nonetheless, he still wishes peace to be maintained among people and rewards them with temporal blessings.[22]

Though the reign of God is the real connecting bracket between the kingdoms, their unity becomes visible in human activity, because humans live in both kingdoms. As responsible cooperators with God, humans encounter both ways in which God governs the world, namely, through the law of God shown in the political realm, the family, and church structures, and through the gospel, which is proclaimed to the people through the announcement of God's Word.

The Lutheran notion of the two reigns of God was often judged very negatively, especially under the influence of Karl Barth, because it was argued that it would lead to a status quo. The church and Christians would be concerned

---

21. Martin Luther, *Resolutiones disputationum et indulgentiarum virtute* (1518), in *WA* 1:624.13.

22. Martin Luther, *Whether Soldiers, Too, Can Be Saved* (1526), in *LW* 46:99–100.

with the spiritual realm only, and the worldly sphere would be left to other forces. It then happened that, especially in Protestant Prussia, National Socialism gained the upper hand. Yet this argument against the notion of the two reigns is only halfway true, because Adolf Hitler received his first confessional support from Roman Catholics. Moreover, Lutheran countries in Scandinavia attempted to resist Nazi occupation, though with little success. The origin and establishment of the so-called Third Reich can be attributed to many sources and not simply to the Lutheran doctrine of two reigns. To blame Lutherans for advocating pure pacifism or quietism does justice neither to Luther nor to the Lutherans during the Third Reich.

It has also been argued that the doctrine of two ways of God's reign contradicts the New Testament understanding of the kingdom of God. In Reformed circles this "bifurcation" is often replaced with Christ's kingship. While this terminology is closer to the language of the Gospels, we must be mindful that in this world there are faithful people, less faithful ones, and unbelievers, and also Christians and non-Christians. True, the kingdom of God has already commenced, as Jesus repeatedly emphasized, but it is not yet visible and not yet universally complete. One can work toward the dominion of Christ, as Calvin attempted to do in Geneva when he put the state practically under the supervision of the spiritual authorities. A similar position seems to have been advocated by Karl Barth when he wrote, "The real Church must be the model and prototype of the real State."[23] Since in Western nations all citizens share equal rights (and equal duties), these nations are rightly secular even if our Western culture is undeniably imprinted by Christendom. Therefore, we must distinguish between that part of society that is expressly guided by God's Word and the other part that is consciously secular and therefore must be indirectly ruled by God. This distinction between the two ways of God's reign is indispensable.

In a positive way this notion of two ways of God's reign reminds us that the whole world is under God's authority. The world is not godless, even if it often seems to be. It is not only the place of sin, even if we see sin too clearly in the world, but it also stands under God's protective guidance. On account of his experience during the Third Reich, the Lutheran theologian Walter Künneth (1901–97) published a political ethics titled *Politics between God and the Demonic*.[24] This title captures the tension that characterizes our world between the secular authorities as the ordering power of God (Rom. 13) and the demonic state (Rev. 13). Under careful observation of certain preconditions,

23. Karl Barth, "The Christian Community and the Civil Community" (1946), in *Community, State, and Church*, trans. Will Herberg (Garden City, NY: Doubleday, 1960), 186.
24. Walter Künneth, *Politik zwischen Dämon und Gott: Eine christliche Ethik des Politischen* (Berlin: Lutherisches Verlagshaus, 1954).

Künneth concedes citizens a right to resist the state and its laws. Yet Christian voices should not be raised against everything that society or politics advocates, with the vain assumption that as Christians we know best what serves the common good. Luther himself had a sound distrust not only of the "mighty ones," whether Christians or not, but also of the enthusiastic attempts to Christianize the world. He writes:

> If anyone attempted to rule the world by the gospel and to abolish all temporal law and sword on the plea that all are baptized and Christian, and that, according to the gospel, there shall be among them no law or sword—or need for either—pray tell me, friend, what would he be doing? He would be loosing the ropes and chains of the savage wild beast and letting them bite and mangle everyone, meanwhile insisting that they were harmless, tame, and gentle creatures; but I would have the proof in my wounds. Just so would the wicked under the name of Christian abuse evangelical freedom, carry on their rascality, and insist that they were Christians subject neither to law nor sword.[25]

Christians and non-Christians live in the same world. Therefore, God rules this world by the law so that it does not turn into a godless chaos. But Christians have no need of this law as long as they are Christians. They would let themselves be guided by God through the gospel, which fulfills the demands of the law. This means that no sphere of life is excluded from God's rule, though God rules the two spheres in very different ways. The church, then, must remind society under whose authority it lives and under whose ultimate reign it conducts its business.

If the church wants to get a hearing in the world, it must affirm society by pointing to common orders that are essential for the survival of a community. For instance, behavioral science has shown that certain norms of conduct, which we see in some of the Ten Commandments, must be maintained in virtually every society. Luther, too, emphasized that what God gave to the Jews in the Ten Commandments, God at the same time had inscribed on the hearts of all people. Walter Künneth called these "orders of preservation" since God preserves humanity through these rules from their self-destructive tendencies. As a church we can take these orders as a starting point to sharpen the conscience of society.

With this point we come to the next task of the church, to transform society. The utopian idea has often emerged that church and society should evolve toward the kingdom of God, an idea that certain enthusiasts endeavored to inaugurate during the time of the Reformation. By doing this, they overlooked

---

25. Martin Luther, *Temporal Authority: To What Extent It Should Be Obeyed* (1523), in *LW* 45:91.

the reality and perversity of evil. Nevertheless, one cannot deny that through the gospel the churches have in a decided way contributed to a humanization of society. The so-called human rights of individuals, for instance, are intimately connected with the Judeo-Christian tradition. That a human person is a child of God, that he or she has inalienable rights, that he or she should be treated as a "thou" and not as an "it"—these insights arose from the Judeo-Christian tradition. This transformation process in which the church is involved must take place not only in society but also in the church itself. The church must transform itself more and more into an example of a new community promised by God so that it remains a beacon of hope in the face of oppression and injustice. The representatives of liberation theology have reminded the church rightly that the church is an ambassador of God's salvific activity. We carry a responsibility for all of humanity as living and trustworthy witnesses to the coming kingdom.

If the church is the conscience of society, it assumes a certain role in caring for those who have no advocates. The church must always exist for others and not primarily for itself. Luther rightly emphasized, "If everybody would serve his neighbor, then the whole world would be full of divine service."[26] Luther was reminded here of Matthew 25:40: "Just as you did it to one of the least of these who are members of my family, you did it to me." Church organizations such as Misereor and Caritas on the Roman Catholic side or Bread for the World on the Protestant side help wherever help is needed. This diaconal activity is symptomatic of the church. In catastrophes such as tsunamis and other environmental disasters, the Christian churches are ready to help immediately, whereas one hears very little of diaconal activities by other religions. Churches are not only a refuge for the neglected, but through their actions they point to a time no longer marred by anxiety, poverty, and suffering.

Reminder of the Future

In a secular culture that relies only on itself, the church contradicts the self-understanding of culture by witnessing to a future caused by God and not by humanity. The church has its strength from the Lord who could not be contained by cross and tomb. The symbols of the evident defeat became the signs of triumph over the anti-godly destructive forces. When Christians live in congruence with the Lord, then the cross becomes a sign of hope that the oppressed and the powerless will not remain forever on the seamy side of

26. Martin Luther, *Predigt am 19. Sonntag nach Trinitatis* (September 29, 1532), in *WA* 36:340.12–13, in a sermon on Matt. 22:34–35.

existence, but a time will come when there will be a community in which all have equal rights. As mentioned earlier, the church is an interim institution between Pentecost and the return of Christ. It awaits and hopes for the fulfillment of the heavenly community of all the faithful.

A utopian attempt to bring about already now that which the church anticipates in its future hope destroys the conditions that make possible such an existence directed toward the future. The anticipation of the heavenly city is no human achievement, but a divine gift. We do not create communion; it is pre-given to us by Christ, whose body is not torn apart (cf. Eph. 4:15–16). The anticipation of the heavenly city, however, is not only a spiritual reality of the realization we await, but it must also show itself in daily living. Dietrich Bonhoeffer rightly says, "A purely spiritual relationship is not only dangerous but also an altogether abnormal thing."[27] What is preached in the Christian community must translate into the everyday life of the people, and what is essential in the church must permeate the world. For instance, we cannot preach love and reconciliation and conduct ourselves inside and outside the church in a loveless and irreconcilable manner. The church would contradict its task to be a beacon of hope if it were in itself always torn apart by dissension. Therefore, the message of reconciliation must be carried beyond its own walls. The mission of the church goes hand in hand with the rediscovery of its own unity, because only a unified Christian church can be a symbol and instrument for the unity of humanity.

The engagement of the church in the world has a twofold purpose. On the one hand, the church serves those who are in need. On the other hand, the church knows that even with its most strenuous attempts, it cannot solve all the problems of the world. Its work always remains piecemeal. The activity of the church must be seen in analogy to that of Jesus. With his healing miracles Jesus helped people in need. Yet his miracles not only met people's needs. Besides being concrete help for humans, they were also pointers to a new creation in which there will be no more suffering and no more tears. In a similar way the ministry of the church points to a completely new world. The two main sacraments of the church, the Lord's Supper and baptism, also function as pointers to the new future. The reference in the Lord's Supper "Do this in remembrance of me" (1 Cor. 11:24) is not only a summons to us to remind ourselves of Jesus' sacrifice, but it is also an indicator that this sacrifice was not in vain but will find its fulfillment in the creation of a new world. Similarly, baptism into the death and resurrection of Christ would be an empty sign if it did not find its fulfillment in the kingdom in which there

---

27. Dietrich Bonhoeffer, *Life Together*, trans. John W. Doberstein (New York: Harper, 1954), 38.

will be no more death. Even the Lord's Prayer, the most important prayer of Christendom, contains in each of its petitions a reference to the future fulfill-ment of the kingdom of God. When we pray, for instance, that God's will be done, we remind ourselves of the promise of the universal rule of God. In its liturgical celebrations and prayer life, the church is a symbol of the future. Power and encouragement for the anticipation of the end-time realization is derived from the experience of Christ. Through the presence of Christ and the power of the Spirit, the church realizes that the life and destiny of Jesus Christ is the main example for our own lives and destinies. Beyond any doubt, the church knows that history will ultimately lead to the triumph of the kingdom of God.

Anticipated joy of this triumph is shown in the music, the hymns, and the art of the church. While the world is interested in efficiency, the church, whether in liturgy or in designing its worship spaces, unfolds a splendor with which it glorifies the one whom it serves and who will lead the church to the final glory. Liturgy is largely a holy drama in which God's salvational activity is exemplified through symbols and then put into words. While the Roman Catholic Church maintained the Latin liturgy until Vatican II, for Luther and the other Reformers it was a matter of course that the faithful should under-stand the text of the liturgy and therefore that the text be translated into the respective language of the land. This shows the emphasis of the Word in the work of the Reformers over against the picturesque and architectural splendor of the Roman Catholic Church. At the time of the Counter-Reformation, this splendor also served as a visible expression of power. With Lutherans it was especially hymnody with which they expressed their faith. Deserving of special mention here is German pastor Paul Gerhard (1607–76), who un-waveringly confessed his Lutheran faith against the Reformed side, and next to Luther is still the most popular Lutheran hymn writer. In the German Protestant hymnal (*Evangelische Gesangbuch*) he is still represented today with twenty-nine hymns, for instance, the passion hymn "O Sacred Heart, Now Wounded" (*Evangelical Lutheran Worship*, no. 351) and "Evening and Morning" (no. 761), which praises God's creation. Luther is represented in the same hymnal with twenty-four hymns, for which he wrote the complete text or part of it. For sixteen of these hymns he also composed the melody, and with two others the tune but not the text is from him. The hymnal of the Evangelical Lutheran Church in America, *Evangelical Lutheran Worship*, still contains nineteen hymns by Luther. In 1620 the Jesuit Adam Conzenius wrote, "Luther's hymns had killed more souls than his writings and lectures."[28]

28. "Hymni lutheri animas plures quam scripta et declamationes occiderunt," as quoted in Karl Anton, *Luther und die Musik*, 3rd ed. (Zwickau: Johannes Herrmann, 1928), 11.

Music and song served for Luther to proclaim the gospel and therefore to praise God. This was continued in the cantatas, motets, oratorios, and great passions of Johann Sebastian Bach (1685–1750) and the oratorios of George Frideric Handel (1685–1759). It is understandable that Bach concluded all of his compositions with the note *Soli Deo gloria*, "Glory to God alone." Ultimately, this is the motivation of music as far as it recognizes itself as a gift of the Creator and in turn praises the Creator with this gift.

It is especially the gift of music that brings many people to the church that otherwise would never attend a church service. They are moved by the music of the great composers. For instance, in the city of Regensburg, Germany, where I live, people want to hear the Regensburg Cathedral Boys' Choir (*Regensburger Domspatzen*), and their concerts, whether in church or in an auditorium, are always sold out well in advance. While perhaps "the church as the reminder of the future" in the traditional sense will not draw many people, through the sung word the gospel of God's future still gets a hearing in the secular world. The same can be said about "the church as the heart of the present." When the church organization "Bread for the World" asks for donations many people inside and outside the church will support this cause which every year in Germany will fetch one of the largest donations of any organization. In the United States too I have heard people saying they will leave a particular congregation if the benevolence budget will be cut. The same attractiveness can be said for church "preserving the past." What would a trip to Europe be without visiting the impressive cathedrals built to praise God? Even in East Germany where often church membership is less than ten percent of the population most village churches have been nicely renovated because people who will not cross the threshold of that church demanded its preservation as "their church." While organized religion may have a difficult time in Europe and parts of North America, allegiance to the spirit of Christianity cannot be that easily erased. In order to survive and thrive the churches must use these interests and permeate them with the gospel.

EXCURSUS: LUTHER AND MUSIC

Martin Luther had a good music education, and he loved to sing, compose songs, and play the lute. For him it was important that the text of a hymn corresponded to the gospel. Therefore he said, "We are concerned with changing the text, not the music."[29] He did not want to be an innovator, but he reformed the faith according to the gospel. "We want the beautiful art of music to be properly used to serve her dear Creator and his Christians. He is thereby praised and honored and we are made better and stronger in faith when his holy Word is impressed on our hearts by sweet music." Music should serve to spread the gospel and to strengthen the true faith. It should draw humans toward God and the gospel and away from themselves. Luther emphasized, "Music is an excellent gift of God and closest to theology."[30] He saw a relationship between music and theology, and believed that music had a theological and a pastoral function. Music makes the human spirit happy, drives away the devil, and refreshes us. Luther also said, "The gift of language combined with the gift of song was only given to man to let him know that he should praise God with both word and music, namely, by proclaiming [the Word of God] through music and by providing sweet melodies with words."[31] Humans have the gift of speech so that they can join together melody and text, and praise God in this fashion.

Luther connected with the tradition and translated Latin hymns, but he also took profane songs and gave them a new text in rhymes. Important also are his hymns of psalms, for instance, "A Mighty Fortress Is Our God," a musical adaptation of Psalm 46. He encouraged others to compose hymns from the Psalms, and psalm adaptations were already regularly in use in Strasbourg in 1524. John Calvin learned of them and in 1538 began to compose the Geneva Psalter. In contrast to Luther, Calvin was much more a biblicist and judged the common singing of the congregation as an inappropriate self-manifestation of Christians and as vanity. Therefore, he restricted congregational singing to that of psalms, as is still today the case in many congregations of the Reformed tradition.

---

29. Martin Luther, "Preface to the Burial Hymns" (1542), in *LW* 53:328, for this and the following quotation.

30. Martin Luther, *Table Talks* (no. 3815, Lauterbach, April 5, 1538), in *WA TR* 3:636.5.

31. Martin Luther, "Preface to Georg Rhau's Symphoniae iucundae" (1538), in *LW* 53:323–24.

$$\boxed{12}$$

THE MEANS OF GRACE

The means of grace are the means that the Lord entrusted to his church to spread the good news of the reconciliation of God with humanity. They are the Word and the sacraments.

The Word of God

Words play an important role in all religions and in every meaningful communication between one human being and another. This is not different in the Christian faith. But there the Word is not a word about God, our future, or the world but a means of God's self-disclosure. Therefore, we read right at the beginning of the Letter to the Hebrews, "Long ago God spoke to our ancestors in many and various ways by the prophets, but in these last days he has spoken to us by a Son" (Heb. 1:1–2). God's self-disclosure in the human being Jesus Christ enables us to recognize *the* Word among the many words and to distinguish between the verbose elements of the Judeo-Christian tradition that accidentally surface in its history and the Word of God that has been spoken into a certain historic situation. The Word of God, as it is preserved in the Christian community and encounters us today in the doctrine and the proclamation of the church, usually assumes one of three basic functions: (1) it judges and condemns, (2) it liberates and affirms, and (3) it guides. The first function is that of the divine law, the second is that of the gospel, and the third is that of a guiding function for human life and is connected either to law or to gospel. We must not equate the term *law*, as it is used in the distinction between law and gospel, with the law contained in the Pentateuch or even in the Old Testament as a whole. The term *gospel* is also not synonymous here with the proclamation of Jesus or the New Testament *kerygma*. Law and gospel are rather two different functions of the same Word of God, with which it either accuses or liberates us. The respective function depends on our grasp of the Word of God and our reaction to it.

The Relationship between Law and Gospel

The law has a twofold function for humanity, one civil and the other theological. According to the civil function, God preserves creation through the law and prevents chaos. This means that the law is known to all people. This view of the law is maintained by the natural law tradition and has received renewed attention by ethicists who claim that basic norms of moral conduct are binding in all societies whether human or animal. As mentioned, Luther, too, asserted that the law has been inscribed onto the hearts of all people. It largely coincides with the Mosaic law, meaning the Ten Commandments, and must be distinguished from the positive laws of a respective country and also from the Jewish ceremonial law.

Paul's remark "But law came in, with the result that the trespass multiplied" (Rom. 5:20) sounds strange. How can the law in its second theological use cause sin and even increase sin's power? Of course, sin existed even before we were confronted with the law. But Paul is not wrong. As Jesus shows in the Sermon on the Mount, the trespasses against the law are often done unknowingly. But God wants sin to be recognized as an attack against God. The announcement of the law, for instance through the call to repentance by John the Baptist, causes this subconscious sin to surface and makes it, so to speak, stronger. The more one tries to consciously fulfill God's will, as for instance Martin Luther attempted in the monastery, the more the law shows our imperfection and our sinfulness. For the one who does not care about the law, however, sin is virtually nonexistent. Paul continues in the same line: "but where sin increased, grace abounded all the more, so that, just as sin exercised dominion in death, so grace might also exercise dominion through justification leading to eternal life through Jesus Christ our Lord" (Rom. 5:20–21). The law leads toward Christ. Therefore, Paul can even call the law the "disciplinarian" toward Christ (Gal. 3:24). Through Christ we realize that the law is not the total Word of God, but next to it there is the gospel.

Law and gospel have different functions. The law meets us as God's demanding Word that says something must be done and something else must not be done. It accuses us of not having fulfilled God's will. The gospel, however, announces that God's will has been fulfilled in Christ. It shows us a God who meets us in Christ and who discloses to us that God is gracious and that God has forgiven us our sins. The salvational aspect of God's Word becomes most clear in the life and activity of Jesus Christ. But already the law and the prophets point to the gracious God, as Paul himself never tires of emphasizing.

Guidelines for Christian Living

During the time of Jesus, many people understood God's Word as a set of rules with the guarantee that they would be justified before God if they simply kept these rules. Jesus corrected this misunderstanding in the Sermon on the Mount and in many other places. But the same attitude still prevails today among many people. They assume that an ethically unblemished life will ultimately be rewarded by God. The German poet Johann Wolfgang von Goethe (1749–1832) expressed this in his dramatic poem *Faust* in this way: "Whoe'er aspiring, struggles on, for him there is salvation."[1] Such a misunderstanding of God's guidelines enslaves humans who think that if they literally fulfill God's Word, then they are justified. This self-righteousness often erects new barriers of injustice and inequality over against other people. One assumes that one is better than others and continually pushes ahead to prove to oneself and others that this is true. Therefore the law, if it is separated from the gospel, can lead to enslavement instead of liberation. But if Christ is the end of the law, there should be liberation. Christ has fulfilled for us God's will and has done justice to the law.

But the law has not simply been abolished, because it still contains God's guidelines for life. It is no longer something that oppresses us or shows us our sinfulness, but it guides us to a godly life. John Calvin writes, "The third and principal use, which pertains more closely to the proper purpose of the law, finds its place among believers in whose hearts the Spirit of God already lives and reigns."[2] To support this statement, Calvin refers primarily to Old Testament texts such as Psalm 19:8: "The precepts of the LORD are right, rejoicing the heart." Philipp Melanchthon, Luther's coworker, pursues a similar line of thinking when he says that "the keeping of the law must begin in us and then increase more and more."[3] We must admit that Christians, too, need moral

---

1. Johann Wolfgang von Goethe, *Faust*, trans. G. M. Priest (Chicago: Encyclopaedia Britannica, 1952), 290.

2. John Calvin, *Institutes of the Christian Religion* 2.7.12, ed. John T. McNeill, trans. F. L. Battles (Philadelphia: Westminster, 1960), 1:360.

3. Philipp Melanchthon, *The Apology of the Augsburg Confession* (art. 4, "Justification"), in *The Book of Concord*, 142. Cf. *The Epitome of the Formula of Concord* 4, where the third use of the law is defended.

guidelines for their lives. They need to recognize God's will so that they can live their lives properly. When we are confronted with the gospel and understand how gracious God is to us, our answer to God's grace does not follow from some guidelines by which we orient ourselves, but we live in thankfulness by living according to God's precepts. We do not live according to the law because obedience to the law is expected of us, but out of thankfulness for God's unmerited love. We remember here the introduction to the Decalogue, which does not start with certain admonitions but with what God has done for Israel (Exod. 20:2). Therefore, Luther advocates a twofold use of the law, one theological and the other political, while Calvin teaches a third use of the law in those who are born again. Following Calvin, Karl Barth writes, "As the doctrine of God's command, ethics interprets the Law as the form of the Gospel."[4] Here the law is embraced, so to speak, by the gospel, and the danger of a new legalism arises as is often seen in Calvinistic and pietistic communities. In a similar way, many secular people today live under the continuous pressure exerted by society or themselves to obey the ruling laws and to meet the expectations of society.

In contrast to the existence oriented by the law that many people pursue, a Christian lives continuously between two poles. As Paul's imperatives indicate (Rom. 6:12–14), the Christian existence is marred over and over again by sin. Therefore, a Christian is often described as a sinner and, at the same time, as having been justified. Justification before God, through which God no longer holds us accountable for our sins, does not change our essence. We are still the same people with our imperfections. If those imperfections begin to rule over us, God's Word reveals itself to us as the law, which accuses us and pushes us back to the gospel. Therefore, not only the gospel but also the law is proclaimed in the Christian community. If we cling to Jesus, then we live from the gospel and in union with God. But as sinners we live under the law and forget about God's grace. Like children, we need not only God's love but also his authority and discipline so that we stay on the right track. As Luther says in a sermon, "The law uncovers the disease, the gospel gives us the medicine."[5]

To become healthy again, we need not only the gospel, the word of God's gracious compassion, but also the realization that we are actually not worthy of that compassion. The Lutheran theologian Dietrich Bonhoeffer writes: "Grace interpreted as a principle, *pecca fortiter* [sin boldly] as a principle, grace at a low cost, is in the last resort a new law, which brings neither help

---

4. Karl Barth, *Church Dogmatics* II/2, ed. G. W. Bromiley and T. F. Torrance (Edinburgh: T&T Clark, 1957), 509.

5. Martin Luther, "Sermon von den Heiligtumen" (Holy Cross) of September 14, 1522, in *WA* 10/3: 338.9–10.

nor freedom. . . . So they said, thinking that we must vindicate our Lutheran heritage by making this grace available on the cheapest and easiest terms. To be 'Lutheran' must mean that we leave the following of Christ to the legalists, Calvinists and enthusiasts—and all this for the sake of grace. We justified the world, and condemned as heretic those who tried to follow Christ."[6] In the same way as grace became possible only by Jesus' offering his whole life, so can it be effective only when we dedicate our whole lives to Jesus. Luther spoke in his *Small Catechism* about daily repentance through which the old Adam must be drowned. Where the old Adam and the old Eve are no longer taken seriously, one slides into libertinism, and ultimately even sin is justified for the sake of love. This casuistic thinking that the goal justifies the means has nothing to do with the gospel.

Confession and Absolution

The pronouncement of law and gospel assumes a particular form in the office of the keys, also known as confession and absolution. The Roman Catholic tradition maintains the sacrament of penance, which includes confession and subsequent atonement. Lutherans, however, see penance as closely associated with the sacraments but do not actually consider it to be one. In the Augsburg Confession the article of confession and absolution follows that of baptism and the Lord's Supper. In Luther's *Small Catechism*, however, the office of the keys comes between baptism and the Lord's Supper to indicate that there is a close connection between the office and the two sacraments. In Melanchthon's *Apology of the Augsburg Confession* absolution is called one of the three sacraments,[7] while the Calvinist tradition acknowledges only two sacraments, baptism and the Lord's Supper. This shows that confession and absolution are closely connected with the proclamation of law and gospel as the one Word of God.

We find the main New Testament reference to the function and office of the keys in the Gospel according to Matthew. There Jesus says to Peter, "I will give you the keys of the kingdom of heaven, and whatever you bind on earth will be bound in heaven, and whatever you loose on earth will be loosed in heaven" (Matt. 16:19). According to John 20:22–23, Jesus says to the disciples, "Receive the Holy Spirit. If you forgive the sins of any, then they are forgiven; if you retain the sins of any, they are retained." Loosing and binding on earth

---

6. Dietrich Bonhoeffer, *The Cost of Discipleship*, rev. ed., trans. Reginald H. Fuller (London: SCM, 1959), 57–58.

7. Philipp Melanchthon, *Apology of the Augsburg Confession* (art. 13: "The Number and Use of the Sacraments"), in *The Book of Concord*, 219.

means the authority to accept someone into the Christian community, or to exclude someone from it, or to conclude then that someone has excluded himself or herself through un-Christian conduct. The Christian community assumes this authority because it sees itself in continuity with the apostles. The office of the keys is closely connected to the proclamation of the Word of God. When Jesus sent out his disciples, he admonished them: "If anyone will not welcome you or listen to your words, shake off the dust from your feet as you leave that house or town. Truly I tell you, it will be more tolerable for the land of Sodom and Gomorrah on the day of judgment than for that town" (Matt. 10:14–15). Since the rejection of the proclamation of the Word of God is a decision for death, those who are entrusted with the proclamation should shake the dust from their feet as a sign that they have separated themselves from those who refuse to listen to God's Word. Those who proclaim God's Word show by this sign that the acceptance or rejection of the gospel has eternal consequences for the hearers.

Those who administer the keys to the kingdom of heaven are empowered to make clear to their listeners the consequences of the Word of God by either absolving them of their sins or leaving them in their sins. In the early church this led to the formation of the sacrament of penance because the Christian community had soon noticed that the forgiveness of all sins at baptism did not lead to a sinless life, even if the baptized attempted to live the Christian faith as seriously as possible. This meant that subsequent sins needed to be forgiven. Luther describes this process in the following manner: "It signifies that the old person in us with all sins and evil desires is to be drowned and die through daily sorrow for sin and through repentance, and on the other hand that daily a new person is to come forth and rise up to live before God in righteousness and purity forever."[8] The phrase "is to come forth" shows Luther's realism. The baptized person intends to live as a new being but will again be misled by sin. Confession of sins and absolution must be a daily process and cannot be relegated to special occasions.

While in the Roman Catholic tradition the sacrament of penance consists of four main points (repentance, the actual confession of one's misdoings, absolution, and restitution), in the Lutheran tradition the last point, restitution, is missing because absolution is of no value if there is no indication that the person has really changed and is leading a new life. Strictly speaking, we cannot even make restitution for our sinful actions. We cannot turn back the wheel of history to undo our negative actions by which we also affect others. If we have hurt someone, even a well-meant restitution leaves the person

8. Martin Luther, *Small Catechism* ("The Sacrament of Holy Baptism").

damaged at least for the period during which no restitution has yet been made. Nevertheless, the Word of God as a freeing word should not be taken lightly. It expects us to respond and to live appropriately as God's sons and daughters.

In our own history the issue of guilt, sin, and restitution has taken on special meaning in connection with the cruelties and unjust actions that occurred during the second World War (1939–45). After the war the Federal Republic of Germany made sizeable financial payments of "restitution," not just to Israel, but also to other countries in whose territory cruelties had been committed by Nazi soldiers. The Council of the Protestant Churches in Germany confessed to representatives of the World Council of Churches at the end of the war the so-called Stuttgart Declaration of Guilt (1945). It confessed guilt for its insufficient resistance to the National Socialist regime of injustice. Similar confessions of guilt were made by ecclesial office bearers in other countries. For instance, before being instituted into his office, the Romanian Orthodox Patriarch Teoctist (1950–2007) issued a declaration of remorse over his collaboration with the Communist regime. And yet those who collaborated with the Communist regime in East Germany have not issued a general admission of guilt. The former presiding bishop of the Protestant Church in Germany, Wolfgang Huber (d. 1942), stated in a public radio address in 2006 that it is disconcerting how the former *Stasi-Mitarbeiter* (collaborators with the Communist surveillance system) were still not ready to admit the extent of the injustice that occurred during Communist rule. Therefore, it is even more necessary to contribute to a culture of remembering, "which at least does belated justice to the victims."[9]

In the fall of 2006 the Protestant Academy in Thuringia met in the former East German town of Guthmannshausen to discuss the "clearance of the Stasi entanglement in the church of Thuringia."[10] The study documents from this meeting point out that in cases of injustice the focus is usually on the culprits and on how to deal appropriately with them, but much less on the victims themselves. One can forgive the wrongdoings, but one must also clarify "how to deal with the real and remaining consequences of the wrongdoings."[11] Sin is not simply eliminated by justifying the sinner, because then one would be confronted with cheap grace. For instance, the Commission on Reconciliation in South Africa attempted to collectively deal with the guilt by consciously incorporating the victims into the reconciliation process. There must also be a

---

9. "SED Unrecht. Bischof Huber warnt vor Verharmlosung," in *EPD-Wochenspiegel* 17 (2006): 2.

10. Cf. *EPD-Dokumentation* 16 (April 17, 2007).

11. Michael Haspel, "'Stasi-Aufarbeitung in der Thüringer Landeskirche' / Einleitung," in *EPD-Dokumentation* 16 (April 17, 2007), 6.

distinction made between sin and guilt, because the forgiveness of sin, which is given to each repentant sinner on account of the graciousness of God, does not eliminate guilt. Rainer Stahl (b. 1951), formerly from East Germany and presently secretary general of the *Martin Luther Bund* in Germany, states: "Forgiveness granted by God does not undo the wounds which were inflicted on other people. To the contrary: If God forgives someone's sins, then this enables that person to deal responsibly with the destruction of communion which was caused by his wrongdoings and therewith also with his guilt."[12] It is important for the evildoers that they do not lose sight of their victims. But we should not forget that sometimes the evildoers were forced by the regime in power to comply, and therefore they collaborated in order to avoid evil being done to their own families. These were situations of mental conflict that could lead to guilt and sin regardless of how the individual person decided. We live in a fallen world and are always drawn into its sinfulness. As Luther stated in the first of his Ninety-Five Theses of 1517, it is indispensable for the Christians to repent daily of their wrongdoings and to push forward to a new life.

EXCURSUS: THE ISSUE OF INDULGENCE

Indulgences developed from the ecclesial practice of penance. The early church dealt severely with sinners and punished them with long fasting or temporary exclusion from the Lord's Supper. If one did serious penance, then the duration of these punishments could be shortened. In addition, the idea was introduced that through the intercession of exceptionally pious Christians, the time span of penance could be abbreviated. One could also call on martyrs, because it was thought that their deaths were a substitution for other Christians, thus achieving atonement for other Christians. This view of a substituting penance led to the notion starting in the eleventh century that the merits of Christ and of the saints were accumulated into such an immeasurable treasure of grace that the church, in the succession of Christ, was allowed to mete them out and apply them to sinners. Through these means, not only the time of penance here on earth but also the time of punishment in purgatory could be shortened or dispensed with. According to the medieval

---

12. Rainer Stahl, "Kontakte zu Geheimdiensten als theologische Herausforderungen: Blicke aus und in die Partnerkirchen," in *EPD-Dokumentation* 16 (April 17, 2007), 24.

view of life after death, a person had to atone in purgatory for the sins he or she had not done penance for on earth. At the time of the Reformation the church and the papacy conducted an actual business by selling indulgences without demanding any repentance from the sinner.

Luther was very much concerned about the indulgences being sold by the Roman Catholic Church. During his time, St. Peter's Basilica in Rome was being rebuilt and the pope needed money for the construction. Therefore the pope offered letters of indulgence, which he promulgated through special indulgence preachers. Especially successful was the Dominican preacher Johann Tetzel (1465–1519), who conducted the indulgence business in the territory of the electoral cardinal Albrecht of Mainz (1490–1545). Tetzel coined the phrase, "As soon as the money in the coffer rings, the soul from purgatory springs."[13] People came to Luther with certificates of indulgence in their hands and asked him for absolution without really having repented of their sins. When Luther noticed that Albrecht of Mainz approved of this and that one needed neither to show repentance nor to confess anything, and that one could even purchase indulgences for people who had already died, Luther could not remain silent. As a responsible teacher of the church, he composed his Ninety-Five Theses. In his very first thesis he stated that repentance should not be a singular act. To the contrary, our Lord Jesus Christ "willed the entire life of believers to be one of repentance."[14]

Today the praxis of indulgence in the Roman Catholic Church has been radically changed, but not the arguments that made indulgence possible. We read, for instance, in the *Code of Canon Law*,

> An indulgence is the remission before God of temporal punishment for sins whose guilt is already forgiven, which a properly disposed member of the Christian faithful gains under certain and defined conditions by the assistance of the Church which as minister of redemption dispenses and applies authoritatively the treasury of the satisfactions of Christ and the saints. An indulgence is partial or plenary in so far as it partially or totally frees from the temporal punishment due to sins.[15]

Though the guilt is already forgiven through Christ, there is "before God" still temporal punishment that can be remitted through the indulgence of the church "under certain and defined conditions" (prayers, pilgrimages, etc.).

13. Quotation according to Nikolaus Paulus, *Johann Tetzel, der Ablassprediger* (Mainz: Kirchheim, 1899), 139.

14. Martin Luther, *Ninety-Five Theses* (1517), in *LW* 31:25.

15. *Code of Canon Law* (1983), 992–93, http://www.vatican.va/archive/ENG1104/_P3I.HTM.

The church as the institution of salvation affirms and rewards the serious penance of the faithful and documents this through the indulgence. Justification "by grace alone" as affirmed by Lutherans is quite different. Therefore, one need not be surprised that in Augsburg in October 1999 the Roman Catholic Church and the Lutheran World Federation signed a *Common Declaration on Justification*, and that Pope John Paul II almost simultaneously issued for the "Holy Year" 2000 an indulgence for the whole Roman Catholic Church. In that church one knows about the necessity of God's grace, but one also emphasizes the church as an institution of salvation and the efforts of the faithful to obtain salvation.

The Visible Word (Sacraments)

Word and sign are closely connected to each other. Jesus often accompanied his teaching with signs, usually miracles, and in a similar way the Old Testament prophets accompanied their announcement with explanatory signs. Signs are a means of interpreting the Word. This shows the nature of the so-called sacraments as visible words. Augustine writes, "The word is added to the element, and there results the Sacrament, as if itself also a kind of visible word."[16]

The Nature of the Sacraments

Among the churches there is agreement that the sacraments have the character of signs. They symbolize something in "sign language." Sacraments are visible signs of the proclamation of God's salvific Word. They render picturesquely the grace that is proclaimed in them. For instance, in baptism one is immersed in water (signifying the dying of the old person) or sprinkled with water (signifying the washing away of one's sins). In analogy to the Word of God, sacraments express the will of God. Article 13 of the Augsburg Confession states: "Concerning the use of the sacraments it is taught that the sacraments are instituted not only to be signs by which people may recognize Christians outwardly, but also as signs and testimonies of God's will toward us in order thereby to awaken and strengthen our faith."[17]

There are still considerable differences among the churches in understanding the sacraments apart from their commonly acknowledged character as signs.

16. Augustine, *On the Gospel of St. John* 80.3, in *NPNF*[1] 7:344.
17. *The Augsburg Confession*, in *The Book of Concord*, 46.

For instance, the Heidelberg Catechism of the Reformed Church states that there are only two sacraments, baptism and the Lord's Supper; only these were instituted by Christ. Luther's line of thought goes in a similar direction, and he therefore also arrives at two sacraments. Melanchthon, however, considers sacraments as rites ordained by God and to which the promise of grace is given. He therefore mentions three sacraments: baptism, the Lord's Supper, and absolution. According to the Second Vatican Council, the sacraments have a threefold purpose: to sanctify people, to build up the body of Christ, and to give worship to God.[18] Both in the Roman Catholic Church and in the Orthodox Church there are seven sacraments: baptism, confirmation, penance, Eucharist, Holy Orders, marriage, and anointing of the sick. Since the number seven is a "holy" number, it expresses the completeness of these rites. Therefore, they are called in the liturgy of the church the seven activities necessary for life that lead toward salvation. They are not necessary for salvation, but help to obtain salvation.

Historical Origin of the Sacraments

Since baptism and the Lord's Supper are intimately related to the Christ event, they were from the very beginning the two most important sacraments. Gradually, the other five were added. These five are not necessary for salvation, and participation in the sacrament of Holy Orders even excludes participation in the sacrament of marriage and vice versa. Celibacy for the priest has only been rigorously instituted by the Roman Catholic Church since the Counter-Reformation. In the Orthodox Church the decision of the Council of Nicaea is still valid that a deacon can be married, and therefore one can marry before one is ordained as a priest. In the early church, too, the concept of sacrament was used much more imprecisely than today, so there appeared a multitude of sacraments. Finally, during the Counter-Reformation the Roman Catholic Church decided at the Council of Trent on the seven sacraments.

Neither the term *sacrament*, which we use in the West, nor the term *mystery* used by the Orthodox churches, occurs in the New Testament. The term *sacrament* has its origin in military language and signifies the pledge of allegiance to the flag. It also occurs in juridical language, where it means the deposition of bail prior to a trial. The term *mystery* is connected to the mystery cults of antiquity. Therefore, in the East the sacraments could be considered as cultic rites in which the destiny of the Godhead (Jesus Christ) is celebrated in front

---

18. *Constitution on the Sacred Liturgy 59*, in *The Documents of Vatican II*, ed. Walter M. Abbott (New York: Guild Press, 1966), 158.

of the faithful in such a way that they participate in that destiny. The church fathers recognized the problem of foreign thoughts entering the Christian faith with the use of the term *mystery*. They considered the mysteries, for instance, those associated with the cult of Mithras, as diabolic inventions. The term *mystery*, however, opened the possibility to consider the sacrament as a reality pertaining to one's being through which a Christian is more and more incorporated into the being of Christ. The Eastern Church still emphasizes *theosis*, in which a Christian will become less and less like the world and more and more like God, or godlike. In the West one was interested not so much in humans becoming godlike, but much more in the legal consequences of being a Christian; that is, through the sacraments one was absolved from one's sins and therefore freed from those sins. In this context the work of the Finnish Lutheran theologian Tuomo Mannermaa (b. 1937) is of special interest. In dialogue with the Orthodox Church, Mannermaa pointed out that there is an analogy between the Lutheran doctrine of justification and the Orthodox doctrine of *theosis*.[19] This idea is based on the real presence of Christ in God's Word, in the sacraments, and in the worship service. Yet one should not forget that (1) *theosis* always has the tinge of a "theology of glory" in contrast to a "theology of the cross," and (2) for Luther the passive justification is always given through Christ behind which all earthly and active justification must subside. Outside Finland the theses of Mannermaa have been accepted by just a few theologians. Mostly they have encountered a high degree of skepticism. For instance, Bernhard Lohse (1928–97) writes, "Though we cannot dispute a deification motif alongside others, we must be cautioned against overestimating this line of tradition."[20]

Efficacy of the Sacraments

The sacraments are the visible signs of God's redeeming Word, and therefore their efficacy is to be seen in analogy to the Word. The Augsburg Confession rightly states in article 5 that God has given the Word and the sacraments "as through instruments the Holy Spirit is given, who effects faith where and when it pleases God in those who hear the gospel." Sacraments are powerful instruments of God's grace and should not be administered lightly but according to

19. For the following, cf. the thoughts of Kurt E. Marquart, "Luther and Theosis," *Concordia Theological Quarterly* 64, no. 3 (July 2000): 182–205; and Tuomo Mannermaa, "The Doctrine of Justification and Christology: Chapter A, Section One of The Christ Present in Faith," *Concordia Theological Quarterly* 64, no. 3 (July 2000): 206–39.

20. Bernhard Lohse, *Martin Luther's Theology: Its Historical and Systematic Development*, trans. and ed. Roy A. Harrisville (Minneapolis: Fortress, 1999), 221.

the gospel. Since they are God's means of grace, their efficacy does not depend on the righteousness of the one who administers them. The Augsburg Confession explains in article 8, "Both the sacraments and the Word are efficacious because of the ordinance and command of Christ, even when offered by evil people." The sacraments even retain their validity when they are administered by heretics. Therefore, rebaptism is very rare when one converts from one church to another, even if neither church recognizes the other as equally valid. The sacraments are not the property of a person or a church, but they are Christ's gifts to us. Luther says in his lectures on the prophet Isaiah, "In the New Testament baptism and the Lord's Supper are so to speak God's garments in which God shows God's self to us and acts with us."[21] Not the priest or the church but God is acting here. Since God has shown God's self in Jesus Christ, it is only consequential when Luther states, "The Holy Scriptures have only one sacrament which is our Lord Christ himself."[22] Luther stands here as a successor to Augustine, who writes in a letter, "There is no other mystery [i.e., sacrament] of God except Christ."[23] Christ is God's gift to us and gives himself to us with all that he has worked for our salvation, namely, forgiveness of sins and eternal bliss.

Yet what about those who receive the sacraments? Here the Council of Trent declared that the sacrament is efficacious in those who put no obstacle in the way of the sacraments. On the side of the Reformation this was often understood as if humans would be summoned to cooperate with God toward their salvation. Such an idea would be foolish because salvation comes only from God. But we should not entertain the idea that there occurs some kind of automatic cause-and-effect sequence. This notion that once a sacrament is executed, the corresponding grace is automatically given is still widespread in popular piety. Many years ago when I was a young vicar, the parents of a baby whom I was to baptize asked me whether evil spirits could play any tricks on the child after baptism. They thought the act of baptism would be like an insurance policy. Yet God's activity always necessitates our "cooperation." Therefore we read in article 5 of the Augsburg Confession that God "as through instruments" gives the Holy Spirit "in them that hear the gospel." God does not give it to those who close their ears before the gospel. In his *Small Catechism* Luther argued in a similar way concerning baptism in response to the question, "How can water do such great things?" He answered, "Clearly,

---

21. Martin Luther, *In Esaiam Scholia ex D. Martini Lutheri praelectionibus collecta* (1532/34), in *WA* 25:127.41–42.
22. Martin Luther, *Disputatio de fide infusa et acquisita* (1520), in *WA* 6:86.7–8.
23. Augustine, *Letters* 187.34, in *The Fathers of the Church: A New Translation*, vol. 4, *Saint Augustine: Letters (163–203)* (New York: The Fathers of the Church, 1955), 249.

the water does not do it, but the word of God, which is with and alongside water, and faith, which trusts this word of God in the water." Sacraments do not have an automatic effect; they are effective only if one faithfully trusts God who is working in them. On the one hand, the sacraments are offered to us, but on the other hand, we ask for baptism and we participate in the Lord's Supper. Of course, one could object that this does not pertain to infant or baby baptism, because it is the parents who usually request the baptism of the infant. Yet there again it shows how God acts with us: God takes the first step and receives the child or baby to be baptized as God's own, whereupon the parents can answer. This answer is then repeated by the baptized one at the person's confirmation. Unfortunately, for many people this rite has lost its meaning and has been reduced to a nice ceremony that does little to confirm the faith of the confirmand.

God's Presence

Baptism and the Lord's Supper are the two sacraments of God's visible presence. Here individual Christians are addressed by God, and through the pastor God mediates to them the gift of salvation.

Baptism

The original place of Christian baptism was mission and conversion. At baptism something occurs with the person who seeks baptism. There can be no compulsory baptism but only voluntary baptism, though regrettably at certain times in history non-Christian groups have been forcibly baptized. Two things come together at baptism: the activity of God and the passive receptivity of the one who is baptized. For those who are baptized, baptism is the visible sign of renouncing the old person and affirming the faith. Therefore baptism and confession of faith belong together. Whoever wants to be baptized seeks baptism. The formula, "What is to prevent me from being baptized?" (Acts 8:36), which occurs several times in the New Testament in connection with the baptism of conversion, perhaps indicates an examination of possible reasons for an obstacle to baptism.

Decisive for our understanding of baptism is what occurs to the one who is baptized. Since the middle of the second century, baptism has been conducted in the name of the Triune God. Because of Christ's death and resurrection, baptism is an act of God. Through baptism one is submitted to the Triune God, who receives the person in grace and accepts that person into God's communion (cf. 1 Cor. 1:9). The baptized person is cleansed by the water from all sinful impurities. The original rite of submersion dramatically depicts the death of the old Adam and the resurrection to new life. Since we are baptized into Christ's death and resurrection, the emergence from the water demonstrates new life. We become part of the new covenant community. Questions may arise as to whether after baptism one ought to be immediately admitted to the Lord's Supper and whether the appropriate place for baptism should not be the Eucharistic service. While the latter question can be immediately affirmed, the first question demands further discussion.

The grace that God grants us is not dependent on our faith. Otherwise the validity of baptism would always remain uncertain. If we do not answer God's gracious gift with an active Christian life, we are not actualizing baptism. As mentioned, baptism is not an automatic ritual of salvation. In analogy, if a lamp is connected to an outlet, it must always be switched on in order to give light. Though baptism does not depend on us, we must, as Luther always emphasized, actualize baptism. The Christian life, as we learn from Luther, is a daily baptism by which we continually acknowledge what God has done for us.

Baptism also means a change in our allegiance from being a child of this world and its sinfulness to becoming a child of God and God's promises. To express this, the one who was baptized traditionally received a Christian name at baptism. The old heathen name was given up, and the new Christian name was assumed. Even today we should consider what we want to say with the name we give to a newborn baby.

During the Reformation the so-called magisterial Reformers such as Luther had heated discussions with the Anabaptists concerning infant baptism. The Anabaptists emphasized that baptism presupposes faith. Luther, too, saw in the command to baptize (Mark 16:15–16) an intimate connection between faith and baptism. Yet he never claimed that infant baptism was founded on the existence of a faith in that infant, though sometimes he asserted that such a faith already existed. Ultimately, Luther's rationale was that infants are to be baptized not because we can ascertain that they believe but because infant baptism is based on Scripture. One should also not baptize infants with respect to their future faith. For Luther baptism calls to faith, and its reality and validity do not depend on the faith of the one to be baptized. Baptism is totally God's work even though God expects the assent of the one who is baptized. Luther writes in his *Large Catechism*: "'I build on this, that it is your Word and Command.' In the same way I go to the Sacrament [of the Altar] not on the strength of my own faith, but on the strength of Christ's faith."[24] Faith is

---

24. Martin Luther, *The Large Catechism: Baptism* (56), in *The Book of Concord*, 463–64.

not unimportant, but all-decisive is God's word of promise. Therefore, Karl Barth's rejection of infant baptism is mistaken when he sees the attempts of Luther and Calvin to justify infant baptism as unconvincing arguments brought forth with exegetical and practical "artifices and sophisms."[25] In his later work Barth completely follows the line of the Anabaptists and their emphasis on confessional baptism.[26]

Here Barth also takes the side of the Baptists, because for them "the personal and conscious faith prior to baptism is indispensible."[27] In general, Baptists cannot accept infant baptism as true baptism. In the eyes of Lutherans it is therefore doubtful "whether Baptists understand baptism as the means of grace" or rather as a confessional act of the faithful. But in baptism the one who is baptized does not do something; rather, something happens with that person. He or she does not baptize himself or herself, but is baptized. The confession, spoken either in a representative way by the congregation or by the one who is baptized, comes before the actual baptism.

By baptism we become children of God and members of the kingdom. There is no additional baptism with the Holy Spirit; otherwise water baptism would be just a symbolic act without any deeper significance. The Holy Spirit is promised to us in water baptism, even though it is an end-time gift. Through baptism we realize that we have already received something of the fullness we may expect to receive at the end. Baptism opens for us the gate to the kingdom of God, and we become heirs of eternal life. But baptism is also the incorporation into the visible church. Therefore, baptism is always conducted in the context of a congregation and not somewhere in private or in a corner. When we read in Mark 16:16, "The one who believes and is baptized will be saved," this does not indicate a sequence but affirms that faith and baptism cannot be separated. Baptism, however, does not depend on our faith but is a gift of God. Faith precedes the act of baptism insofar as someone asks for baptism. Faith is connected to baptism because in the context of the baptismal act the baptismal creed is usually affirmed in the form of the Apostles' Creed, and faith follows from baptism because one's new life is continuously realized in faith.

25. Karl Barth, *The Teaching of the Church regarding Baptism*, trans. E. A. Payne (London: SCM, 1948), 49.

26. Cf. Karl Barth, *Church Dogmatics* IV/4, trans. G. W. Bromiley (Edinburgh: T&T Clark, 1969), 195, where he writes, "Baptism [is] the first step of the Christian life which is to be taken in a free and responsible human act."

27. Baptist-Lutheran Joint Commission, *A Message to Our Churches* 33, in *Growth in Agreement II: Reports and Agreed Statements of Ecumenical Conversations on a World Level, 1982–1998*, ed. Jeffrey Gros et al. (Grand Rapids: Eerdmans, 2000), 161, for this and the following quotation.

The Lord's Supper

The Lord's Supper or the Eucharist is in many ways the central sacrament of the Christian community. In the New Testament we find the words of the institution of the Lord's Supper four times. First Corinthians 11:23–25 is probably the oldest text, dating back to the spring of AD 55. There Paul writes, "For I received from the Lord what I also handed on to you." This means that Paul handed on a tradition. The second oldest source is probably Mark 14:22–25, with small changes rendered in Matthew 26:26–29. In Luke 22:15–20 there is a shorter and a longer version of the words of the Lord's Supper. Often John 6:51–59 is also adduced, though there the Lord's Supper is not expressly mentioned. While we know that Jesus celebrated with the disciples the Last Supper and that he often shared a meal with his disciples and even with sinners and those who were excluded from society, we are separated from all of those meals by Jesus' death and resurrection. The faith in the resurrected One, with the expectation of his return and the completion of salvation, has decisively shaped the Christian understanding of the Lord's Supper.

Since the Lord's Supper is the main sacrament of Christ's presence, often the question arises how this presence is to be understood. On the one side, we have the extreme symbolism of Huldrych Zwingli, while on the other side is the Roman Catholic doctrine of transubstantiation, and in the middle is the Lutheran doctrine of the real presence. On the Reformed side, only rarely is an extreme symbolism advocated today. Instead, the mediation of Christ's presence through the Holy Spirit is emphasized. Therefore, in 1971 the *Concord of the Reformation Churches in Europe* (*Leuenberg Concord*) was agreed upon. There we read: "In the Lord's Supper, Jesus Christ, the risen One, bestows himself in his body, given into death for all, and his blood through his promising word with bread and wine."[28] But what does such an assertion that intends the real presence actually mean?

The *Heidelberg Catechism* of the Reformed branch of the Reformation points out that "although he [Christ] is in heaven and we are on earth, we are nevertheless flesh of his flesh and bone of his bone, always living and being governed by one Spirit, as the members of our bodies are governed by one soul."[29] Though perhaps we could discern in this statement a "sacramental realism," the answer points to the communion with Christ through the Holy Spirit since it is believed that Christ is only present in heaven. This does not

28. *Leuenberg Concord* 15, *The Springfielder* 35 (March 1972): 245.
29. *The Heidelberg Catechism*, trans. A. O. Miller and M. E. Osterhaven (Philadelphia: United Church Press, 1962), 129, in the explanation of question 76; the term "sacramental realism" is used by the commentator on this question (cf. 130).

mean that Christ is only symbolically in and with the elements of the Lord's Supper. Reformed theologians emphasize that we drink his blood and eat his flesh as is indicated by Scripture.[30] Though it says in a qualified way that "Christ is in heaven and we are on earth," the Catechism also asserts that we "become more and more united to his sacred body."[31] But is this the real presence of Christ in the fullest sense of the word? Here the Lutheran side much more clearly affirms the real presence of Christ in the Lord's Supper.

In the Augsburg Confession we read "that the body and blood of Christ are truly present and are distributed to those who eat the Lord's Supper." How this happens and whether the Holy Spirit is the mediator is not elaborated. The doctrine of transubstantiation officially pronounced at the Fourth Lateran Council in 1215 seems to separate the Protestants from the Roman Catholics. There it was said that "the bread (changed) into His body by the divine power of transubstantiation, and the wine into the blood."[32] At the Council of Trent this was reasserted in the decree on the Sacrament of the Eucharist in 1551 with the following words: "By the consecration of the bread and wine a conversion takes place of the whole substance of bread into the substance of the body of Christ our Lord, and of the whole substance of the wine into the substance of His blood. This conversion is appropriately and properly called transubstantiation by the Catholic Church."[33] What is asserted here is a change of a substance (the invisible inner substance), while the accidents (the visible outer appearance) remain the same. This presupposed two points: (1) the philosophical distinction introduced by Aristotle between substance and accident, which today is no longer followed; and (2) the belief that the bread and wine are not simply bread and wine, but become the body and blood of Christ in which he is really present. We notice that basically the same conviction is expressed as we noted with the Lutherans, though Roman Catholics do it with philosophical concepts. This basic agreement was also affirmed by the bilateral dialogue between Lutherans and Roman Catholics.

As Christ shared his daily meals with his disciples and invited sinners and outcasts to eat with him, so now he invites us as his disciples to gather at his table to have communion with him. Yet it is no longer the earthly Jesus who invites us but the resurrected and exalted Christ. Important here is the presence

30. Cf. *The Heidelberg Catechism*, 130.

31. *The Heidelberg Catechism*, 129, in the explanation of question 76.

32. Fourth Lateran Council (802/430), http://www.catecheticsonline.com/SourcesofDogma5.php.

33. Council of Trent, Session 13 (1642/877), http://www.catecheticsonline.com/SourcesofDogma9.php.

of the resurrected and exalted One, while the memory of the earthly Jesus recedes into the background. Since Christ offers his presence and communion in the meal, he demonstrates that in Christ God is no longer a distant God but is present in and with us. The sinful estrangement from God is overcome at the Lord's Supper, and forgiveness of sins and communion with God become visible. But the Lord's Supper is not a sacrament for individual people. It is always a community meal that we celebrate with our Lord. The Lord's Supper has an ecclesial aspect in that the members of the community enjoy the meal with their Lord. Though Eucharistic communion between churches is always seen as the high point of union, we should not forget that the Lord's Supper is not the property of an individual church, but it is always Christ who gives himself. He invites us to his altar, and we cannot be so presumptuous as to invite others to the altar, or to reject them, without turning this meal of Christ into our own supper. The Lord's Supper is not only the end point of union but also a possibility of celebrating the way to union. It is as wrong to expect that Eucharistic communion would automatically induce ecclesial communion as to think that Eucharistic communion is only possible if ecclesial communion is already attained. The Lord's Supper refers to the union with Christ that already exists, and because Christ is the one acting in the meal, it has a unifying character and rightly can be celebrated as being on the way to union. We dare not become more Christian than Jesus himself, who did not reserve the meal for the "saints" only, but offered it to people with whom the "saints" did not want to associate.

Next to the ecclesial aspect we must also mention the christological aspect, which, theologically speaking, is the presupposition for the former. The decisive gift in the Eucharist is Christ himself and all that he has worked for us. This is the main reason that the church has always so stubbornly insisted that Christ is really present in the meal. While the sacrament of the body and blood of Christ reminds us of Christ's sacrifice on the cross, decisive is his presence because through this he sanctifies those who participate in the sacrament. If he were not really present, nothing would happen on the side of Christ and everything would come from us. But he is present as the living and resurrected Christ who has overcome death. Therefore, he wants us to turn to the future because there his sacrifice will find its completion in a new life. Since the Spirit is called upon at the Eucharist, we are sanctified and renewed by him. In this way new life is opened for us.

Finally, we must touch on the end-time dimension of the Eucharist. The early church called the Eucharist the medicine of immortality. On the one hand, this means personal sanctification, and on the other hand, through Christ's presence, it is a step toward the final goal of his sacrifice, unrestrained union with God. The end-time marriage feast is in some ways already anticipated in the Lord's Supper. It is a meal of praise and hope, and therefore the Eucharist has a festive note. We celebrate Jesus' victory over death and rejoice in his living presence when we assemble around the table. Since we look forward to the end-time fulfillment, the burden is taken away from us to understand ourselves already as a perfect end-time community. We can admit our weaknesses because we know that Christ will complete all our half-hearted endeavors. The expectation that God will one day live among his people inspires us ecclesiastically to share with each other the union we already enjoy as the body of Christ. We are summoned to show solidarity around Christ's table. Since the Eucharist contains so many important aspects of the Christian faith and hope, it is good that this celebration is not restricted to special occasions but in many churches is part of the regular worship service. In this way we approach the early Christian practice and also remind ourselves that worship means more than singing a few hymns, praying for each other, and listening to a sermon. Christ and his presence belong at the center of each worship service.

So far we have not talked about one aspect of communion that is practiced in the Orthodox Church, namely, the communion of infants. If someone is baptized, he or she is a full member of the church. Yet this does not mean that the person is given immediate access to all the sacraments, such as marriage, ordination, and anointing of the sick. We should think about admission to the Lord's Supper in a similar way. Before people participate, it is important that they understand what this meal stands for. Therefore, on the one hand, it is not altogether appropriate that we admit people to the Lord's Table only after they are confirmed. On the other hand, the Lord's Supper should not be given indiscriminately to babies and small children if they do not yet understand what they are receiving. I remember with horror the time when a pastor gave our infant daughter a communion wafer. She looked at it with curiosity since she had no idea what it meant. The aspect of deification through participation in the Eucharist emphasized in the Orthodox communion is as important as the more juridical aspect of forgiveness of sins emphasized in the West. If it is so important that we proceed directly from baptism to the Eucharist, the question must be raised as to why so few adults participate in the Eucharist in churches that practice infant communion. Perhaps it is the strict practice of penance demanded of adults before they participate in communion that wrongly leads to the overwhelming praxis of infant and children communion. However, this deification of infants seems to be more a symbolic than a real act. When Christians increase in age and wisdom, they may participate in certain rites that count as sacraments so that they may receive help in attaining the goal of sanctification. If not on theological grounds, then at least on pedagogical grounds, Christian children should be excluded from certain rites for which they are not yet mature enough. Here more flexibility would be in order. Maturity and participation could be coordinated so that in the Christian life there is actual growth in maturity and sanctification.

13

THE CHRISTIAN HOPE

When we now in conclusion talk about the Christian hope from a Lutheran perspective, we must first remember that our situation is in many ways completely different from that of Martin Luther and his time. When Luther died before he even reached sixty-three years of age, he was stricken by diseases and was old and fragile. Shortly before his death he signed a letter to his wife with the words: "Your loving Martin Luther, who has grown old."[1] Today's senior citizens live a full life unencumbered by the duties of their former professions and usually in relatively good health. Yet for his time Luther was old when he died, because life expectancy then was not even half of what it is today. Moreover, infant mortality was exceedingly high, and of the six children that the Luther family had, two died in infancy, another one reached only age thirty-four, and the other three grew to a mature age. At the end of the Middle Ages, death was all-pervading. Life on earth was short and a drudgery. It is not surprising that people wanted to secure a pleasant hereafter. The question that first made Luther join the monastery and then made him a Reformer, "How do I obtain a gracious God?" illustrates the yearning of the people in the late Middle Ages. People went on pilgrimages, made huge endowments to the church, and bought indulgences. The primary underlying concern was salvation in the hereafter.

Luther's reformatory breakthrough occurred when he recognized two points: (1) God is not a wrathful and angry God but has disclosed God's love in Christ,

---

1. Martin Luther, "Letter to Mrs. Martin Luther" of February 1, 1546 (no. 4195), in *LW* 50:292.

and (2) we cannot justify ourselves before God, but God has already justified us in Christ. This trust in God's grace shown to us in Christ induced in Luther a relaxed attitude, which at that time was rare. Many believed that with our death we approach judgment day, which was usually understood as the day of God's wrath. In contrast to that, Luther saw that day as a day of salvation and expressed in many of his letters the desire "that this day of our salvation may come soon."[2] How little he was afraid of that day and how ready he was to return to his Lord can be seen from a "table talk" that took place two days before he died. Luther said, "When I go home again to Wittenberg, I will lie down in a coffin and give the maggots a fat doctor to feast on."[3]

In many parts of the population there was an intensive expectation of the immediate approach of the day of judgment often intensified by ignorance and superstition. Thunderstorms, floods, and severe hail, and unusual appearances in the sky such as solar eclipses, comets, and shooting stars—all these natural events were interpreted as signs of God's wrath and of the approaching judgment. No doubt, Luther was a child of his time and accepted some of these prevailing fears. Monsters, such as the Freiberg calf of a monk, and the papal ass that supposedly was found in the Tiber River, were seen as portents of a great war and pointers to the nearness of judgment day.[4] When in 1531 Halley's Comet appeared on the sky, Luther saw nothing good in this "portent." Yet he added immediately: "Christ rules."[5] If Christ is the ruler, ultimately nothing bad can occur, and world history will come to a good end. Though Luther often emphasized that one cannot calculate the end of the world, sometimes he indulged in speculations. In his chronology of the world, for example, he expressed the conviction that the world will end before the sixth millennium is completed (in the year 2040).[6] In one of his table talks of 1538 he calculated from the book of Daniel that it will take another twenty years until the end of the world arrives. But then he ended his speculations with the words: "Only God knows how God will do it. It is not our task to prophesy at what time God will free his people, but to pray and to repent."[7]

2. Martin Luther, "Brief an Anton Lauterbach in Pirna" of April 2, 1540 (no. 3861), in *WA BR* 10:284.22. Cf. more extensively Paul Althaus, *The Theology of Martin Luther*, trans. Robert C. Schultz (Philadelphia: Fortress, 1966), 420–21.

3. Martin Luther, *Table Talks* (no. 6975, February 16, 1546), in *WA TR* 6:302.12–14.

4. Martin Luther, "Brief an Wenzeslaus Link in Altenburg" of January 16, 1523 (no. 573), in *WA BR* 3:17.2–7.

5. Luther, "Brief an Wenzeslaus Link in Altenburg," in *WA BR* 6:165.5–8.

6. Martin Luther, *Supputatio annorum mundi* (1541–45), in *WA* 53:171. Counted from the presumed date of the creation of the world.

7. Luther, *Table Talks* (no. 3831, April 10–11, 1538), in *WA TR* 3:646.10–12.

Though Luther was a child of his time, his theological convictions are not influenced by the prevailing views. Quite the opposite! He asked: "Why should the believers be afraid and not rejoice in the highest? Since they trust in Christ and in the judge who will come to their salvation and who will be their portion?"[8] Then he turns against the "Godforsaken preachers of dreams" who attempt to make people pious and do satisfaction for their sins by preaching sermons on the final judgment. If Christ were really the stern judge, nobody could pass before him. Yet Luther had recognized that Christ is the gracious Savior. Therefore he could approach the future relaxed, trusting in God. The Lutheran theologian Friedrich Beisser (b. 1934) writes: "In Luther actually all the topics of his theology are influenced by eschatology. The eschatological moment is omnipresent in him."[9] Many people today are far away from Luther's insight as to the significance of eschatology and his unshakable trust in Christ.

In our modern lifestyle most people, whether young or old, have very tight schedules. There is no "empty space," and if such a gap emerges, it is immediately filled up with new appointments. Instead of a relaxed retirement, one often hears about the restlessness and the stressful situations of senior citizens. People are continuously busy and never stop to rest or even to think. Even vacations are often only a continuation of work. Many people have backed away from a "divine intervention," and their thoughts and dreams focus on how they can shape the planet on which they live according to their own predilections. This means that eschatology in the sense of a completion of nature and history seems antiquated. But is this really true? We must admit that modernity has caused a deep-going secularization of all facets of life. Even death itself is largely understood as a biological phenomenon, and in many countries most older people no longer believe in a life after death. Nevertheless, two phenomena are remarkable: anxiety and hope.

When the year 2000 came around, there was not just rejoicing. The prophecies of the French astrologer Nostradamus (1503–66) were best sellers, and many people feared for the worst, from airplane crashes to financial catastrophes. The Federal Reserve System in New York demanded that all its workers stay at their workstations on New Year's Eve so that they could meet a potential catastrophe. Ever and ever again anxiety spreads with fear of climate change, a worldwide financial crisis, or terrorist attacks. Though we tell ourselves the opposite, we have no control over our future, and therefore fear haunts us. The dream of an earthly paradise or of eternal peace has not become reality.

8. Martin Luther, *Adventspostille* (1522), in WA 10.1/2:110.31–33 and 112.23, in a sermon on Luke 21:25–36.
9. Friedrich Beisser, *Hoffnung und Vollendung*, in *Handbuch Systematische Theologie* (Gütersloh: Gerd Mohn, 1993), 15:33.

All security measures and scientific prognoses notwithstanding, our future has not become more secure. To the contrary, it has become less secure and less predictable than ever. Many agree with this assertion and consequently live according to the cynical fatalism quoted by Paul: "Let us eat and drink, for tomorrow we die" (1 Cor. 15:32). Yet humans do not live in the present. They always stretch toward the future through their plans, through that which they still hope to achieve and acquire. All this would be without any meaning if there were no hope for the future.

Hope is as important for human life as oxygen. When a person has no hope, often physical and psychic problems emerge. But it is difficult to describe exactly what the content of the Christian hope is. On the one hand, it should not degenerate into some kind of fantasy with no connection to the promised reality. On the other hand, we should not express the Christian hope so timidly that it becomes anemic and has no convincing power. Moreover, the Christian hope is always in danger of becoming secularized. During the time of the Reformation enthusiasts such as Thomas Müntzer (ca. 1490–1525) wanted to establish the kingdom of God on earth. In the nineteenth century in a very different manner, Friedrich Engels (1820–95), the coauthor of the *Communist Manifesto*, summoned the nations of the world to a holy war at the end of which there should emerge a millennium of freedom. Similarly, Adolf Hitler was greeted with "*Heil!*" (salvation) because he promised a "Thousand-Year Reich" that would encompass the whole world. All of these utopias collapsed in confrontation with the earthly reality. What, then, gives us assurance that this is not also true for the Christian hope?

As scientists tell us, our earth has been around for several billion years and will continue to exist for a considerable time. Yet we are confronted with the continuous cycle of growth and decay, not only through the sequence of summer and winter, but also through being born, growing, aging, and finally dying, a fate that we share with all other living beings. In that situation it is difficult not to agree with the aforementioned maxim that comes from Hellenistic paganism: "Let us eat and drink, for tomorrow we die." The excessive interest in eating, drinking, and sexuality in our present time could indeed be caused by the fact that many people do not know what the future will bring and therefore limit themselves to enjoying the here and now. Moreover, we must seriously keep in mind that Jesus lived on this earth approximately two thousand years ago. Have we come any closer since then to the realization of the kingdom of God, or has the Christian faith simply become a fringe phenomenon in many countries of Europe and North America?

Indeed, the direct influence of the Christian faith in many countries has greatly diminished. Yet we should not overlook the indirect influence of that faith, which documents itself in many secular and religious movements. We need only think here of Marxism and National Socialism. These ideologies gleaned their messianic features from the Judeo-Christian tradition. Much more important, however, is the progressive spirit of the present, which is directly derived from the Judeo-Christian faith. Other religions such as Hinduism and Buddhism are largely indifferent to earthly reality or are even world-denying. In the Judeo-Christian faith, however, the conviction grew that God is not just the creator of the world, or the redeemer, but that the one God is creator, sustainer, and redeemer. God created this world, and with it God also created us. God protects us in the present through the natural orders, from the destructive chaos, and will guide the creation toward a new creation. This gives us a trustworthy basis on which we can stand and move. On our pilgrimage from creation to salvation, this earth is entrusted to us so that we can use it as a proving ground toward the eternal goal.

The secular spirit that is noticeable everywhere eliminates God deliberately and allows only for the continuous progression from yesterday through today to tomorrow. We see this, for instance, as productivity is continually increased, the stock market goes up and up, and the employed capital expands (or should expand) from year to year. But what is the significance of this continuous expansion and this unceasing march forward if we no longer have an unmovable goal before us? Moreover, any responsible scientist tells us that continuous expansion is an unrealizable dream. As the philosopher Plato recognized, everything that has a beginning also has an end. Our rapidly diminishing nonrenewable resources remind us: it will not become better and better so that at the end we will enter paradise. No, seen from our side, at the end there is nothing, there is death. Even Paul writes, "If for this life only we have hoped in Christ, we are of all people most to be pitied" (1 Cor. 15:19). We know from the tradition of late Judaism that the resurrection of the dead is an end-time event. Consequently, the resurrection of Christ indicates that the end is not moved into an infinite distance. The resurrection of Jesus has endowed the apocalyptic idea of the resurrection of the dead with reality. Since Jesus Christ anticipated through his own resurrection the goal of the history of this world and of our destiny, he has provided us with a foundation for hope.

The Resurrection

We must refute the idea that humans consist only of matter. But the converse idea is also wrong, namely, that we have eternal or divine qualities, such as immortal souls, that can give us hope beyond death. Of course, we must distinguish between the material side of our human existence and the more spiritual side. The material side comprises our bodily existence, while the latter refers to our spirit, our reason, and our soul. Yet the spiritual side is no epiphenomenon of the material, and conversely, the body is not the prison house of the soul as Plato thought. We are humans and thereby creatures of a finite world. All our divine or eternal qualities are only a gift, not a genuine part of ourselves. Even in the funeral liturgy it is stated, "From dust you are taken, to dust you return." If something survives death, it is not because of our innate possibilities but only because of God's grace.

A pure survival existence after death, as the Old Testament faithful imagined in sheol, the netherworld or abode of the dead, is not desirable. There is no real life and no personal identity. The dissipation into a world-soul or into the all-one, as announced by Asian religions, also denies the preservation of personal identity. The Judeo-Christian tradition has recognized the personal relationship between God and humanity as indispensable. In the sacraments God in Christ addresses us as individual persons. We are relational beings, and our renunciation of our relationship to God or to other living beings makes us into less than what we really are. With these thoughts in mind, individualism should not be advocated as it is implied in the idea of a personal immortality. What is decisive is the overcoming of our sinful estrangement from God and from our fellow human beings. The communion of fulfilled persons who have been freed from this estrangement is seen in the resurrection of the dead. Therefore, our own resurrection cannot be separated from the certitude of the resurrection of Jesus Christ.

The Resurrection of Jesus Christ

Though the earliest Christian community was certain that Jesus had been raised from the dead, they could not empirically prove his resurrection as they could his death on the cross. Death, the end of a human life, can be dated in space and time. We can even date a revivification historically in space and time, because the one who is revived continues to live until he or she finally dies. Resurrection, however, is something entirely different from a revivification as is reported, for instance, about Lazarus in John 11. The resurrection of Jesus does not end with his later death but is the beginning of his eternal life in a new kind of existence. Even the report of the empty tomb will not help us to prove the resurrection of Christ. First of all, if we look just at the empty tomb, Christ could have been revivified instead of actually resurrected. Moreover, the empty tomb story allows for different interpretations. As we can gather from Matthew 28, the disciples were convinced that Jesus had been resurrected, while other people claimed on account of the empty tomb that the disciples had stolen Jesus' corpse. Even Paul, who wants to make the congregation in Corinth understand the resurrection of Jesus, can only adduce the witness of other people and of Scripture, meaning in both cases witnesses of faith. The reason that we cannot obtain a proof of the resurrection is founded on the fact that with the resurrection we are not encountering a rising up of Jesus, suggesting an act of a human being, but a resurrection, meaning an action of God. Such an act can only be witnessed to; it cannot be empirically proven. If it could, then we could also prove empirically that God exists.

Through his resurrection Jesus was vindicated by God. God affirmed that Jesus is indeed the one he said he was, the eschatological savior who was called the Messiah (Acts 2:31). Therefore, he is now called the Lord (*kyrios*) as is seen in Philippians 2:5–11. This title *kyrios* shows that indeed Jesus Christ represents God and is identical with God. Death is no longer a possibility for the resurrected Christ. The resurrection of Jesus becomes the first point of the new creation, a creation in completion. This new creation becomes evident with the body of the earthly Jesus. The corpse disappeared, not through theft, but through a transformation from the present creation to a new imperishable kind of existence.

Christ's Resurrection and Our Resurrection

As we have seen, the Christian faith in the resurrection of the dead did not result from the development of the idea of the resurrection within the Jewish tradition. The resurrection is fundamentally centered on Christ. Christ is not only the firstborn of those resurrected, as is suggested in apocalyptic thought, but he is the presupposition of our own resurrections. Therefore Paul writes, "If Christ has not been raised, then our proclamation has been in vain and your faith has been in vain" (1 Cor. 15:14). Through the resurrection of Jesus Christ the apocalyptic idea of a general resurrection was transformed into the Christian hope of the resurrection of the dead. Therefore, the New Testament does not just announce Jesus as "the firstborn from the dead" (Col. 1:18), but also as the one with whom we are united in a resurrection like his, so that "we too might walk in newness of life" (Rom. 6:4). Our hope is not based on mere ideas; it is based on the resurrection of Jesus alone.

Resurrection of the Body

Our resurrection hope is expressed in the Apostles' Creed with the reference that we believe in "the resurrection of the body."[10] This does not imply

10. The original Greek and Latin versions say "the resurrection of the flesh."

an awakening in a strict biological way. If that were so, we would immediately be confronted with the problem of corporal identity, namely, how we would retrieve our body parts that had decayed and now had been transformed into other forms of life. Moreover, a regaining of our same body would mean that we would be confronted with the same limitations that we have now. When the early church confessed in its creed the resurrection of the body, the intention was to refute the idea of only a spiritual resurrection or a spiritual immortality. Not the soul or some kind of divine spark in us continues to live in eternity, but we ourselves are resurrected as is expressed with the drastic metaphor of the resurrection of the flesh. Resurrection is not a continuation of our present life, not even on a different level. To the contrary, our whole present life must cease. When Paul talks about the resurrection, he purposely uses antonyms, such as perishable and imperishable, dishonor and glory, weakness and power, physical and spiritual (1 Cor. 15:42–44). He wants to show that nothing is exempted from this drastic change. This does not mean, however, that the resurrected person is different from us. Of course, there will be a radical change because we will have a totally new spiritual bodily existence and we will encounter a new creation. Yet even now we are already undergoing a steady change from childhood to youth to old age and finally to senescence. This often causes in us considerable identity crises, but we always remain the same person.

Intermediate State?

If death brings our personal life to an end, and the resurrection occurs beyond death, then one may ask what occurs in between. While not all die at the same time, the Judeo-Christian tradition affirms a general resurrection of the dead. When Paul was confronted with these questions, he did not mention immortality, reincarnation, or purgatory, though he knew of these ideas, but instead pointed out that there is no privileged status. Whether we are still alive when Christ returns or whether we have been dead for a long time, our destiny lies alone in the encounter with the returning Lord (1 Thess. 4:15). It is neither necessary nor appropriate to speculate about an intermediate state between death and resurrection, because time is a purely this-worldly category. God is not subject to time. But he has created this time-bound world, and through its transitoriness we can observe time. When we think of God, we must abandon the time concept that Luther affirmed.[11]

---

11. Cf. Martin Luther, *Notes on Ecclesiastes* (1526), in *LW* 15:49–50, in his explanations of Eccl. 3:1.

Eternity cannot be equated with infinity in the scientific sense. Eternity is the dimension of God and therefore stands in contrast to our world time, which is limited by creation and has a beginning and a completion. If time will be completed through God's redeeming power, then all life-threatening powers will be overcome.

But when will this completion be reached, at death or some "time" afterward? The Bible does not give us a definite answer. Death is described as something that leads toward the final state or as something from which ensues a transitional state. In the New Testament the dead are often described as those who have fallen asleep (1 Cor. 15:20; Luke 8:52). They sleep until judgment day and then will be resurrected. With death they have not yet arrived in heaven or hell as their final end. Other New Testament passages, however, suggest that with death the end is reached. In Jesus' parable of the rich man and poor Lazarus, both men arrive immediately after their death at their final destinies, either Hades or Abraham's bosom (Luke 16:19–31). Similarly, Jesus promises the one criminal on the cross, "Today you will be with me in Paradise" (Luke 23:43). The Gospel according to John seems to attempt to bridge the gap between a transitional state and the goal. There we hear Jesus say, "Very truly, I tell you, the hour is coming, and is now here, when the dead will hear the voice of the Son of God, and those who hear will live" (John 5:25).

The writers of the New Testament knew that the response to the encounter with Jesus and his message would decide the final result, acceptance or rejection by God. Yet they did not conclude that those who had lived their lives in congruence with the "Word made flesh" would immediately enter heaven once they left this life. The writers knew that at the end of their earthly life Christians would have to die. When they talked about a sleep after death, they wanted to imply both the transition and the final goal. In Jesus Christ they encountered God's ultimate Word, which allowed them already to participate in a proleptic way in the new creation. They perceived death as an interruption of this proleptic participation, which pointed to something beyond death. Whether finality or transition, one thing was clear to them: there is no vacuum in death; we do not fall into nothingness, but are received by God. Therefore, the New Testament is very hesitant to paint in vivid colors what will meet us between death and resurrection.

In contrast to late medieval speculations about an intermediate state, especially about purgatory, Luther retained this New Testament restraint. He was convinced that an intermediate state after death would intimate in advance something of our acceptance or rejection by God. Yet it could not be a final state, otherwise the still outstanding fulfillment and completion through the resurrection would be fully realized. Luther described this state often as a deep sleep without dreams, consciousness, or feelings. To illustrate this intermediate state, he said that he had often attempted, though without success, to observe himself when he fell asleep. He thought it was this way with death. "As one does not know how it happens that one falls asleep, and suddenly morning approaches when one awakes, so we will suddenly be resurrected at the Last Day, not knowing how we have come into death and through death."[12] On another occasion he said: "We shall sleep until he comes and knocks at the tomb and says: 'Doctor Martin, get up!' Then in one moment, I will get up and I will rejoice with him in eternity."[13] Although Luther follows the tradition of his time and maintains an intermediate state, this state is unimportant for him. Decisive is the biblically founded certainty that in and with Christ a new eternal life is waiting for us beyond death.

Death is not only the border of this life but also the border of time. Beyond death there is no time, but only God's eternal presence. Though people meet their deaths at different points in time, we know that the last judgment occurs at the end of all possible and actual time, though it does not coincide with these various time points. If it were otherwise, then we would talk about an individualized last judgment that occurs at many different points, depending on when one leaves this life. Since people go beyond the time boundary at different points, we can use the New Testament metaphor of the sleep of the dead. Yet we know that when we are before God, all time differences dissipate. In God's eternal presence there is no difference between past, present, and future. These exist only for us time-bound creatures. When we go beyond the limits of time and death and encounter God's eternal presence, we are present not only with God but simultaneously with all other people. Regardless of when we go beyond this timeline, we appear on the "other side" in "the same moment" as all others. The transition from life to death leads immediately to the last judgment.

The End of History

The end of history and therewith of the world is closely connected to the concept of the last judgment. For many people such a divine judgment day seems antiquated. Yet we should not overlook the fact that through the relentless competition in our world we are already, in the here and now, continuously evaluated and judged. In these daily evaluations we are measured by external

12. Martin Luther, *Fastenpostille* (1525), in WA 17/2:235.17–20.
13. Martin Luther, *Predigten* (1533), in WA 37:151.18.

criteria, but the last judgment is a judgment according to our own possibilities. "To whom much has been given, much will be required; and from the one to whom much has been entrusted, even more will be demanded" (Luke 12:48). Since this judgment occurs at the return of Christ, it is clear that Christ will be the judge of the world. He judges us in God's name and as God, and therefore his verdict is binding and cannot be overturned. Since Christ is also our redeemer, in all its seriousness this judgment has a comforting aspect. By his example Christ has shown us the direction our lives should take, and through his dying and rising he has made it possible for us to live in communion with God. Therefore, the early Christian community was not afraid of the final judgment, though it handed on to us all the fear-causing apocalyptic images of judgment day found in the Bible. The early Christians realized that judgment is a necessary entrance to a new life. Therefore "Our Lord, come!" (*marana tha*) was a well-known saying in the early Christian community (cf. 1 Cor. 16:22). The book of Revelation closes in a similar way: "Amen. Come, Lord Jesus!" (Rev. 22:20). Martin Luther resumed this New Testament confidence in the face of judgment. In contrast to the widespread sentiment of the Middle Ages when people feared the day of wrath, Luther could say that we "may be ready for it, hope for it with joy, and hasten to meet it as the Day which delivers us from sin, death, and hell."[14]

Since death also brings our earthly lives to an end, our lives here on earth will be fully known to us only at the end. In the last judgment our lives will be confronted with the eternal will of God and with what we "could have" made out of them. Therefore, the fragmentariness of our lives becomes visible and with it the discrepancy between the possible and the actual, a discrepancy that we will experience with sorrow as God's final judgment. In reality we will have long ago spoken this verdict over our earthly lives. If we have been connected in this life with the eternity in time, that is, with Jesus Christ, we are assured that the discrepancy will be overcome between what could have been and what actually took place. We have the assurance because Jesus Christ, though human, never allowed this discrepancy to develop in his own life. If we cling to him, our death will issue not only into a resurrection to judgment but to eternal life.

Beyond Pure Justice

The issue of a universal homecoming, in which all people will obtain eternal bliss, becomes especially urgent when we realize that on judgment day not

14. Martin Luther, *Sermons on the Second Epistle of St. Peter* (1523/24), in *LW* 30:197, in his comments on 2 Pet. 3:12.

everybody will be saved. Jesus affirms a twofold outcome of history when he says, "The gate is wide and the road is easy that leads to destruction, and there are many who take it. For the gate is narrow and the road is hard that leads to life, and there are few who find it" (Matt. 7:13–14). But there are also passages in the New Testament that imply that God wants all people to be saved. As Paul wrestles with the destiny of Israel, he utters the conviction that "God has imprisoned all in disobedience so that he may be merciful to all" (Rom. 11:32). Both cosmological history and salvation history aim at a common history that comprises the destiny of all, both Jews and gentiles. We are confronted with the paradox that God in God's love wants all to be saved while God's justice requires that all who are disobedient be punished. We could attempt to solve this paradox by assuming that God's justice and love correspond to each other just as law and gospel do, that when God threatens with justice we flee to God's love. But such an interpretation would neglect references in Scripture that affirm that the opposition between us and God will not be bridged by God's love if our way of conduct continuously runs counter to that love. By talking about God's justice and love, we do not describe God's own self but rather how God is experienced by us. We must remind ourselves that God confronts us with a decision-demanding word when God calls us through Jesus: "Repent and follow me." If we accept God's offer and direct our lives accordingly, then the issue of a universal homecoming loses its urgency for us. The issue of a universal homecoming stems from the speculation about the ultimate destiny of others. Yet the gospel is not a theory about other people. It meets us as an existential encounter that demands our decision. How God meets other people, we must leave to God. We can only hope and pray that God's never-ending grace will finally win them over.

The End of the World

Now we must look beyond ourselves to the world that surrounds us, to the categories of space, time, and matter. It is one of the convincing affirmations of the New Testament that this world will come to an end. Curious people have always sought to find out how such an end could occur, perhaps through a collision of our earth with other planets, through a cosmic nuclear reaction, or through global environmental pollution that would make life on earth impossible. But, as Pierre Teilhard de Chardin cautions, such a cosmic disaster would only affect part of our universe and not the universe as a whole.[15]

---

15. Cf. Pierre Teilhard de Chardin, *The Future of Man*, trans. Norman Denny (New York: Harper, 1969), 321–22.

Moreover, it would lead only to destruction, not to a new world. Paul envisions the end of this world and the creation of the new world of God when he talks about the "eager longing" of creation, which "will be set free from its bondage to decay and will obtain the freedom of the glory of the children of God" (Rom. 8:19, 21).

Salvation will extend to the whole cosmos and to the whole creation. Whether initially it will pertain only to the part of creation in which we find ourselves, that is, our solar system and its closer environment, or our galaxy, we do not know and need not know. This issue has no existential relevance for us. It could very well be that in our part of the universe a complete change and perfection of creation will take place or that this transformation will even extend to the whole cosmos. Whatever may happen, the boundaries of space, time, and matter, which keep us confined here, will no longer be limiting. We have had a foretaste of this in the appearances of the resurrected One, who showed himself within these boundaries to his disciples and to other people, but who was no longer confined to them. Thus we have finally reached the subject of the new world of God.

The New World of God

When we talk about the new world of God, we should neither talk in generalities nor indulge in wishful dreams. Jesus and the New Testament writers emphasized that to some degree we can already anticipate this ultimate future in our present life. The new world has already shown itself in a preview in and with Jesus Christ. When, for instance, Jesus relieved sick people from their suffering, his actions were pointers to a new world of God in which the destructive forces could no longer exercise their power. This means that the powers of darkness and everything that pertains to them will be excluded from God's new creation. We will encounter heaven as God's new creation and hell as the dimensional separation from God. Often heaven and hell were thought to be geographic, cosmological places. As mentioned, Luther quipped about the enthusiasts who understood heaven in a local sense. Since the visible heaven (sky) continuously moves, Luther concluded that this would mean that Christ could not sit still for one moment. According to Luther, Christ is not up there like a stork in his nest, and hell is not somewhere down here.

The seer of the book of Revelation writes, "I saw a new heaven and a new earth." There God will dwell with God's people, and "they will be his peoples, and God himself will be with them; he will wipe every tear from their eyes.

Death will be no more; mourning and crying and pain will be no more; for the first things have passed away" (Rev. 21:1–4). Here we are confronted with a situation that is the complete opposite of our own. Since Jesus Christ has shown us through his death and resurrection that such a state is really attainable, we know that this is not wishful thinking. Through Jesus Christ and the promise contained in the Christ event, the hope for an ultimate realization of such a promise is realistic. It shows us that our immanent and continuous yearning for self-transcendence, for deification, for the elimination of death, and for progress toward perfection is not a utopian dream. It will find its fulfillment in life eternal.

But what about hell? Only in the world of fantasy is hell the realm of the devil in which unfortunate people are continuously tortured. According to the biblical understanding, at the end everything will be under God's reign, even hell. Hell shows the dimensional separation of God from those who do not accept God. For them God and the destiny of those who are with God will remain an unobtainable desire. They will have excluded themselves from unity with God and refused the offer of salvation. Therefore Luther writes: "I am not sure what hell is like before the Day of Judgment. The notion that hell is a specific place, now tenanted by the souls of the damned, as artists portray it and the belly servers preach it, I consider of no value."[16] In the Nicene Creed we read nothing about hell; instead we read, "We look for the resurrection of the dead, and the life of the world to come." For us hell serves only as an admonition that we reach our eternal destiny. Since we already know that our future is assured through God's grace as it appears in Jesus Christ, we can relax and realize something of this new world and continue to hope for its full inauguration. We need not be saviors in miniature form, as if the destiny of the world and of each individual human being depended on us. We can trust in the God who appears to us in Jesus Christ for the salvation of the world. Therefore, we look confidently toward the future. Luther writes in the same vein: "We do not sing any dirges or doleful songs over our dead and at the grave, but comforting hymns of the forgiveness of sins, of rest, sleep, life, and of the resurrection of departed Christians so that our faith may be strengthened."[17] And then he composes a hymn in line with John 11:25–26, almost as the summary of his faith:

> Christ is the truth, he is the life,
> And resurrection he will give.

16. Martin Luther, *Lectures on Jonah* (1526), in *LW* 19:74, in his exegesis of Jon. 2:2.
17. Martin Luther, "Preface to the Burial Hymns" (1542), in *LW* 53:326.

> Who trusts in him will obtain life,
> Though he may in the grave have lain.
> Who lives and trusts, will never die,
> But praise him in eternity.[18]

This can also stand as the summary of the Christian faith in general as we praise the God of our Lord Jesus Christ.

---

18. Luther, "Preface to the Burial Hymns," in *LW* 53:330–31.

INDEX